1959

Irene Ledbetter
Memphis Housing Authority

THE VALUATION

OF

RESIDENTIAL REAL ESTATE

THE VALUATION

OF

RESIDENTIAL REAL ESTATE

by

ARTHUR A. MAY

*Professorial Lecturer in Land Economics
American University*

Second Edition

Englewood Cliffs, N. J.

PRENTICE-HALL, INC.

L. C. Catalog Card No. 53–7783

First printing .... May, 1953
Second printing .... February, 1954
Third printing .... December, 1954
Fourth printing .... April, 1956
Fifth printing .... April, 1957
Sixth printing .... December, 1957
Seventh printing .... August, 1958

PRINTED IN THE UNITED STATES OF AMERICA
93998

"*Write me as one who loves his fellow men.*"

— Abou Ben Adhem

. . . and I, the more so, because it was their advice, help, counsel, and tolerance which have made this book possible.

To them I dedicate it, with thanks.

Preface

A book of this kind finds its way into print because: (1) the author cannot suppress a desire to teach something to someone or (2) he wishes to record, for whatever interest it may have to the reader, the lessons taught by an interesting experience.

Or perhaps the author looks upon his mission in much the same way I once heard expressed by my learned friend, Dr. Thurston Howard Ross, of Beverly Hills, California. Addressing a real estate valuation class, one of whose students complained of what the student mistakenly thought was an irrational appraisal technique, Dr. Ross replied: "I am not here to teach or to force upon you any of my pet dicta or dogma; my purpose is to explain methods which work for me. Perhaps they will for you. But you are under no obligation to accept or to use them."

This idea, I think, is the underlying theme of this book. I have no desire to force my teachings on anyone. What follows, beginning at Chapter I, is simply the recorded impression of an experience of many years, during which the appraisal of all kinds of real estate was my daily task. This book records in detail the methods and techniques that have assisted me in my work in the residential field.

And although I have been mindful that my colleagues might find some note of interest in that record, this book has not been written for them. Rather, I have been thinking of the savings and loan institutions whose funds are invested in real estate mortgages; of the host of real estate brokers and employees of federal agencies whose stock in trade is the single-family dwelling; of the banks and insurance companies as lenders of mortgage funds; of estate and property managers; of attorneys-at-law specializing in matters appertaining to real estate; of the students of real estate valuation in the schools and colleges, as well as those who attend the special courses sponsored by the Society of Residential Appraisers, the Savings & Loan Leagues, and the American Institute of Real Estate Appraisers; and all of those who contact the commodity of residential real estate in the business of making a living. This book is for all of them.

This is a "case" book. It combines the theoretical and the practical. The first sixteen chapters discuss valuation theory. In Chapters 17 and 18, eight specific properties are described in considerable detail. Four of these are new buildings, the remaining four are used buildings, varying in age from ten to twenty years. After these eight case properties have been described, they are subjected to appraisal treatment. In each case, a solution of the problem follows its definition. Thus, valuation method as actually used in the field is applied to the case problem.

The real estate business is an indigenous business; it cannot be transacted nationally because the commodity is not transportable. Thus the profession of real estate appraisal is also an indigenous one; the geographic scope of the real estate and appraisal commerce is native to the area in which the commodity lies.

In this edition, two new case properties are presented as reflecting the popular demand for a new architectural type, namely the "ranch house" or the "rambler." The past few years have witnessed a growing demand for this type of dwelling, offering as it does the convenience of a one-floor plan. An effort was made to obtain a design which differed from the usual production type of "rambler" — to select one that had more than the usual individuality of style and pleasing facade.

Incidentally, no attempt has been made in Chapters 17 and 18 to record actual, current construction costs or value; the figures used are entirely hypothetical, although they reflect current levels.

My debt to those who have assisted in the development of this book is hereby acknowledged. Space will not permit mention of the entire list. Special mention should be made, however, of Eugene G. Betzold, who provided floor and plot plans and the physical descriptions of the case-properties except Case Property No. 3.

Finally, and because of the nature of the commodity with which we deal here, let the reader remember that the principles laid down in the pages that follow are *general* in their application.

Exceptions can be taken (and valid ones), in more or less remote instances, to anything the author states. Thus the reader should be mindful of the words of the philosopher who said, "No general statement is ever completely true; *not even this one.*"

A. A. M.

Contents

THE VALUATION
OF
RESIDENTIAL REAL ESTATE

CHAPTER 1

The Purposes to Be Served

At the very beginning, let us be frank. Any book on such a subject as this, no matter how earnest the author may be in his desire to present his message in readable style, is bound to be rather heavy going in spots.

On the whole, this is an interesting subject. Real estate is interesting if for no other reason than that it represents the principal source of our national wealth. Any study of valuation method is extremely fascinating. Here is one phase of real estate operations that presents a bold and vigorous challenge to the inquiring mind because of the simple fact that no solution to any real estate valuation problem has as yet recorded all of the pertinent information obtainable.

Yet, despite the challenging nature of this subject, certain unexciting preliminary steps leading up to the discussion of valuation techniques are necessary in order to provide an understandable approach to the study of residential real estate valuation. This first chapter, for example, is purely elementary but it is the *raison d'être* for what comes after, the prelude to more interesting action.

The Objective

The objective of this discussion is to deal with the mass appraisal problem; that is, the problem of valuating residential properties.

The single-family home represents the bulk of the real estate economy of the nation. It is the principal mortgage business of the lending agencies of the country. It is the principal business of most real estate brokers. And, in the number of appraisals made, it is by far the greatest part of the work of the professional appraiser. Because the single-family home makes up the largest

1

volume of the real estate business, it should be accorded specialized, scientific treatment in the appraisal process.

The field of single-family residential appraisal work is the fresh-
man phase that leads to the Master's Degree. The top men who
specialize in valuation work and whose reputation for skill is
nationwide in this business (this profession, if you please, for
that is what it has become in twenty short years), did not get their
start by appraising properties like the Empire State Building.
They started out by appraising single-family homes. This is the
type of property which brings into play ALL of the techniques
that must be applied in the valuation of any type of property. In
this indoctrination course are learned the rudiments — the funda-
mentals — that must be employed in the appraisal of any kind of
real estate. That man who has served his apprenticeship in single-
family residential appraisal work and who has achieved the status
of journeyman is amply qualified to estimate the value of a sky-
scraper, a chain of hotels, an iron mine, a gas transmission pipeline,
a shipyard, or an atomic energy plant.

The appraisal of a single-family home may appear to be prosaic
when compared to the appraisal of a department store, hotel,
multistory garage, or any number of special kinds of properties
where, because "big money" is involved, the problem takes on
glamor.

However, let us not underestimate the single-family home as
an appraisal problem. The statement has been made before, and
can be repeated now, that it is easier to appraise the Waldorf-
Astoria Hotel than to appraise a single-family home in a twilight
neighborhood on the fringe of a downtown retail district where
no sales have been made for many years, where the property has
undergone a succession of declining uses, and where indicia in the
form of statistics in the market place are conspicuous by their
absence. Many a good appraiser, well versed in the field of appraising income property, has fallen flat on his face when faced
with this type of problem.

This is because the single-family home is subject to a type of
deterioration not characterized by investment properties in the
same degree. In other words, the single-family home is always
subject to sociological peritonitis. "Peritonitis," says the dictionary, is "acute inflammation of the peritoneum or lining membrane of the abdomen." No one has more cause to fear peritonitis

than the skilled surgeon who knows that once infection attacks this membrane which surrounds the viscera, there is little hope for the patient.

So it is with the single-family home. Once the forces of social decay have begun to eat into the "peritoneum," or the neighborhood surrounding the property under appraisal, it is not long before the value begins to tumble, despite all of the intrinsic construction quality and excellence of design. This is the basis for the old saying, "More houses are torn down than fall down." This is also the reason that the single-family residence in mid-life, in a neighborhood which is undergoing social change, presents a problem to the appraiser which is difficult, intricate, and challenging.

The mass appraisal problem is of daily concern to the mortgage lender, the real estate broker, and the owner, institutional or individual, with the exception of the individual owner of a single parcel. In discussing the mass problem, therefore, it seems desirable to consider only those purposes of valuation most common to the people who deal with the single-family dwelling as a part of their daily activities.

Knowledge of the purpose essential. The appraisal of real estate is a problem. The value estimate is its solution. There can be no logical solution unless the problem has been defined. That definition consists of a clear-cut statement of the reasons for making the appraisal and the objective to be sought. Under any other conditions, there can be no intelligent application of the appraisal process. Thus the principal asks the appraiser to make an appraisal of property to find:

1. Market value
2. Sales price
3. Purchase price
4. Fair rental value
5. Fair trading value
6. Insurance coverage
7. Fair compensation for damages suffered

In each of these instances a different result may be obtained (not, by the way, a different "value"). And in each of these instances a different appraisal pattern will evolve. Thus the purpose of the appraisal points the path to be followed in the accumulation, analysis, and interpretation of the data used to fashion the valuation conclusion. The means must serve the end. The process must fit the problem, and the nature of the problem is disclosed by its definition — the purpose for which the appraisal is to be made. This is the primary step in the appraisal process.

Appraisals for the Mortgage Lender

The reason for the real estate debacle of the early thirties is now generally known. Artificial values brought about by excessive costs of financing, overexpansion of mortgage credit, and faulty appraisals helped to precipitate one of the worst real estate crashes in history. If we intend to profit by the lessons of the past, the desirability of sound values as a basis for the lending of mortgage funds is obvious. These funds represent, in the case of banks and savings and loan associations, the savings of the depositors and shareholders of these institutions — their hedge against adversity. In the case of loans made by insurance companies, they represent the savings of policyholders. Basically, they are the funds necessary to pay death claims and annuity benefits.

It follows, then, that the valuation of properties pledged as security for loans of this type carries heavy moral responsibility, for in the lending operation are involved the financial safety and security of millions of people whose lifetime savings have been — or will be — indirectly invested in real estate mortgages. This should call for expert treatment in the appraisal process.

The appraiser's responsibilities. The appraiser for the mortgage lending institution has two responsibilities: (1) to the institution he represents, which calls for a sound appraisal comprising all the known factors affecting the property in order to protect his principal from making an unsound loan; and (2) his moral responsibility to the investing public as reflected by his unwillingness to undervalue or overvalue the security property. In fact he may, with logic, consider himself a sort of governor atop the spinning flywheel of the machine of mortgage finance, a control on the possibility of disintegration of the machine itself.

The trend of lending practice. The mortgage loan appraisal of today reflects the changes that have occurred in mortgage lending practice. Prior to the thirties, the five-year nonamortizing mortgage was much in vogue. Commonly, mortgages were made for ten years requiring payments of principal at semiannual intervals. Today, the bulk of residential lending is characterized by the direct reduction feature — the payment of a prorata share of the principal monthly (to include taxes and insurance), the whole to be amortized over fifteen to twenty-four years. Loan tenures have been extended. The period of repayment is now three or four times as great as it was.

This change in lending practice lays far greater emphasis on the necessity for expert appraisal treatment than once was the case. The property must stand as security for the loan over a longer period of time. The objective of this type of appraisal must contemplate the possibility of default, and in that event the ability of the *then* value of the real estate pledged as collateral to satisfy the mortgage debt. Obviously, therefore, the "catch-as-catch-can" market price at the time of appraisal is not the answer to the problem. Rather, the valuation of the property to be used as a sound lendable basis should contemplate the future benefits and services and the detriments and disservices that will flow from the ownership of the property over that period of time for which the loan is made.[1]

The position of the lender in this instance is somewhat different from that of the real estate broker. The broker handling the sale or purchase of a parcel of real estate for his client completes the transaction, and there's an end to it. But the lender must "live" with the security property for the tenure of the loan. The property is his anchor to windward. In the event of default by the borrower, it is the instrument of liquidation. The mortgage loan appraisal therefore must reflect, in so far as possible, the risks environing the security property over a long period of time into the future.

As will be shown later, the risks to investment lie principally in the factors surrounding the property, rather than within the physical structure itself; this being so, there devolves upon the mortgage loan appraiser the responsibility for analyzing these

---

[1] It is not to be implied that the appraiser, in the process of making an appraisal for mortgage loan purposes will arrive at a "market value" lower in amount than the figure at which he would arrive for the purposes of estimating "fair sales price" or "fair purchase price." Should he do so he is departing from his role as the disinterested technician operating in the same advisory sphere as the company lawyer — and is impinging his actions and his findings on the lending policy of the institution for which he is acting. His judgment having been swayed by this influence, his professional attainments have but little value to his employer or his principal.

factors and interpreting their meaning as reflecting the relative degree of risk.

This business of forecasting. There will be those who, noting the foregoing remarks, will say that this procedure compels the appraiser to forecast coming events, else how can he predict the "future benefits and services" which the property may render through the years to come?

The appraiser is not being asked to perform any feat of the supernatural. All that we ask him to do is to apply his experience and to tell his principal what he believes the trend of events will be in the instant problem. He is (it is assumed) well fitted to do this by virtue of his vocation. It can be assumed further than he is as well qualified for his work as any other businessman who is required each day of his business life to make predictions based on his past experience.

Forecasting is a characteristic of ordinary, rational, human conduct. If this were not so, automobiles, radios, electric refrigerators, endowment insurance policies, and a host of other things now sold extensively on the installment plan would enjoy a limited sale, because the decision to purchase them is based originally on the forecast by the purchaser that, considering the events of the past (meaning his past income), he will be able to buy and pay for them in the future, and further that he will live to enjoy their benefits.

This is exactly what we ask the appraiser to do. We ask him to forecast, as best he can, what the future holds for the property. The value of the forecast will be in ratio to his experience. It will be dependable only to the extent that he may assume the future trend of the real estate cycle will be like the past or that the future trend of a residential district will be like that of other residential districts. And the length of the projection into the future will affect the reliability of the forecast; the longer it is, the less accurate it will be.

With these limitations in mind, we ask the appraiser called upon to make an appraisal for mortgage lending purposes to measure as best he can the probabilities in the present situation, thus informing the lender of the probable risks involved and the future benefits that the property may hold during the tenure of the loan about to be made.

Appraisals for the Real Estate Broker

The operations of the general real estate office divide themselves into several chief activities, as follows: sales of property; purchases of property; negotiations of leases; residential rentals; insurance; and property management. In the analysis of all these operations will be found the interplay of the appraisal process. The whole fabric of real estate operations is shot through with the thread of it. In many cases, there can be no sound decision made until the process has been invoked. Witness the following category of questions asked of the real estate broker almost daily:

I want you to sell my property for me. What is it worth?
I want you to purchase this property for me. What is its fair price?
I want you to lease my property for me. What fair rental should it command?
I want you to handle the renting of my house. What shall I ask for it?
What is the fair amount of insurance coverage I should carry on my property?
I want my property to return 8 per cent net. What rentals must I establish and on what value?
I want to trade my property for another. What value shall I establish as a fair basis for the trade?
Part of my property has been condemned by the city to accommodate a street-widening project. What is the amount of damages to which I am entitled?

There can be no reliable answer to these questions until the appraisal process has been invoked in some form. Facts not at hand must be gathered; analyses must be made; data must be interpreted; some of the tools of the process must be applied; and a value estimate must be fashioned that evolves as the answer to the client's problem.

But more important than anything else to the broker is the control that the appraisal process exerts on the choice of potentially salable listings. Time was when the broker would accept any listing proffered him. But experience has taught him that the property sales operation will be conducted at a loss or profit, depending upon judicious selection of the properties on which the broker is to expend sales effort and advertising expense. Very few of the large offices will now accept a property listing until the property has been inspected and an appraisal (of some sort) made to determine if the price asked by the client is in line with marketing possibilities.

In fact, some real estate boards and trade associations using the system of multiple listing (by means of which the listing is circulated to all of the members) process all potential listings through an appraisal committee before acceptance and distribution to the membership.

The effect of this is twofold: (1) to insure the broker against the unwise expenditure of time and money in attempting to promote the sale of a property that is not salable because the price asked is too high; and (2) to protect the client against offering the property at a price so low as to demoralize the market.

Appraisals for the Owner

In discussing appraisals for the owner, we have in mind the following two classes of owners:

1. The individual as the willing owner usually of one parcel of real estate — his place of abode.

2. The business institution as the unwilling owner of many parcels of real estate of which it has become possessed because of the default of mortgages made by it, or through the purchase or merger of assets.

The circumstances occasioning the appraisal of real estate for the first class of owners are substantially the same as those outlined for the real estate broker; for example, appraisals are desired to determine:

1. The fair purchase price

2. The prospective selling price

3. The equity of tax assessment

4. The measurement of damages resulting from actions in eminent domain (condemnation)

5. The equitable settlement of estates containing real property

For the second class, the institution as the unwilling owner, the appraisal serves two purposes: (1) it forms the base for determining the book value; and (2) it establishes the liquidation value of the asset.

It is important to note, in this latter instance, that the appraiser's objective may vary with the management policy of the institution he represents. In a rising market, the management may elect not to sell but to hold for a rise in price. Or, conversely, it may elect to dispose of the property assets with dispatch. In the former case, the appraiser's object is to arrive at the pure concept of market value (as discussed in the following chapter), defined as the "present worth of all the rights to future benefits." In the latter case, the objective is the going price at the moment. Indeed, it may develop as the "knockdown" price, depending upon the degree of urgency of the management in liquidating its real estate account.

There are many more individual purposes for which appraisals are made. Two authorities catalogue forty.[2] Our discussion, however, is aimed at appraisal circumstances most frequently encountered by those engaged in some form of the real estate business, and we have intentionally confined our enumeration to purposes that represent the mass of the problem.

---

[2] Frederick M. Babcock, *The Valuation of Real Estate* (New York, McGraw-Hill Book Company, Inc., 1933); The American Institute of Real Estate Appraisers, *The Appraisal of Real Estate,* Chicago, 1951.

CHAPTER 2

Market Value: the End Product

The term "value" originates and has its being in the field of economics. It follows, then, that the appraisal of property which has "value" as the end product of the process is an experiment in the field of economic thought. Although it is not the intention here to engage in any ponderous discussion of economic philosophy, it does seem advisable to recite certain fundamental economic concepts that provide an intelligent approach to what we are trying to do. Furthermore, as we shall see later, certain of these basic precepts provide the original structure on which have been erected the three principal valuation techniques — cost, market, and income — the tools used by the appraiser in estimating value.

Economics has been variously described as the science that seeks to explain all business phenomena, the science of business, the social science that treats of human activity in the business of making a living, and the science of human behavior. For our purposes we shall consider that aspect of economics that deals with the behavior of human beings in relation to the acquisition and manipulation of wealth in the form of real property. This is a field in which the application of dogmatic theory does not produce as precise results as in the field of the physical sciences such as physics or chemistry. Alfred Marshall, in his general introduction to the *Cambridge Economic Handbook* says:

The theory of economics does not furnish a body of settled conclusions immediately applicable to policy. It is a method rather than a doctrine, an apparatus of the mind, a technique of thinking, which helps its possessor to draw correct conclusions.[1]

---

[1] Quoted from Alexander Gray, *The Development of Economic Doctrine* (New York, Longmans Green and Company, 1931).

10

This absence of a "body of settled conclusions" imperils any assertion that economic causes always produce economic results in like volume at like times. Thus, it does not follow that because a bushel of wheat was once worth two bushels of corn that this will always be so. The intensity of human desire for the bushel of wheat may vary from time to time. It is well known that it does, as evidenced by the exchange value (in terms of money) of wheat in the market place.

Economics studies the behavioristic tendencies of people in the mass in the pursuit of livelihood. These tendencies and movements are not "settled"; they are not characterized by method, by habit, or by definite cyclical frequencies. This so-called "science," therefore, while recording with commendable accuracy what people *have* done in the pursuit of their wants and desires may fail to tell the truth as to what they *will* do. Or, as Alexander Gray says in his *Development of Economic Doctrine:*

> To say that economics is a method rather than a doctrine, that it is not a body of concrete truth, but an engine for the discovery of concrete truth, is to express with great felicity the view that economic truth, as such, is unattainable.[2]

From all this, we may make this generalization: since the instrument we must employ to discover value is one that lacks precision, the end product of the process must also lack precision; if the tools and the processes with which we must work are inexact in their application, the result — that is, value — must be inexact. It is axiomatic in the study of real estate valuation that the optimum value cannot be found; it can only be estimated.[3]

The zone of error. Appraisal technicians of experience and good judgment respectfully acknowledge a "zone of error" in every valuation of property. This amounts to a tacit admission of the principle enunciated above — namely, that exact and precise value cannot be measured. Somewhere between the upper and lower limits of this zone is supposed to lie the value optimum. One of the objectives of the appraisal process is to reduce these limits to the narrowest possible confines. The type of property under appraisal and the peculiarity of its environment, however, do not

---

[2] *Ibid.*

[3] "What people expect from the economists is beyond the power of any mortal man." Ludwig von Mises, *Human Action* (New Haven, Yale University Press, 1949).

always permit these limits to be squeezed to the point where they will bear on the core of practical accuracy. Where this is true, two appraisals made by two appraisers on the same property on the same day may produce varying results.[4]

This circumstance does not invalidate the process. The correct estimate of value will eventuate from the comparative experience of the appraisers with the type of property involved and their comparative ability to interpret correctly the data pertinent to the problem.

The Desideratum: Market Value

Value, according to the economist, is the power of a good, or commodity, to command other goods, or commodities, in exchange. "Value," says the American Institute of Real Estate Appraisers,[5] "is the *relationship* between a thing desired and a potential purchaser." "Value," says von Mises, "is the importance that acting man attaches to his ultimate needs." [6] What, then, is "value" in reference to real estate? As noted in the preceding chapter, it has been defined as the present worth of all the rights to future benefits arising from the ownership of property. This is a good definition. It contemplates that, in the process of appraisal, there will be an attempt to measure the worth or size of the volume of benefits or services flowing from the property. But there are many conceptions (and many misconceptions) of the term. There are many definitions; one text lists thirty-eight.[5] "Fair," "present," "insurable," "economic," "sound," "assessed," "taxable," and a host of other kinds of "value" have all been defined, discussed, and are alleged to have their specific application to the problem and the field of usage in which their proponents are engaged.

We shall not pause to debate the logic of such practice, although a sizable volume might be written around the thesis that real estate has, or has not, more than one "value." The bull's-eye of our target is "market value," and we must have specific and clear-cut delineation of the target, or we shall be wide of the mark. To aim

---

[4] Many laymen still think, mistakenly, that the market value of real estate is measured with the engineer's "slip-stick" and are inclined to condemn two appraisers who, acting concurrently, differ nominally in their estimates of value of the same property.

[5] American Institute of Real Estate Appraisers, *Appraisal Terminology and Handbook* (Chicago, American Institute of Real Estate Appraisers, 1950).

[6] Von Mises, *op. cit.*

at a variety of "market values" is to get nowhere in the discussion that follows. No discussion of the appraisal process can proceed upon an intelligent basis past this point unless "market value" has been defined and accepted by the reader as the foundation on which the valuation process is premised. And so we proceed to a definition.

Market Value Defined

The American Institute of Real Estate Appraisers, in its *Appraisal Terminology and Handbook,* says:

Market Value: (1) As defined by the courts is the highest price estimated in terms of money which a property will bring if exposed for sale in the open market, allowing a reasonable time to find a purchaser who buys with knowledge of all the uses to which it is adapted and for which it is capable of being used. (2) Frequently it is referred to as the price at which a willing seller would sell and a willing buyer would buy, neither being under abnormal pressure.) (3) It is the price expectable if a reasonable time is allowed to find a purchaser and if both seller and prospective buyer are fully informed.

An analysis of this definition shows that, while a money transaction in the market place is the probable root of "market value," all transactions in the market place are not indicators of that same "market value" *unless* they exhibit all of the limitations and characteristics with which the definition is equipped. Inability to understand these limitations and willingness to accept without reservation the phenomena of the market place as indexing market value have resulted in a confusion of tongues by comparison with which the Tower of Babel becomes insignificant. By this process of faulty reasoning, the man in the street assumes that "value" is synonymous with "price." No economist — for that matter, no appraiser (perforce, an economist of parts) — who values his professional reputation will agree with this idea; yet it persists because the transactions in the market place are not subjected to analysis nor related to the requirements of the definition.

The "highest" price is sought, obviously because the market calibrates "market value," or the intensity of the desire of the prospective purchaser, with the yardstick of dollars — meaning, of course, the most dollars.

Intelligent action is required. Justification of the price asked is based on an assumed "intelligence" of the contracting parties.

The requirement that the buyer and seller be "fully informed" determines the quality and quantity of their "intelligence." "To be informed" apparently implies to be supplied with a knowledge of the present and potential purposes for which the property may be, and is capable of being, used.

The mortgage loan that follows an appraisal to determine market value is not made for a day or for a year. It is usually made for fifteen or twenty years. The home that is purchased following the appraisal of its market value is not bought by the purchsaer for temporary occupancy; it is bought for the enjoyment of himself and his family for a period of many years, perhaps a lifetime. In either of these two appraisal instances, the mortgage made or the purchase price paid contemplates an intelligent, informed estimate of the value of *future* benefits, amenities, services of convenient living, and utilitarian capacities of the property.

If there were any question as to the sufficiency of the Institute's definition, it would arise from the use of the phrase "a reasonable time." What is a reasonable time? This will vary according to:

1. The type of property involved (cottage or mansion)
2. The condition of the market at a particular time (and the ebb and flow of demand)
3. The seller's idea of a "reasonable time" (more accurately stated as the multitudinous ideas of a multitude of sellers)

The definition further requires that the action of buyer and seller shall be a voluntary one. Neither shall be under abnormal pressure. There shall be no element of duress or coercion in the transaction. This is important; for if the action of buyer or seller is forced, the resulting price will be less or more than the golden mean of market value, and the plus or minus figure will represent the penalty of enforced action.

This principle illustrates what has been said above concerning the confusion between market price and market value. Where the feature of free and competitive trading is absent in the transaction, market price is bound to result. As an example, imagine the owner of a residential property suddenly forced to sell in order to realize cash with which to meet an immediately pressing obligation. The urgency of his needs at that moment may force him to sell his property at a price so far below market value as to make the relationship absurd. Conversely, there is the situation where, because of exorbitant demand for shelter and scarcity of supply of housing, the builder, taking advantage of a seller's market, may decide to increase his margin of profit beyond any conscionable amount. The resulting price to the consumer under these circumstances cannot be considered "value."

During the boom period of the twenties, when demand for housing outran the supply and when, as a consequence, discount rates for junior financing and second mortgages reached 25 and 30 per cent, properties were freely traded in the market place at figures approximately 40 per cent in excess of actual reproduction costs.

This moot question of market value versus market price has been treated by one author [7] as follows:

Certain economic forces and changes have a pronounced effect upon the market price with negligible influence upon the justified value, while the reverse is true as to other economic changes and forces. Still other forces will affect both price and value. As a result of these varying effects upon the price and value it is seldom that the market price and justified value exactly coincide.

The famed "Brewer" decision. There is another definition that enjoys a distinctive place in the lore of valuation practice and that is widely quoted by appraisal authorities. This emerges from a decision of the United States Supreme Court in the case of the C.C.C. and St. Louis versus Victor M. Backus. The opinion of Mr. Justice Brewer says in part:

But the value of the property results from the use to which it is put and varies with the profitableness of that use, present and prospective, actual and anticipated. There is no pecuniary value outside of that which results from such use.[8]

In writing this opinion into the law of the land, the Supreme Court made three valuable contributions to appraisal thought:

1. "Value results from use." This is, of course, basic economic precept. Real estate would have no value in exchange unless it had value in use as a prerequisite. Value and utility go hand in hand, and when coupled with scarcity, the combination produces optimum values. Thus, the value aspect of real property is one which arises basically from the use concept.

---

[7] Philip W. Kniskern, *Real Estate Appraisal and Valuation* (New York, The Ronald Press Company, 1933), Ch. IV, p. 66.

[8] U. S. Supreme Court Reports: Book 38, 151-154 at page 439.

2. Value is derived from the profitableness of use — the money profit in the case of rental properties; the amenity profit (or income) in the case of owner-occupied homes.

3. The profit derivable from use is not only the present profit. It is the profit now and into the future; the immediate benefits and the future benefits; the present money income and the future money income; the present flow of living comforts and the future flow of the same amenities.

Importance of the legal concept. These decisions by the courts [9] must be accorded considerable weight by appraisers in their selection of a particular definition of "value." In the appraisal of property, we value the rights of ownership. The legal character of these rights is defined by the courts, and since this is so, their interpretation of the value of property rights must form a solid foundation for appraisal procedure. Definitions are easily coined by combining a glib tongue with a few mental gymnastics, but when argument ensues, recourse must finally be had to established opinions of record in the field of jurisprudence that have withstood the test of adjudication and bear the imprimatur of the bench. Disputes as to the value of property rights must eventually be settled at law; the courts have defined the value of these rights many times. It must follow, then, that any safe definition of the "value" of real estate is one that is akin to those that emanate from decisions of our higher courts.

Governmental Definitions of Value

The policies of governmental agencies that are involved in the field of real estate have considerable bearing on appraisal thought and practice. Most important of these, in its effect on the real estate economy of the nation, is the Federal Housing Administration. In the years between 1935 and 1952, this agency acted as the insurer of nearly three million mortgages for a total of more than 22 billion dollars. In the course of its operations, it has had to appraise more than three million properties, both single and multifamily. Obviously its policies affect the mortgage market, the real estate market, and appraisal methods. Because this is so, its definition of "value" (or "market value") is of considerable significance to appraisers.

---

[9] See Orgel, *Valuation Under Eminent Domain* (The Mitchie Co., Charlottesville, Va., 1936).

The word value as used by the Federal Housing Administration refers to a price which a purchaser is warranted in paying for a property, rather than the price at which the property may be sold, and is defined as: The price which typical buyers would be warranted in paying for the property for long term use or investment, if they were well informed, acted voluntarily, and without necessity.[10]

The War Assets Administration (now liquidated) was organized after World War II for the purpose of disposing of property, both real and personal, that became surplus to the needs of a peacetime economy. Its portfolio of real estate included some 2400 locations (largely industrial in character) having a cost to the government of approximately 7.8 billion dollars. This disposal program involved a mass appraisal operation for the purpose of estimating the prices at which the properties should be sold. WAA's definition of value is of interest to appraisers.

"Fair Value" means the maximum price which a well informed buyer, acting voluntarily and intelligently, would be warranted in paying, if he were acquiring the property for investment or for use with the intention of devoting such property to the best or most productive type of use for which the property is suitable or capable of being adapted.[11]

The Veterans Administration, to fit the language of the legislation authorizing its loan guaranty program (the insuring of loans to veterans), was obliged to coin a definition of "reasonable value."

That figure which represents the amount a reputable and qualified appraiser, unaffected by personal interest, bias, or prejudice, would recommend to a prospective purchaser as a proper price or cost in the light of prevailing conditions.

The General Services Administration, through its constituent Public Buildings Service, is more directly involved in volume real estate operations than any other agency of the Government. Its activities comprise the acquisition of sites for new public buildings, the disposal of real estate determined to be surplus to the needs of all Federal agencies, and the leasing of space for governmental operations throughout the country. Its definition of "fair market value" is as follows:

"Fair Market Value" is defined as the amount in cash, or on terms reasonably equivalent to cash, for which in all probability the property would be sold by an owner willing but not obliged to sell to a purchaser who desires but is not obliged to buy. In ascertaining that figure, con-

---

10 Federal Housing Administration, *Underwriter's Manual* (Washington, D. C., Revised 1947).

11 War Assets Administration; Regulation 5, 1948.

siberation should be given to all matters that might be brought forward and reasonably given substantial weight in bargaining by persons of ordinary prudence.[12]

All of these definitions (although coined by the particular agencies to fit their specific purposes and programs) follow closely that of the Appraisal Institute quoted on page 13. All of them encompass a "warranted" price; "prudent" or "informed" buyers and sellers; an awareness on the part of the contracting parties as to the present use of the property as well as the uses to which it might be adapted; the presence in the exchange of the element of free and competitive trading. Because these definitions have the sanction of several large Government agencies concerned with real estate, they are deserving of respectful consideration by appraisers. They indicate concepts of real estate value as viewed by important branches of the Government.

Transaction Terms and Market Value

The question is frequently raised by appraisers and others in the real estate and mortgage business as to the effect of transaction terms on market value, and the assertion is sometimes made that variation in the terms of purchase will to some extent control the quantum of dollar value as indexed by sales and purchases in the market. Can this be true?

In the process of answering this question, let us look at the following example:

Assume that we are dealing with two residential properties in two different cities, which we shall call City A and City B. Both of these cities, we shall assume, have the same population history and trend, the same social and economic background, and the same supply and demand ratio. In each city, we have a residential property to appraise. Each of these properties is similarly environed, of the same size, quality, utilitarian capacity, and cost. The only factor of difference in the problem is the local custom concerning terms of sale, which we may assume are 25 per cent down and 5 years to pay the balance in the case of City A, and 10 per cent down and 15 years to pay the balance in the case of City B. Does it now follow that, because of this difference in the terms of sale, the property located in City A may conceivably be valued at $10,000, and the property located in City B at $12,500? The

---

[12] Public Buildings Service, *Real Estate Manual* (Washington, 1948).

answer is, no; value is the same in each case, but the price differs because the price as finally fixed in each case stems from the terms agreed upon.

In support of this reasoning, the reader is asked to reconsider the economist's definition of "value" — the ratio at which goods exchange. If at the moment a bushel of wheat is worth two bushels of corn, value is established when the owner of the bushel of wheat passes it to the owner of the corn and receives the two bushels of corn in exchange. It is implied that all of the corn and all of the wheat changed hands; there is no inference that one trader gave *all* of the wheat and got back the corn in installments.

Theoretically, this is what happens in the real estate transaction. The seller offers a chunk of property; the buyer offers a bag of cash; the exchange is made. But in the practical sense, the buyer, not having all of the money in his possession necessary to complete the transaction on a cash basis, must borrow it, pledging the property as security (for his note, mortgage, land contract, or deed of trust) and agreeing to pay interest on the loan. In effect, therefore, this is a cash transaction; inferentially, the buyer has transferred a bag of cash to the seller and has then borrowed from him the difference between the amount of the initial payment and the balance yet to be paid.

It will be observed that the value figure in this instance is not synonymous with the price paid, for actually the total price paid is value plus the cost of securing the money to complete the cash transaction.[13]

The price paid, therefore, may be of as many different amounts as there are variations in terms. But if value has its genesis and its being in utility, the quantum of value, or the use capacities of the property (to include the amenity content), cannot be made more or less by the terms of sale. From this it may be deduced that the pure concept of "value" in exchange as applied to the commodity of real estate makes the clear-cut implication that, in every case, a cash transaction is involved.

Value in the Absence of a Market

The term "market value" implies the existence of a market. It is a well-known fact, however, that there are segments of the real

---

[13] This evokes the thought that, if every buyer were to include the payment of interest in computing the actual cost, the effect on the real estate market for homes would be paralyzing.

estate cycle in which a market does not exist in the popularly accepted sense of the term.

It has been said that if a parcel of real estate is correctly priced, a buyer will always be found; yet the depression of the thirties records with admirable fidelity the complete absence of buyers for real estate at any price.

And instances may be found currently of those cities that have in the past drawn their sustenance from extractive industries — such as quarrying, mining, and lumber — where, because of the failure of these industries from exhaustion, there is now a vast oversupply of housing that cannot be absorbed regardless of the extent to which prices may be reduced. In the face of that situation, where supply has suffocated demand, does value disappear?

Let us examine two examples in which, at first glance, that may appear to be the case:

1. This is the case of a large apartment house which (including the land on which it sets) cost $1,000,000. Assume that it is being appraised during the depths of a real estate depression, when, because of the depletion of rentals, an operating statement shows that the annual income is $40,000 and the operating expenses (to include fixed charges such as taxes, insurance, and so forth) are $40,000.

Question: Is the value zero?

2. This is the case of a small Midwestern city that in the past existed on one industry — namely, quarrying. Assume that because of changing construction styles, the use for this product has disappeared, and that of 900 residential units within the city, more than 300 are for sale by the occupying owners, with no buyers.

Question: Is the value of these 300 housing units zero?

The answer in each case is that value exists despite the absence of a market. That value is one which is derivable from use. The use value may well be the "anticipated" or the "potential" use, as quoted by the Supreme Court in the famed Brewer decision noted above. Or, it may be that future value which the Supreme Court of the State of Wisconsin had in mind in rendering the following decision in 1933:

In theory, a thing that cannot be sold has no value, and so with a parcel of real estate that is offered for sale on foreclosure. It may be argued that it is worth what purchasers will pay for it, and no more,

and that if the only price offered constitutes but a negligible part of its
theretofore assumed value, it nevertheless represents the value of the
real estate at that time. Such a conclusion is shocking to the conscience
of the court. . . . Certainly the land has value so long as it or the buildings upon it may be used . . . however difficult it may be to translate
this value into terms of dollars. Furthermore, this real estate, which is
suffering from the consequences of a period of readjustment through
which we are now passing, has potential or future value which may
legitimately be taken into account.[14]

It is an admitted fact, of course, that any value thus found will
lie well within the field of opinion, which opinion will stand or fall
on the reputation and experience of the one who utters it.

In conclusion, it seems wise to premise the discussion that follows on the definition of "market value" of the American Institute
of Real Estate Appraisers (see page 13).

The reader may not agree with this definition. If so, let him
stop here and save his time. Nothing could be more futile than
an attempt to prove valuation theory based on the many definitions
of "market value" extant. Nothing could be more confusing than
to launch upon a discussion of appraisal techniques without first
having established a solid basis on which to erect our valuation
theorem. Furthermore, the AIREA definition has been uttered
by one of our higher courts.[15] Thus, we have the assurance that
we are in accord with legal precept. Since appraisal literature is
so liberally barnacled with definitions of "value" and "market
value," we had best chart our course with the aid of a "market
value" definition that bears the approval of the organized appraisal
profession and that has been tested in the courts.

---

[14] Wisc. 489 (1933) 246 N.W. 557. Cf. Northwestern Loan and Trust Co. v.
Bidinger, 276 N.W. 645 (Wisc. 1939).

[15] The Supreme Court of The State of California.

CHAPTER 3

The Appraisal Process

We have said that the appraisal of property is an adventure in economic research. We have agreed that economics is an inexact science, and that the tools of that science, in their application to the present problem, may achieve inexact results. To the amateur appraiser, this may present a dismal outlook until the nature of the problem is clearly understood. The character of the problem is abstract. This is true as it pertains to all properties, but it is particularly true of the single-family home. The valuation conclusion is drawn out of the information that has been gathered, weighed, and judged.

In some types of properties, the method of abstraction is easier than in others. In the appraisal of a large income or investment property, where the test of value lies in the calculation of the net income, the facts are ofttimes fairly easy to discover. Many properties in this class are the subject of good management, which implies accurate accounting practices. Operating statements compiled by reputable accounting, auditing, or management firms are frequently available for the use of the appraiser. This simplifies the problem, both from the standpoint of availability of accurate data as well as method. The profit derivable from use can be readily exposed. Once exposed, it can be transmuted into capital value by the process of mathematics.

The Amenity Factor

The profit derivable from the ownership of a single-family home is less susceptible to accurate analysis. This arises from the fact that an owner-occupied home has no *actual* rental income. "In-

22

come" in the money sense does not come into being until the home passes from the status of owner occupancy to tenant occupancy. Meanwhile it has a theoretical rental income based on a comparison with other similar properties that are in actual rental status. But there exists another kind of income to the homeowner, evanescent in character and elusive of estimation. This is referred to in appraisal practice as the "amenity income" arising out of the conditions of agreeable living. These are the things that make homeownership more enjoyable than any other kind of housing, more pleasurable than tenancy. They consist of such enjoyments as freedom from a harassing landlord, an abundance of sunlight and fresh air, the congeniality of social intercourse, the urge to participate in the political life of the community, the prestige that attaches to the adage of "having a stake in the community," a preferred credit rating, and all those attributes that are inherent in the saying that "a man's home is his castle."

These amenities are difficult to measure in terms of dollars. For example, one individual will pay $10,000 for a home that may have a rental value of $100 per month, while another will pay the same purchase price for a home that may have a rental value of only $75 per month. Why does this happen? The answer lies in the fact that, in the latter instance, the property exerts greater appeal to the homeowner. The amenities are present in greater volume than in the former case. While the theoretical money income is less, the psychic or mental income is greater. In other words, the conditions of agreeable living exist in larger volume in the second case than in the first.

The income from a home, therefore, is of two kinds: (1) the rental it would bring if used for tenant occupancy, and (2) the psychological profit to be derived from the satisfaction that comes with homeownership. The ethereal form of these amenities and their variable factor of value to one owner as against another (often in respect to the same property) make for difficulty in the appraisal of residential property as compared to investment or commercial property when viewed from the concept of income. In fact, it may be claimed that valuations of the single-family home in mid life or late life are the most difficult problems of the appraiser because of his inability to measure the dollar value of the amenities.

The Nature of the Commodity

There is yet another facet of the problem that must be scrutinized. This has to do with the nature of the commodity with which we deal.

In the first place, real estate is immobile. It is fixed and stationary. It cannot be picked up and brought to the store of the merchant (that is, the real estate broker) and placed on his shelves, where all the possible buyers may come to shop for it. As one writer says:

Since there is no common trading place for real estate, the estimation of the market value of real property is not the simple matter that attends the evaluation of listed stocks, bonds and other commodities commonly dealt in in a centralized market. In the stock exchange, buyers and sellers are brought together at a central point. All of the prospective purchasers are informed as to offering prices, the quantities offered and the quantities and prices of recent sales.

These conditions are not true of the real estate market, however, although some semblance of them has been attained in the multiple-listing activities of various real estate boards. When buyers and sellers are brought together at a central point — the stock exchange — there is little danger that the seller will lose the highest price by the action of missing the buyer who would pay it. The seller is dealing with all the prospective purchasers who, collectively, regulate the price that will be paid. With real estate, unfortunately, there is little certainty of finding the purchaser who would pay the highest price. For this reason the market value of real estate is variable, within limits, owing to the absence of the balancing influence of such a focal point.[1]

This characteristic of immobility creates a market limited by the number of possible buyers who may see and be attracted by the newspaper advertisements concerning it, and the number of possible purchasers who may be prevailed upon by the broker to visit the property and examine it.

Second, single-family homes in the mass are not manufactured to one standard specification. There is no standardization of the product. We cannot think of parcels of real estate as packages of sugar on the shelf of the grocer or as automobiles rolling off the assembly line. We are dealing with a commodity that is never alike in any two instances. Fundamentally, it is dissimilar as to location because no two parcels of real estate are located alike. Land is affixed to the earth; hence exact similarity in any two parcels could not exist unless one were superimposed on the

---

[1] George L. Schmutz, *Condemnation Appraiser's Handbook* (New York, Prentice-Hall, Inc., 1949), Ch. I, p. 4.

other. We may conclude, therefore, that "similar" properties do not in fact exist.

These two characteristics, immobility and dissimilarity, argue for an appraisal process that will explore all the possible fields of information and an appraiser who will approach the problem with an open mind and a willingness to use all the tools at his command. They negate the preachment that there is no such thing as an organized process and that the appraisal of property results from the kindergarten method of matching market prices. Market prices must indeed be matched in the exploration of the market approach, but fortunately this is not the only tool to be used; if it were, how, then, could we appraise real estate during that phase of the market cycle when there is no "market" and when there is more demand for expert appraisals than during the boom period?

The Method of Production

The new automobile, rolling off the sales floor for the first time in all its sleek beauty, was born on the draughting board of the engineer. The new home, glistening in the sun with shining paint and well-tailored facade, was born on the drawing table of the architect. From a simple line sketch, there evolved a master scale drawing; approval of the design was followed by the assembly of materials; tools in the hands of skilled workmen fashioned all of the component parts into the finished product. All this started with a well-conceived plan.

We are about to fashion an appraisal of a property. Our datum point is the same as that of the automobile manufacturer or the builder of a home — namely, the plan. In the building of an appraisal, there must be a well-planned continuity — a carefully plotted survey and investigation — necessary in gathering the materials to be tooled into the finished product. In shaping the appraisal, the same ingredients are involved as in the manufacture of the house or the automobile.

1. The working plan
2. The materials
3. The tools
4. The labor

The working plan. The process to be used must represent a planned continuity of action. There must be a definitely, logically routed itinerary of investigation. This calls for intelligent planning — for the delineation of a series of successive steps that will lead toward a sound conclusion of estimated value. These steps are shown in the chart in Figure 1.

In step 1, the problem is defined. Its location is fixed by street address, as well as by legal description, in order to avoid mistake or misunderstanding as to what is actually being appraised. The *type* of property or class of usage into which it falls is also stated, and the *purpose* of the appraisal is made known for reasons previously stated.

Step 2 involves a preliminary approach to the problem. This may require a visit to the property and the neighborhood for the purpose of determining the character of each. The present and potential uses are observed and studied, and a tentative selection is made of the technique or approach that appears best to fit the problem. The information plant of the appraiser may contain ample comparative factual data as to the neighborhood and the properties similar to the one under appraisal, in which case the preliminary visit is unnecessary.

The assembly of the data commences with step 3. Actual field work has now begun. All of the factual information pertaining to the real estate economy of the city and the neighborhood, as well as those data inherent in the subject property, are gleaned from all possible sources — from survey and investigation in the field; from comparative and pertinent records in the files of the appraiser.

Once assembled, these data are brought together on the appraiser's desk in step 4 for purposes of analysis and classification — analysis as to the extent to which they relate to the problem in hand, their pertinency to the property study before him; classification in respect to their relation to each of the three approaches to value estimation. Thus, certain data will be classified as market data, such as:

1.   Recent sales and offerings of comparable properties
2.   Delay factor involved in consummating such sales (or length of time the offerings were exposed to the market)
3.   Terms of sale (as an indicator of the difference between "price" and "value")
4.   Vacancy ratio
5.   Buyer and seller motives (if discoverable)
6.   Occupancy and use maps of the particular area

7. Reports of interviews with owners, brokers, mortgage lenders, and other appraisers

Other data will be classified as relating to the cost approach, such as:

1. The comparative costs of land
2. The comparative costs of buildings
3. The estimate of depreciation

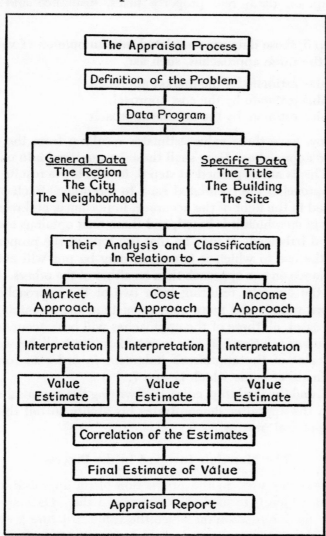

Figure 1

Still other data will relate to the income approach, such as:

1. A survey of current rental levels
2. Analysis of the trend of past and future rents
3. Analysis of the ratio between the supply and demand for rental housing
4. Comparison between the rents being paid and sales prices (as an index to the rate of capitalization)
5. Expense data; real property taxes, insurance and maintenance

In step 5, these data are translated into an opinion of value by each of the three approaches, such as:

1. Value estimate by the market approach
2. Value estimate by the cost approach
3. Value estimate by the income approach

We now have three value estimates resulting from the use of the three approaches. How shall these be rendered into one estimate? This is accomplished in step 6, in which the results of the three approaches are correlated each to the other. Each opinion is weighed in the light of the accuracy, importance, and relevancy of the data on which it is based, and these final opinions are compared and balanced. It may be that the type of the property, its age, or the use to which it is now or may be put will evidence more reliance on one approach than on either of the others. It may be that the opinions resulting from two of the approaches will offer more weight and more conviction than the remaining one. In some cases, all three of the approaches will bear accurately on the valuation solution. In any event, they must all be weighed in the scales of the appraiser's judgment in order to form the final estimate of value which is step 7.

Step 8, and the final step, consists of writing the appraisal report, in which the appraiser demonstrates his ability to tell the story of the appraisal process.

The Materials Involved in the Process

The materials used in the production of an appraisal are the data from which is formed the opinion of value. Data are facts. They are the information on which the value structure is erected.

In the data program, a wide field is investigated. Because of the inexact nature of the appraisal process, we cannot tell at the outset of the problem how much information we shall need nor what avenues must be explored. The sound procedure seems to be first to use the "umbrella" technique, to accumulate all possible information, even that which may appear to be of only slight interest to us, and then to subject this mass of information to analysis in order to sift the relevant from the irrelevant. Thus, all available facts or semifacts that relate to the problem must be gathered.

These data may be divided into two classes: (1) data of general character; and (2) data of specific character. General data usually relate to those facts that surround and influence the property under appraisal, such as the real estate economy of the city and neighborhood, the supply and demand factors, and the public attitude toward property ownership. Specific data have to do with the character of usage of the subject property, its floor plan and layout, cost of replacement, potential rental, and those facts that are inherent in the property itself. Information relative to the title to the property is also classed as specific data.

The Tools Involved in the Process

The tools of the process are the mechanical means used to shape the materials into the finished product — that is, the estimate of value. They are the techniques of the appraisal process usually referred to as the "three approaches." The first of these is called the "market approach." This approach, as its name implies, relies on the data of the market place to prove the value estimate. In its application, the records of sales and offerings of properties that are presumed to be reasonably similar to the property under appraisal are examined, and from this process of matching and comparing transactions in the market, an estimate of value is deduced. This is often spoken of as value by the purchasing public.

The second of these approaches is called the "cost approach." While cost is not value, it is an element of value. In the solution of the appraisal problem, we are interested in the cost of the property as a possible index to the value estimate. Based on the principle of substitution, a property cannot be worth more than that amount necessary to replace it.[2] The cost of duplication is

---

[2] Provided the substitution can be made without costly delay.

said to be the upper limit of value. In the application of the method, an estimate is made of the cost necessary to reproduce the building. From this, there is deducted the dollar penalty of decreased desirability (depreciation). To that remainder, there is added the present-day demand price of the land, and the result is an estimate of value via the cost approach.

The third of the approaches is that of income. In this method, a study is made of the income stream flowing from the property — the actual rental income in the case of the single-family home occupied by a tenant; the theoretical rental income *plus* the amenity income in the case of the home occupied by the owner. The method compares the value of the flow of services from the property under appraisal to that of the "ideal" property in the process of measuring the present and future income stream. By the mathematics of capitalization, this income is translated into capital value, and a third value estimate is produced.

The variable application. We are given three tools with which to measure value. All should be used. This does not mean that all can be used with equal facility. Some will fit better than others, depending upon the type of property that is being appraised. Sometimes a preliminary survey of the problem and an examination of the type of property will indicate which of the approaches will require the most exhaustive treatment. Again, this may not be discernible until the data program is well under way. But the appraiser who is a finished technician will exhaust all three approaches in the assembly, analysis, and classification of the data, in the hope of discovering that one or more of these techniques have developed conclusions that give substantiation to the value estimate. The type of property will vary the scope of application, as shown in the following examples:

1. The new residence being appraised as of the completion date of construction where the building on the land represents the highest and best use; an active market with the supply of housing finding quick absorption by owner-occupants in the market place. The indicated approach of greatest reliability: cost.

2. The used residence being appraised at middle age; tenant-occupied; majority of properties in the district in rental status; few sales, many listings, stagnant market. Indicated approach of greatest reliability: income.

3. A small estate, consisting of several acres of land and a residence of twenty-five rooms, with caretaker's lodge, guest cottage, swimming pool, stables, and other outbuildings, being appraised at middle age; an overstuffed market with many offerings and few sales; many like properties rented at varying figures, depending upon what desperate (and unwilling) owners can get — in short, a tenants' market. Indicated approach of greatest reliability: market.

In these examples, the fact that one approach indicated a more reliable set of conclusions than either of the others was not discovered until all three had been explored. All should be explored in the appraisal process to the point of correlating each to the others in order to determine which set of facts will best support the value estimate.

The interdependence of the techniques. The necessity for the thoroughgoing use of all the tools of the process is also emphasized by the nature of the tools themselves. Each is to some degree dependent on the other. Seldom is it possible to use one alone, to the exclusion of the others. Each has its advantages as well as its limitations, its weaknesses as well as its strong points. Thus, the cost approach is to some extent dependent on the market approach, on the theory that the cost (of a new residential property) is to some extent indicative of the value that will be placed on it by the public. The income approach is to some extent dependent on the cost approach on the ground that there will always exist, in the valuation of residential property, a relationship between cost and income. All through the appraisal process, there is revealed the interdependence of these three techniques. They lean on each other, and as a consequence, the appraiser must of necessity investigate all three in his approach to value.

The Quantum Value of Experience

If, in the manufacture of a motorcar or a house, we were to take the materials and the tools and place them in the hands of an inexperienced workman whose only background consisted of having read a book on the subject, the result would be technical pandemonium.

So it is with the appraisal process. The classroom cannot turn out the finished technician. A well-rounded theoretical background is essential, but even more essential is the background of experience. This is true because the housing industry has long been characterized by a lack of statistical control. Except in small communities and in some states where statutory regulations require the recording of all transfers of property, the figures pertaining to production, in ratio to consumption, are rarely known. The volume of construction of new family units can usually be ascertained from the city engineer or other municipal officer who has authority to issue building permits. This provides us with information as to the number of new units being offered in the market.

The picture is different, however, as it affects the volume of consumption, for, with the exception of statistics that reveal the number of mortgages recorded, there is no central recording agency that gathers information reflecting *all* the purchases of new residential property.[3]

In the case of used housing, the problem is even more difficult. There is no central agency that can be depended upon to keep the industry informed of the current relation between supply and demand. Occasional surveys are made by local institutions or by government agencies active in the field of housing. Aside from these, the industry is sadly lacking in that type of statistical information which records the current volume of used housing in the market and the number of units being currently withdrawn by purchase.

In the large urban center, there is almost a complete lack of centralized statistical information affecting the mortality of districts. Residential neighborhoods are born; they grow to economic maturity; they undergo a succession of declining uses, from good to fair, from fair to poor, and from poor to downright bad; and then they die. What is this life span? Obviously, it varies according to the economic complexion of the city itself. In those cities that are nurtured by a stable economy, the life span is long. In those cities where, because of the peculiarity of the industrial background, there is a high degree of economic instability, the life span is short. But the devices for recording this information and keeping it up to date are meager in the extreme.

This lack of compiled data as to supply and demand and as to

---

[3] Except in those few cities and states where there are statutory control and recordization of all real estate transfers, or private firms that supply these statistics.

the age characteristics of districts and neighborhoods places a premium on the practical experience of the appraiser. He usually records in some fashion the vital statistics pertaining to the commodity of real estate for his own community. Daily work at his specialized task will in time develop an information plant of incalculable value, and the study of this information will enable him to understand the present scene and to interpret its meaning in reference to the present appraisal problem. With all due respect to the efficacy of the tools of the appraisal process, there is no instrument that can supplant an ample experience in the field of valuation practice.

The Qualitative Value of Judgment

A well-worn axiom states that the appraisal is no more accurate than the experience of the appraiser is great and his judgment sound. What is this thing called "judgment"? Generally, we think of it as "taste" or "discrimination." The latter synonym connotes with more precision what we require as a control on the entire appraisal process. "Discrimination" implies an ability to sort the good from the bad, the relevant from the irrelevant.

In making an appraisal, we deal with two kinds of data: factual and inferential. The size of a building and the number of cubic feet within it are factual data. The appraiser's estimates of the cost at which it may be reproduced are inferential data and are based on a comparison with costs of similar buildings.

The information that residential districts similar to the one under appraisal have an optimum use life of twenty-five years is a fact; the conclusion that the district in which the appraisal is being made will have a life span of the same length is inferential. The movement of a retail district toward the district in which the subject property is located is a fact; the conclusion that, within a certain period of time, it will reach out and enfold the property under appraisal is inferential.

Certain facts point with definite accuracy at that which is so; others only hint at their application. It is in the interpretation of these inferential data that the appraiser's sense of discrimination is brought into play. Here judgment is brought to bear as a curb on wishful thinking.

The judgment is for the greater part employed in throwing stumbling blocks in the way of imagination, in dissipating the scenes of its enchantment and in tying us down to the disagreeable yoke of our reason.[4]

The difference between the finished appraisal technician and the "saw-and-hatchet" apprentice lies in this delicate quality of cool, dispassionate discrimination that is schooled to revere the basic and to discard the unimportant.

The appraiser's judgment, sharpened and tempered in the school of experience, helps him to avoid the pitfalls which entrap the neophyte, who, intrigued by the ingeniousness of the tools at his command, relies upon them utterly, letting them lead him where they may. Not so, however, the seasoned technician. Intriguing as are the mathematics of the valuation process, and despite his ability to use them accurately, always he sees ahead of him the *reasonable answer* to the problem. The ability to see this reasonable answer reflects the impact of his judgment on the appraisal process.

The type of judgment needed in the appraisal process is not learned in the classroom. Nor can it be learned from books. It comes with a well-rounded career in the field of real estate valuation. It is the recorded result of trial and error and the corrective measures taken to avoid repetitious mistakes. It is the means used to weigh all of the data in the scales of experience and courageously to report the result.

The appraisal plan may be well conceived; the materials may be ample in amount and of good quality; the tools may be instruments of the finest precision; the quantum of experience may be vast. But all of these are of no avail in helping to solve the valuation problem in the absence of good judgment. Of all the ingredients, this one is priceless!

In conclusion, the appraisal process is a method of producing an estimate of value. It proceeds with a definite scheme. The finished product results from the transmutation of raw materials into finished goods. There must be: (1) the plan — the appraiser's blueprint showing the work he is to perform; (2) the materials of the process — namely, the wealth of data that is accumulated, analyzed, classified, and interpreted; (3) the tools of the process — namely, the three techniques of cost approach, market approach,

---

[4] Edmund Burke, *"Taste," The Harvard Classics* (New York, P. F. Collier and Son, 1909).

and income approach, all of which are given exhaustive treatment; and (4) the skilled mental labor necessary to fuse these ingredients.

If the plan has been carefully followed; if the necessary volume of materials has been diligently accumulated, carefully sorted, and intelligently fitted into the pattern; if the tools have been skillfully used; and if there has been a sufficient application of expert labor in the process — then the result should be an estimate of value that is well fashioned, durable, and invulnerable.

CHAPTER 4

The Data Program

*Knowledge is of two kinds; we know a subject ourselves or
we know where we can find information upon it.*

SAMUEL JOHNSON

Reference to Figure 1, Chapter 3, page 27, shows that we are
now at step 3 in the appraisal process. The materials are about to
be gathered. What are they? They are the facts that form the
premises on which the opinion of value is constructed.

Assembling the Materials

The necessity for an adequate volume of informative data in
the appraisal process is obvious. One writer has said:

It has been said that the greatest failure of mankind is in arriving at
a conclusion without first validating the premise upon which the conclusion is based; and that this failure is more pronounced in those having a knowledge of mathematics than in those lacking such knowledge.
That this accusation is warranted is hardly open to dispute. The crying
need of the times is greater attention to the validation of premises (such
as income and expense) and to the analysis of data, and less attention
to mathematical processes until our reasoning reaches its proper level.[1]

Value is not a fact. Neither are the premises upon which the
value opinion is erected. However, the basis from which the
premises are formed must be — and is — factual. We say that the
home under appraisal is worth a certain sum of money because
similar houses have sold in the market place for a like sum or because they have like costs or like rentals. The information as to
costs, selling prices, and rentals of the similar houses is factual.
That we know; the evidence is conclusive. The costs represent

---

[1] Schmutz, *op. cit.*

actual expenditures; the sales have actually been made and are of record; the rentals are actually being received. But from this point on, the various premises as to cost, market, and income evolve as an implication of value. This, while developing finally as an opinion, must derive from the evidence of probability supplied by a vast fund of facts in the form of appraisal data.

Volume required. How much of this is necessary? Enough at least to support the final conclusion. And the requirement is one, not of quantity, but of quality. The fund of available information, particularly during an active real estate market, is practically inexhaustible. What we must aim at, however, is a selection of facts that bear on the problem. At the outset, we cannot tell which data are relevant and which are not. So we take no chances. We collect all data that even hint at a relationship to the problem.

Sources. Where shall we go to secure this information? From the owners of property; from residents of the district in which the subject property is located [2]; from real estate brokers who handle and sell comparable properties; from mortgage lending institutions; from the mortgage departments of banks; from real estate boards; from the local chapters of appraisal societies; from municipal and state bureaus responsible for the recording of facts pertaining to real estate transfers; from public libraries; from chambers of commerce; from the agencies of the Federal Government active in the field of housing.

The most reliable type of "information plant," however, is the appraiser's own, built up from the transactions that have passed through his hands over a long period. There is available in the files of real estate brokers, banks, insurance companies, and savings and loan institutions a vast fund of information that, once properly organized and classified, provides an efficient and valuable appraisal laboratory. The value of this kind of statistical storehouse lies in its specific application to the problem of the particular lender or appraiser, for it furnishes a large volume of exact information in the particular field in which the appraiser or the institution specializes.

The classifications. How shall we classify these data? Into two broad general classifications first: (1) data of general ap-

---

[2] The author can remember but few instances where he failed to get information by the simple process of asking for it and stating the reasons why he wanted it.

plication; and (2) data of specific application. The general data have to do with facts and information related to the nation, the region, the metropolitan area surrounding the city, the city itself, and the neighborhood. Data of specific application have to do with the building and the site on which it stands.

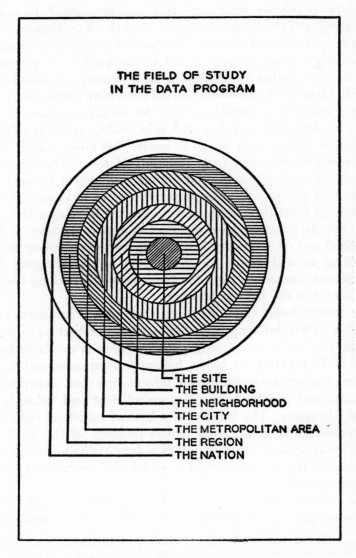

THE FIELD OF STUDY
IN THE DATA PROGRAM

THE SITE
THE BUILDING
THE NEIGHBORHOOD
THE CITY
THE METROPOLITAN AREA
THE REGION
THE NATION

Figure 2

Outline of the Program

While the examination and study of the property under appraisal is the most interesting element in the valuation problem, a great many other facets of the situation must be explored before we get down to the core of the matter. The appraiser examines the setting as well as the jewel before putting the price tag on the merchandise. The factors surrounding and influencing the property must be subjected to detailed analysis. These environmental characteristics, as will be shown, make — or destroy — value. The area of investigation, therefore, extends inward from the outermost fringe of the research area to the radix. (See Figure 2, page 38.)

The field of study, that must be explored in any intelligent appraisal operation is detailed in the following outline of a data program:

General Data

A. The nation
  1. Population growth, present and anticipated
  2. Economic background
  3. Trade and commerce; balance of trade
  4. Degree of economic independence
  5. Political complexion and trends, right or left
  6. Fiscal policies
    a. Taxation
    b. National debt
  7. Attitude toward rights of private ownership of property
  8. Participation in the field of housing
    a. Insurance of mortgages
    b. Slum clearance
    c. "Subsidized" housing

B. The region
  1. Population growth
  2. Economic background
  3. Economic relationship to the city
    a. Raw materials
    b. Agricultural production
    c. Industry and employment
    d. Scope of the trading area
C. The metropolitan area
  1. Satellite communities
  2. Number and size
  3. Population growth, present and anticipated

    4. Economic background
    5. Accessibility

D. The city
    1. Its origin
    2. Population growth, present and anticipated; trend of marriages
    3. Economic pattern
    4. Economic trends
    5. Nature of the inhabitants
        a. Social
        b. Racial
        c. National
    6. Geographic pattern
    7. Government policy
        a. Taxation
        b. Per capita debt
    8. Transportation facilities
    9. Public utilities, adequacy and cost
  10. Recreational and cultural facilities
  11. History of neighborhood shifts; trends
  12. History of the movement of retail districts; trends
  13. Governmental control of land usage
  14. Governmental attitude toward subsidized housing

E. The neighborhood
    1. Physical
        a. Topography
        b. Drainage
        c. Area
        d. Contour
        e. Advantages
        f. Limitations
    2. Utilization of land
        a. Type of improvements
        b. Percentage of each type of improvement
        c. Extent and trend of utilization
        d. Zoning and other types of control
        e. Street pattern
        f. Transportation
        g. Sufficiency of retail stores
        h. Adequacy of recreation centers, parks, etc.
        i. Nature of the terrain
            (1) Rolling or flat
            (2) Wooded
            (3) Subsoil
            (4) Drainage
            (5) Water
            (6) Physical barriers

3. Social factors
    a. Historical background of people — their habits, culture, and institutions
    b. Nationality of people; percentage of each and trends
    c. Special characteristics of people
    d. Civic pride of residents
    e. Cultural institutions
        (1) Schools
        (2) Libraries
        (3) Educational institutions
        (4) Churches (various denominations)
    f. Absence or presence of vice
    g. Nature of local government and politics
    h. Marriages and divorces; trends
    i. Average family size
    j. School enrollment
    k. Attitude toward government and law enforcement
4. Economic factors
    a. Occupation of people by percentages
    b. Wage levels by classes or occupations; purchasing power
    c. Rent levels (minimum rents and maximum rents)
    d. Stability of income
    e. Unemployment
    f. Degree of relief and charity requirements
    g. Tax levels
        (1) Real estate; trend
        (2) Other taxes; trend
        (3) Delinquencies
    h. Public and private debt load; trend
    i. Sales records and asking prices
    j. Vacancy data
    k. Zoning and other restrictions
    l. New building in the area; trend
    m. Building material and labor costs; trends
    n. Mortgage money and foreclosures
    o. Business failures
5. Mortgagee's neighborhood rating; contemplated and assured public improvements
6. Neighborhood depreciation
    a. Physical deterioration
    b. Functional obsolescence
    c. Economic obsolescence
7. General
    a. Number of comparable houses in the neighborhood
    b. Number of comparable houses vacant in the neighborhood

  c. Number of comparable houses sold last year in the neighborhood

  d. Range of prices paid for purchase of comparable houses in the neighborhood last year

  e. Number of comparable houses built in the neighborhood last year; costs

  f. Number of better houses built last year; costs

  g. Number of cheaper houses built last year; costs

  h. Number of comparable houses now for sale and asking prices

  i. Number of better houses now for sale and asking prices

  j. Number of cheaper houses now for sale and asking prices

  k. Is the house now rented and at what rental?

  l. If not rented, what rent would it command?

  m. Monthly rental asked

   (1) For comparable houses

   (2) For better houses

   (3) For cheaper houses

  n. Distance to

   (1) Neighborhood shopping center

   (2) Regional shopping center

   (3) Public or parochial grade school

   (4) Public or parochial high school

   (5) Protestant or Catholic church, or synagogue

   (6) Movie

   (7) Car or bus line, and frequency of schedules

   (8) Through auto highway

   (9) Downtown shopping district, in miles and minutes

  o. Streetcar or bus fare to downtown shopping district

Specific Data

A. Title data

 1. Nature of the estate

  a. Fee simple

  b. Leasehold

  c. Life estate

  d. Mortgagor's or vendee's equity

 2. Legal description

  a. By lot number and name of subdivision

  b. By metes and bounds

  c. By real estate atlas identification

 3. Public restrictions

  a. Zoning

  b. Building codes

  c. Fire ordinances

4. Private restrictions
    a. As imposed by the deed to the land
        (1) Restrictive use
        (2) Restrictive design
        (3) Restrictive cost
    b. Reservations and easements

B. The building
  1. General
    a. Floor plan
    b. Date of erection
    c. Date additions were erected
    d. Base dimensions
    e. Cubical or square foot content
    f. Direction the house faces
    g. Photographs
  2. Architecture and design
    a. Attached or detached
    b. Type
    c. Modern or obsolete
    d. Intelligent placement
    e. Conformity of design
    f. Ample privacy from street
    g. Ample privacy from adjacent houses
    h. Conformity of size
    i. Front and/or side entrance
    j. Garage, built in or detached
  3. Utilities
    a. City water
    b. Private water
    c. Gas
    d. Electricity
    e. Telephone
    f. Garbage and ash removal
    g. Sewerage
    h. Distance to fireplug
    i. Police protection
  4. Excavation and foundations
    a. Basement depth
    b. Size of area excavated
    c. Load-bearing quality of soil
    d. Depth of foundations and footings
    e. Height of foundation wall above grade
    f. Strength of the foundation materials
    g. Condition of foundation walls
    h. Dimensions of the footings
    i. Kinds of sills

  j. Underpinning
  k. Joists
    (1) Dimensions
    (2) Distance between centers
    (3) Bridging
  l. Set of building on foundations
  m. Subflooring construction, first floor
  n. Structural soundness of load-bearing members
    (1) Rot
    (2) Sagging
    (3) Settling
    (4) Termites
  o. Basement floor, quality and thickness
  p. Condition of soil beneath floor
  q. Drain tile, location and adequacy
5. Exterior walls
  a. Height in feet
  b. Thickness in inches
  c. Construction materials
  d. Insulation
  e. Paint
  f. Chimneys, logical placement
6. Roof
  a. Dimensions of
    (1) Rafters
    (2) Jack rafters
    (3) Trusses
    (4) Bracing
  b. Gables; dormers and hips
  c. Valleys
  d. Gutters and conductors
  e. Eaves projection
  f. Type
  g. Construction
  h. Shingles
  i. Composition
  j. Insulation
  k. Age
  l. Condition
7. Porches
  a. Front
    (1) Size
    (2) Exposure
    (3) Drainage
    (4) Construction
    (5) Open or glass-enclosed
    (6) Heated

   b. Rear
         (1) Size
         (2) Exposure
         (3) Drainage
         (4) Construction
         (5) Open or enclosed
         (6) Heated
8. Plumbing
      a. Type
      b. Color
      c. Water closets
      d. Lavatories
      e. Bathtubs
      f. Stall showers
      g. Combination tub-shower
      h. Kitchen sink
      i. Laundry tubs
      j. Clothes dryer
      k. Water heater
      l. Softener
     m. Cistern
      n. Water pump
      o. Connection with sewer or cesspool
      p. Sewage disposal efficiency
      q. Piping, condition and material
      r. Capacity of hot water heater
      s. Age of hot water heater
      t. Condition of valves
      u. Fittings, styles and material
9. Heating
      a. Type; conventional or radiant
      b. Fireplaces
      c. Radiators and grilles
      d. Oil burner
      e. Gas burner
      f. Coal burner
      g. Mechanical stoker
      h. Thermostatic control
      i. Hydrostatic control
      j. Furnace
         (1) Make
         (2) Age
         (3) Condition
      k. Pipes
         (1) Concealed and visible
         (2) Insulated
         (3) Condition

       l. Adequacy of heating system

      m. Ratio of B.T.U. loss

10. Cooling

    a. Refrigerated air system

        (1) Type

        (2) Ice capacity

        (3) Power plant

    b. Exhaust system

        (1) Location of fan

        (2) Size of fan

        (3) Intake grille

        (4) Size and location

        (5) Switches

11. Staircases

    a. Front

    b. Rear

    c. Basement

    d. Attic

12. Built-in features and equipment

    a. Breakfast bar

    b. Kitchen cabinets

    c. Ironing board cabinet

    d. China cabinet

    e. Medicine cabinet

    f. Buffet

    g. Bookcases

    h. Window seat

    i. Clothes chute

    j. Incinerator

    k. Garbage disposal

    l. Dishwasher

    m. Kitchen ventilation

    n. Screens

    o. Storm sash

    p. Shutters

    q. Awnings

   * r. Stove

   * s. Refrigerator

   * t. Washing machine

   * u. Clothes dryer

13. Room layout

    a. Convenience of floor plan

    b. Privacy

    c. Roominess

    d. Livability

* Part of the standard equipment in some urban areas.

14. Analysis of basement
    a. Dimensions
    b. Entrances
    c. Floor
    d. Windows
    e. Doors
    f. Rooms and room sizes
        (1) Furnace room
        (2) Store room
        (3) Recreation room
        (4) Laundry room
        (5) Fuel room
        (6) Workshop
        (7) Bedroom; bath; lavatory
        (8) Garage
        (9) Adequacy
        (10) Convenience of arrangement
    g. Artificial lighting
        (1) Adequacy
        (2) Convenience of switches
    h. Walls
        (1) Material
        (2) Finish
        (3) Condition
        (4) Dry or damp
    i. Ceiling
        (1) Height
        (2) Material
        (3) Finish
        (4) Condition
    j. Ventilation
15. Analysis of first floor
    a. Rooms and room sizes
        (1) Entrance hall
        (2) Living room
        (3) Kitchen
        (4) Counter space
        (5) Library or den
        (6) Sun room
        (7) Lavatory
        (8) Hallways
        (9) Dining room
        (10) Breakfast nook
        (11) Music room
        (12) Bathroom
        (13) Powder room
        (14) Bedrooms

   (15) Closets
  b. Layout
   (1) Convenience
   (2) Attractiveness
   (3) Adequacy
16. Check each room for
  a. Ceiling
   (1) Height
   (2) Finish
   (3) Condition
  b. Floors
   (1) Insulated
   (2) Finish
   (3) Condition
   (4) Materials
  c. Windows
   (1) Ratio of glass area to floor area
   (2) "Thermo-pane"
   (3) Weatherstripped
   (4) Location
   (5) Views or outlook
   (6) Condition
  d. Doors
   (1) Adequacy
   (2) Location
   (3) Material
   (4) Hardware
   (5) Condition
  e. Walls
   (1) Material
   (2) Finish
   (3) Insulation
   (4) Adequate wall space; furniture placement
   (5) Condition
  f. Fixtures
   (1) Adequacy
   (2) Convenience
   (3) Quality
   (4) Condition
  g. Artificial lighting
   (1) Adequacy
   (2) Quality of fixtures
   (3) Condition
   (4) Convenience of switches
   (5) Switches; standard toggle or mercury
   (6) Convenience of outlets; multitelephone; radio and television

(7) Obsolete or modern
　h. Heating
　　　(1) Adequacy
　　　(2) Radiators or radiant piping
　　　(3) Location
　　　(4) Condition
　i. Ventilation
　j. Air conditioning
　　　(1) Type
　　　(2) Adequacy
　　　(3) Condition
17. Analysis of attic
　a. Dimensions
　b. Access
　c. Floor
　　　(1) Finish
　　　(2) Insulation
　　　(3) Condition
　　　(4) Expansion potential
　d. Ceiling
　　　(1) Height
　　　(2) Finish
　　　(3) Insulation
　　　(4) Condition
　e. Walls
　　　(1) Finish
　　　(2) Insulation
　　　(3) Condition
　f. Windows
　g. Closets
18. Analysis of garage
　a. Location
　　　(1) In house
　　　(2) Detached
　　　(3) Convenience of ingress and egress
　b. If detached
　　　(1) Roof
　　　(2) Position on lot
　　　(3) Distance from house
　　　(4) Convenience of outlet; turning space
　c. Walls
　　　(1) Material
　　　(2) Height
　　　(3) Outside finish
　　　(4) Inside finish
　d. Ceiling
　　　(1) Insulation

           (2) Height
           (3) Condition
    e. Floor
        (1) Size
        (2) Drainage
        (3) Kind
        (4) Condition
        (5) Above, level with, or below grade
    f. Doors
        (1) Kind; conventional; overhead; accordion
        (2) Size
        (3) Hardware
        (4) Condition
    g. Water
    h. Heat
    i. Cabinets
    j. Workbench
    k. Windows
    l. Lighting
    m. Special features; automatic electric lighting and door-opening

19. Cost data
    a. Original cost of the improvements
    b. Estimated cost, new, today
    c. Estimated cost of rehabilitation and remodeling

C. Analysis of the lot
1. Dimensions in feet
2. Shape
3. Distance from front lot line to front wall
4. Distance from rear lot line to rear wall
5. Distance from right lot line to right wall
6. Distance from left lot line to left wall
7. Width of parkway between curb and sidewalk
8. Width of sidewalk
9. Width of street
10. Width of alley
11. Location in block
12. Character of soil
13. Character of subsoil
14. Elevation above or below street level
15. Elevation above or below alley level
16. Building restrictions, tenure thereof
17. Setback line
18. Basements
19. Street paving
20. Alley paving

21. Sidewalks on the lot
22. Sidewalks adjacent to the lot
23. Side drive
24. Riparian rights
25. Topography, level or sloping
26. Shrubbery and trees
27. Subsidence
28. Deed restrictions
29. Zoning restrictions
30. Fences, garden, and lawn

The above program appears to be a formidable one; yet no conclusion as to the value of a single-family home may be considered reliable unless these facts have been explored and recorded. Obviously, all of them will not be included in the appraisal report. Data pertaining to the nation, the region, and the metropolitan area will have been investigated by the appraiser or will be known to him. They will bear on his conclusions, although they may not be written into the report. Likewise, in the case of valuations made for local institutions, data pertaining to the city may not appear in the report, but they will be known to the appraiser and will have assisted him in arriving at his estimate of value.[3]

It is not implied here that all of these data are gathered freshly for each appraisal operation. The general data may be used time and again, provided they are kept up to date. They are "stock" information and may be used in repeated operations. The specific data, however, are always a new study, for they apply to the land and building under investigation.

This outline, then, is not a program that must be instituted and carried out for each separate appraisal operation. Rather, it is a catalogue of the laboratory equipment that the appraiser should have in the form of materials, in order that his task may be executed with skill and precision.

---

[3] It is not to be expected that an appraiser, employed by the same local institution in repeated instances, will burden his appraisal report with voluminous city data. Conversely, where the appraiser acts for some client remote from the location under appraisal, the report will contain adequate information as to the political, social, and economic trends pertaining to that particular city on the grounds that the client is not familiar with and needs this information to assist his judgment in making a management decision.

CHAPTER 5

National and Regional Influences on Values

It may seem odd to state that accurate valuation of residential property depends to some extent on the appraiser's knowledge of national affairs. It may seem even more odd to state that the skilled appraiser should be accurately informed on matters pertaining to world politics. Yet a casual study of these statements will show how true they are.

The Nation

Political background. The private ownership of property is an inherent right of free, democratic government. The totalitarian state is a definite threat to this ideology. Totalitarianism and its kindred "isms" teach that the State is more important than the individual; it prescribes "that men must be divided into two classes: the omnipotent god-like dictator on the one hand and the masses which must surrender volition and reasoning in order to become mere chessmen in the plans of the dictator." [1]

This means the abolition of individual rights, and with it the right to own real estate. "Totalitarianism" and "*kommandieren*" abide in the same political dictionary. The latter is the indispensable tool of the former, used to enrich the coffers of the State at the expense of the individual. The pages of current history are replete with records of confiscation of private property in those nations that have junked the democratic form of government for one of the various nebulous forms of state capitalism.

Were we to live under this form of government, the valuation

---

[1] Von Mises, *op. cit.*

of property as an important phase of real estate operations would disappear, as indeed would all commerce having to do with the financing, buying, selling, and management of that commodity as a form of private business enterprise. Because the recent past has seen the development of this new (at least in its modern guise) political philosophy, the student of real estate value is compelled to study these world movements in their effect on our national thinking. The price level of real estate in the United States reflects not only what buyers are willing to pay; it reflects as well the history of a kind of government that still believes in individual enterprise, in the right of the private ownership of property, both real and personal, and in an expressed willingness by the Government to defend and perpetuate these rights. This is the hidden increment in every real estate purchase, and it is so commonplace as to command no attention.

The political complexion of the nation must engage the attention of the valuation expert. The actions of the legislative branch of the Government must be followed with respect to the laws it may enact affecting ownership. The expressed attitude of the executive branch must be followed as to the extent to which it may influence Congress toward the making or unmaking of laws that affect the ownership of real estate. The judicial branch must be observed in its interpretation of the laws that affect the interest of the property owner. And the whole must be watched for any sign of a swing away from a first principle of democracy in government — namely, the right of the individual to own his own home. When that principle ceases to exist, the material between these covers will be of no value to anyone.

The population curve. In the year 1790, there resided within the United States 3,929,000 persons. In the year 1950, the national population totaled 154,233,000.[2]

This extraordinary growth (is) unprecedented in history except possibly for the population increase in China during the sixteenth and seventeenth centuries. . . .[3]

The same period saw an intense urban development. Cities grew and prospered. The demand for urban dwellings (except for periodic lapses in the market cycle) was constantly on the increase.

---

[2] March 1950 Estimate; Bureau of the Census.

[3] Arthur Martin Weimer and Homer Hoyt, *Principles of Urban Real Estate* (New York, The Ronald Press Company, 1939).

This rapid and constant increase in the national population has long been regarded as a reliable instrument in the valuation process, particularly so in the valuation of urban real estate. Until 1950, as revealed by the following chart which indicates per centum increases at each ten-year level, there were evidences that the population growth had slowed down:

Year	Decennial per cent increase
1800	35.1
1810	36.4
1820	33.1
1830	33.5
1840	32.7
1850	36.3
1860	35.4
1870	26.7
1880	26.0
1890	25.5
1900	20.7
1910	21.2
1920	16.2
1930	14.8
1940	7.0
1950	14.9

The 1850-1940 figures indicate that we were headed toward a static population. These figures caused the experts to predict that on or about the year 1960 the nation would stop growing. However, the 1950 census brought a sharp reversal in the forecasts made ten years earlier.[4] It shows that the per centum of increase in population over the year 1940 was 14.9, matching approximately the per centum of increase in 1930 over 1920 and indicating that population increase is again on the march.

This reversal was undoubtedly brought about by a sharp increase in marriages during World War II and immediately thereafter. In 1946 the formation of new families (marriages) reached an unprecedented total of nearly 2,300,000, compared with slightly less than one million in 1932.

There are two basic factors which influence population increase: the formation of new families (as an index to the birth rate) and immigration. These factors should be required study

---

[4] Proving again that prophecy is a dangerous business.

for the appraiser, not only for the nation but also for the city in which he operates. Publications of the Bureau of the Census are readily available to him at small cost. Any prediction of housing necessity must, perforce, be based on an examination of popula- tion trends, and study of the above chart reveals that national trends of the future will not necessarily follow those of the past.

Economic background. The national economy has intimate relation to the value of real property. How does the nation live? Can it sustain itself in times of war or economic stress? The availability of everything necessary to feed, clothe, and house the population — raw materials, agricultural products, textiles, min- erals — and the nation's ability to be self-sufficient, to produce what it needs from within, give stability to the value of real estate.

As an example, it may be claimed that the strength of the British navy bears a direct relation to the values of property within the British Isles. Without a superior armed naval strength capable of preventing an enemy blockade of British ports, cir- cumstances might develop where, because of a shortage of food- stuffs, a palatial English estate might be freely traded for a barrel of flour. As another example, we read that, during the war be- tween the States, the blockade of Southern ports by the Northern navy caused the price of such staple commodities as tea and sugar to soar to several hundred dollars per pound. In these cir- cumstances, the value of property is indexed by the exchange ratio of the bare necessities of life. Thus, it is claimed that the degree of independence inherent in the economic structure of the nation plays an important part in its real estate economy.

Fiscal policies. National financial policies play their part in tipping the scales of value up or down. It is not possible here to give this subject the attention it deserves, but there are two aspects of governmental finance that deserve mention. First, there is the matter of Federal taxes as they affect the prospective homeowner. The type of home that he can afford to own and maintain is proportionate to his income. (Most housing econo- mists agree that he can afford to pay 25 to 30 per cent of his income for shelter.) Federal income taxes are naturally based on his earnings. Thus there exists a per centum relationship be- tween that share of his income which he may expend for housing and that which goes out in Federal taxes. If one of these "agents in consumption" (that is, his liability for taxes) is increased, obviously one of two things must happen: (1) he must increase his income proportionately; or (2) he must decrease his standard of living by decreasing the amount of that share of his income which he spends for housing.

The constantly mounting cost of citizenship in this great country of ours (and the cost is still less in proportion to what we enjoy than anywhere else on earth) claims important attention in our analysis, for it is plain that as national taxes increase, housing standards must decrease.

The second item of interest in this analysis — the national debt — is an offshoot of the first. It is a fact, of course, that the per capita national debt is greater than at any time in history. One school of thought on the subject claims that the country is headed toward national bankruptcy. The opposite school says that one cannot be bankrupted because of a debt owed to oneself, meaning that the national debt arises primarily from defense spending and is evidenced by the obligations owed by the Government in the form of bonds held by its citizens — in short, that the money the Government owes is owed to itself, and not to foreign creditors.

The significance of all this in respect to our investigation has to do with the extent to which the individual citizen may be affected by the possible future increase in taxes necessary to reduce the funded debt of the Government. When and if that happens, the reduction in net consumer incomes resultant from increased taxes will reduce the number of possible home buyers in the market. When demand diminishes, values are affected.

In any event, the fiscal policies of the Federal Government must be subjected to constant study by the appraiser because of their effect on the financial ability of our people to own and maintain their homes.

Government participation in the field of housing. The past two decades have seen the Government enter the housing field in various capacities. Today, its weight and influence are felt in practically every large urban community through the instrumentality of the Federal Housing Administration, the Veterans Administration, and the Public Housing Administration. Because the activities of each of these agencies have a definite bearing on the valuation of all residential properties in the communities in which they operate, their operations must be observed and weighed in respect to their effect on the real estate market.

The Federal Housing Administration. The Federal Housing Administration, set up in 1934, is an underwriting operation designed to insure mortgages on residential properties, thus minimizing the risk to the lender. The principle of mortgage insurance is entirely new and has been readily accepted by lenders, as witness the steady growth of residential construction during the years FHA has been in operation. The significance of its operations to the appraiser is threefold: (1) the currently recorded volume of mortgages accepted for insurance by FHA is a reliable index to the demand for new housing; (2) the extent of its operations tends to "peg" the mortgage interest rate; and (3) the volume of new-house construction currently entering the local market is some index to the resistance created to the sale of used housing.

Let us examine these three points. The first statement is obvious except in so far as a low interest rate may bring about a shift from insured to noninsured mortgages because of a shortage of money in the mortgage market and a consequent demand for higher interest rates than FHA requires. Generally stated, however, an insured mortgage is a *preferred* type of real estate investment and represents a large part of the lending portfolios of large institutions. The demand for insured mortgages, with the exception noted, is therefore an index to the demand factor in the housing market.

The second statement, while not pertinent to the appraisal of single-family homes, does interest the appraiser of multifamily housing (apartments) and commercial, investment real estate. If an insured mortgage at an interest rate of 4¼ per cent is indeed a form of prime real estate investment, this rate is bound to influence all other types of real estate financing, particularly multifamily housing. It may be considered the basis of the rate structure. Any deviation, up or down, from the rate of 4¼ per cent has a bearing on the cost of borrowing for real estate financing.

As to the third statement, the merchandising precept that the more *new* goods sold, the more *used* goods will also be sold is axiomatic, and it has equal application in the field of housing. But the limit of the extent to which used housing can compete with new housing is reached in the long-term purchase contract or mortgage. While it may be fully practicable and financially sound to finance new housing on the basis of mortgage payments extending over a period of twenty-five years, it is doubtful, purely because of its age, if the used house can meet this competition. At the time of purchase, the used house is likely to have lived a substantial share of its useful — or economic — life. The neighborhood in which it is situated has, likewise, lived a substantial share of its useful — or lendable — life. The risks to the investment of mortgage capital are greater.

From an analysis of this condition, we may generalize as follows: the perpetuation of mortgage insurance by FHA with continued low interest rates and long-term financing will tend to accelerate depreciation in used housing of comparable utility, as well as in neighborhoods of comparable attractiveness which have reached construction saturation. Finally, the appraiser of single-family homes would do well to observe closely the operations of FHA in his home community. The volume and trend of its operations are an important weather vane indicating the direction and velocity of the winds of the real estate economy.

The Public Housing Administration is one of three constituents of the Housing and Home Finance Agency established by Reorganization Plan No. 3 of 1947. Its responsibilities cover housing in which the Government has a direct financial interest, either through Federal aid to local bodies or as the owner of Government-built housing. Its responsibilities include five separate housing programs.

U. S. Housing Act program
Subsistence Homestead and Greentowns program
Public War Housing program
Veterans' Re-Use Housing program
Homes Conversion program

The extent to which the Government enters the field of private business in direct competition with the building industry in the construction and operation of low-cost (or as some call it, "subsidized") housing bears directly on the valuation problem. Any time an agency of Government embarking on a program of low-cost housing ignores the principle of a fair return on its investment or functions at a rate of return lower than private business expects and requires, housing values, as we have known them, are apt to be subject to considerable distortion. If and when the Government is found to be in actual competition with the housing industry for tenants or potential homebuyers, the values of residential property are bound to be disturbed. But if low-cost housing is found to be supplying housing needs to the low-income groups where, because of material, labor, and land costs, private business has never been able to supply those same needs, value levels in the remainder market will not be affected.

The Veterans Administration. The loan guaranty program of the Veterans Administration was first authorized by Title III of the Servicemen's Readjustment Act (P.L. 346, 78th Congress) enacted June 22, 1944. Title III authorized the guaranty by the Veterans Administration of loans made to World War II veterans for the purchase, construction, alteration, or improvement of homes, or in connection with farm or business enterprises. The basic purpose of the law was to aid veterans in their postwar readjustment to civilian life by making available to them mortgage financing on liberal equity terms and at low interest costs.

Since the Veterans Administration is another governmental agency that partially insures mortgage loans in volume, it, too, must be the subject of study by the appraiser. Its activities have a definite bearing on the residential real estate economy to much the same extent as the Federal Housing Administration's.

This analysis of data pertaining to the nation should end on the note that the policies of the Government are all-important in their effect on the values of real property. The ownership of wealth in the form of property in this country is no more secure than the avowed and expressed willingness of the State to encourage, perpetuate, and protect these rights.

The Region

The region that surrounds the city — the hinterland — presents a field of study requiring exploration in the data program. Its *population growth* and trend must be subjected to the same type of inquiring analysis as those of the nation and the city. The last decade has seen a considerable shift of people from the rural areas to the cities, brought about by industrial expansion and high wages in the cities as well as by technological advancement in agricultural devices. Less manual labor is required on the farm today than ever before. The surplus of farm labor has drifted into the cities, attracted by "good pay." Moreover, the opportunities for cultural advantages — principally in the field of education — have lured thousands of rural inhabitants to the city. These movements of population between the region and the city demand attention from the student of valuation. They may portend a change in the population status of the city in which the valuation problem lies.

The *economic background* must be accorded intelligent study as to its effect on the ebb or flow of the prosperity of the city within the region. In the case of the commercial or trading center, the scope of the regional trading area and its ability to continue the production of those commodities that sustain the central city bear investigation. In the case of manufacturing cities, the accessibility of raw materials used in the manufacturing process is important in that it indicates the economic stability of the principal city within the region.

Cities sometimes die from natural causes. There is the example of the shipbuilding and munitions cities built during the war years that ceased to exist when the war ended. There are also the examples of the mining and lumber towns that no longer exist because the extractive industries upon which they lived have expired.

The extent to which the subject city depends for its existence on the surrounding area has intimate relation to the appraisal problem. Economically, socially, and politically, the city is an integral part of the regional development, and generally the ebb and flow of the regional economy has a direct effect upon its economic status.

The Metropolitan Area

The satellite communities that hang on the fringe of the large urban area reflect the growth and prosperity of the city whose periphery they compose. As such, they must be subjected to study and their characteristics catalogued in the information plant of the appraiser. These suburban communities may be discussed under two classifications: (1) the noncompetitive suburb; and (2) the competitive suburb.

The noncompetitive suburb. This is the type of suburban community that offers no competition to the city proper because it is not an economic entity in itself. It lives upon and draws its economic sustenance from the urban area to which it attaches. Only a small percentage of its inhabitants are supported by the local community. The majority earns and spends a large part of its income in the large near-by city. These are, in effect, "dormitory" cities; the largest portion of their population comes here to sleep. Economically and socially, they belong to the major city.

This type of community is important to the city and to its growth. As cities increase in size, they become less desirable as a place in which to live. Overcrowding of residential areas, overloading of transportation facilities, crowded schools, and the noises and nuisances that characterize the large commercial or industrial city urge the homeowner to seek the peace and quiet of the near-by suburb, where he and his family may pursue life, liberty, and happiness "far from the madding crowd." Analysis of these communities — their number, size, growth, and accessibility — is necessary as reflecting the future expansion of the growing megalopolis.

The competitive suburb. This is the type of community that is an economic entity in itself. By virtue of location, transportation facilities, availability of labor markets, and complete retail shopping facilities (including regional branches of the near-by city's principal department stores), the competitive suburb is in active competition with the larger city for population, stores, and factories.

The development of the competitive suburb is a phenomenon of recent years. It is the product of a decentralization movement of urban population, retail trade, and industry. The effect of this movement on the city is more fully discussed in the pages that follow. Suffice it to say here that the competitive suburb, promoting as it does the impetus of decentralization, does more than hint at disturbance of realty values in the near-by large city.

CHAPTER 6

Government Regulations
Affecting Value

A prominent industrialist has been quoted as saying, "Time was when my lawyer was the most important adviser I had. Today it's different. What I need most in my organization, and that person on whom I rely the most is someone who can interpret for me the government regulations which affect my business."

This is undoubtedly true. The change in our economic pattern as a result of having passed through two wars within the first half of the twentieth century has been dynamic. Like the nation as a whole, the real estate industry has felt the impact of a planned economy. This, of course, was an attempt to control the law of supply and demand — an attempt during the years between the wars to produce artificial scarcities by plowing under crops, and particularly during the wars to control inflation by pegging the price of commodities. These policies, on the part of the national Government, were aimed at bringing into balance a condition of imbalance in our economy resulting from the violent stresses and strains occasioned by war and depression. They were meant only to provide a stopgap until the nation could revert to its normal economic status. These could be only temporary measures, since the law of supply and demand is immutable and, notwithstanding the man-made controls exerted upon it, will always in the end regulate its own interactive forces.

A war economy has a dynamic impact in the convulsive conversion from peace-time to war-time production. The abrupt diversion of our productive effort gives birth to a number of regulatory bodies within the national Government which prescribe by executive fiat what materials (and to a lesser extent, what labor) may be used for what purposes. This was the primary function of the War Production Board in World War II.

Other organizations are set up to control prices on materials so as to prevent and control exorbitant war-time profits. In the conversion of the flow of materials and labor from peace-time to war-time goods, the effect on the supply of housing, and consequently on the real estate market, is felt immediately. Materials used in the production of houses (and of stores, factories, and office buildings) are diverted into other channels necessary to supply the munitions of war. Furthermore, the segment of the labor market ordinarily involved in building construction is syphoned off into other areas of production; there is an immediate shortage of labor for the construction of real estate properties. This same situation creates a backlog of needed housing, which was clearly manifested during the last two wars in which we were engaged.[1]

Following the close of a war, there comes the reconversion period. New laws and regulations are invoked. The Government attempts to, and does, decontrol prices, and the swing is then back from a war-time to a peace-time economy with a rejuvenating effect on the real estate industry.

Evolution of constitutional law. Our constitutional law has gone through many phases of evolution since the early colonial times. It was first applied to the original thirteen colonies. It was patterned to fit the needs of a new, geographically small nation which was principally agrarian in character. Since that time, however, it has been modified to fit changing social and economic conditions. Examples of this are the regulations covering interstate commerce imposed by the Interstate Commerce Commission; the control by the Federal Trade Commission of trade practices for the purpose of protecting the public; the control of monopolistic enterprises by enforcement of the antitrust laws; the growing use of the power of eminent domain. There was a time in the history of our country when a grant of a piece of land by the Government to an individual was supposed to be absolute. But, with the rapid growth of our country, we have had more and more recourse to the condemnation of private property for public use. All these

---

[1] As a matter of fact, we were well into a housing shortage in the first year of World War II, the degree of which was not made statistically clear until the war was over.

things were necessary to implement the needs of a changing social order.

Important Federal Laws and Regulations

Rent control. The Federal regulation that has exercised the greatest impact on the real estate industry is rent control. This was considered a necessary war-time measure. Whether it remains necessary after the close of a war is debatable. However, it is not the purpose of this discussion to point out the merits or demerits of rent control. What interests us is its effect on the real estate valuation problem. And it has been a problem indeed to the appraiser, for it has had the definite effect of establishing, by law, a ceiling of value. The appraiser has been faced with a situation where, for example, the fair rental value of a residential property is probably $100 a month, but because of rent control regulations it cannot be rented for more than $60 per month; his problem has been to attempt a guess as to when controls would be lifted and the property freed to command a fair economic rental in the market place.

Rent control has also had its effect on the supply of housing because it has tended to accentuate the shortage of multifamily buildings. New housing of this type, free of rent control and with scheduled rents reflecting a fair return on investment found itself at a competitive disadvantage with used housing of comparable utility subject to rent control. The resultant effect was to discourage investment in new housing of this character.

It has had its effect on the demand for investment property. During periods of rent control there was little demand for investment property on the grounds that ascending construction costs, combined with frozen rents, made it unprofitable to build for investment.

It has had its effect on the maintenance of properties. Landlords, having their income frozen under rent control, were reluctant or financially unable to carry out proper maintenance programs, and as a consequence, tenants were left to get along as best they could, some of them being obliged to do at their own expense ordinary items of maintenance, particularly decorating, which the landlord could not or would not do. All of this has had a tendency to accelerate depreciation in investment properties.

Income taxes. Income taxes have their effect on real estate purchasing power, both of the homeowner and of the investor.

But the effect has been more far-reaching in the field of investment real estate where the income tax laws have acted as a deterrent to profit-making sales because the profit might place the seller in a higher surtax bracket.

This same condition ofttimes has discouraged the purchase of leased property because the tenant finds that continued leasing can be charged off as a business expense and may result in larger tax savings to the lessee than the amount he could charge off as depreciation were he in ownership. It may be said in this circumstance that high income taxes discourage real estate purchases.

Another and more interesting effect, however, is the extent to which high taxes have acted as a stimulus to the purchase of deficit properties. The investor has sought and acquired concurrently profit-making properties and properties which have operated for years at a loss, with the object of escaping higher surtaxes.

Foreign aid. Programs involving aid to foreign nations, either in terms of dollars or commodities, may have their effect on the real estate market, particularly in so far as these expenditures increase the income tax dollar. Shortages in the domestic market resulting from the export of large quantities of such materials as steel, may be reflected in the supply of building materials.

Cost ceilings. The imposition of cost ceilings on housing has an important effect on real estate. In a war economy the Government may decide to curtail all but low-cost housing and to prohibit building above a specific level of cost. This further slows the housing market and freezes large quantities of land which could be used for housing but which is of such high value that it cannot economically accommodate housing within the cost limits prescribed by the Government.

Control of materials. The control of critical materials, such as steel, copper, and aluminum, has its effect. This relates to our previous discussion on the principle of substitution, which states that a parcel of real estate cannot be worth more than its duplicate provided the duplication can be made without any extraordinary delay. Ordinarily, this principle postulates also that cost is the upper limit of value. However, when critical materials cannot be obtained, this principle has to be shelved temporarily because the purchaser of a particular property who is not able to get critical materials with which to build a duplicate may choose to pay a price above the cost of production of the property he wishes to acquire at that particular moment. In these circumstances, the upper limit of value is not cost but rather the intensity of the desire of an investor or of a prospective homeowner for a particular property at a particular time.

Social security and unemployment compensation. These regulations and laws have to do with unemployment compensation and old age pensions. The latter may have a dual effect on the real estate market. It has been claimed that the flow of investment capital into the market is reduced because of the sums employers have to pay to maintain unemployment compensation and old age pensions. On the other hand, it has been contended that payment of these benefits tends to maintain and increase the purchasing power of the recipients.

Labor laws and regulations. The extent to which labor laws and regulations are favorable or unfavorable to labor require study. Laws that are extremely favorable to labor have a discouraging effect upon capitalistic enterprise. Laws that are extremely unfavorable to labor usually lead to strikes and consequent loss of production and purchasing power.

Subsidies. Subsidies are of concern to the valuator of real estate, particularly in the field of housing. This matter has been discussed before, but it should be noted here that any time the Government chooses to subsidize housing to such an extent that its program competes with the conventional housing market, private builders, mortgage lenders, and others will tend to decrease their own activities.

Government pegging of interest rates. The Government is all-powerful with respect to pegging the interest rate for money. The instrumentalities involved are the Federal Reserve Bank, the Federal Home Loan Bank, the Federal Housing Administration, the Veterans Administration, the Reconstruction Finance Corporation, and all other Federal agencies in the lending business. The volume of their business is so vast, and their influence so far-reaching, that any fluctuation in the rate by these agencies has its effect upon the entire financial market. This has particularly to do with the mortgage interest rate for housing.

Other Federal Government policies. Other policies of the Federal Government such as the pegging of the price of gold or the pegging of the silver content of the dollar affect the economy, and indirectly the real estate economy. We are mindful, too, of what happened during the era of prohibition in the 1920's to the properties used by industries involved in the manufacture of alcoholic beverages. During that time, breweries and distilleries were a drug on the market and could not be sold.

State laws and regulations. What has been said of Federal income taxes is also true of state income taxes. The larger the share of the consumer's dollar that is taken for state income taxes, the less he has to spend for housing. Thus, states that have exorbitant income taxes are in competition with neighboring states whose income taxes are lower or that have no state income tax.

The appraiser needs to be aware of state laws and regulations governing mortgage loans by insurance companies. Usually these laws specify the exact per centum of loan to value that may be made by the company. As a result, competition arises between insurance companies chartered in different states where the regulations vary in respect to the latitude of lending operations.

Public utility rates fixed by the state are important to the appraiser, as has been previously noted.

Municipal laws, regulations, policies. Building codes, zoning ordinances, taxation policy, governmental cost, efficiency of government, progressive civic spirit and the will to progress within a municipality affect the local real estate market (see Chapter 6).

Conclusions. All of the foregoing indicates that the appraiser must have under constant study the laws and regulations of the Federal, state, county, township, and municipal governments. These laws may from time to time affect the valuation of real estate or the desire for housing. It is not difficult to keep up with these regulations. The *Federal Register* publishes daily laws and regulations passed by the Congress or issued by administrative heads of Federal agencies.

Headlines, the weekly newsletter of the National Association of Real Estate Boards, keeps a watchful eye on Federal legislation.

This information can also be found in Savings and Loan bulletins, the Appraisal Journal, and the Review of the Society of Residential Appraisers, among others. The fact to remember is: in our type of economy, where Federal, state, or city governments can pass laws affecting real estate, the appraiser must be ever watchful of the effect of those laws upon the real estate market and, particularly, upon the demand for housing.

CHAPTER 7

Analyzing the City

. . . a geographic plexus, an economic organization . . . a theater of social action. . . .

MUMFORD

In dealing with the American city, the appraiser is confronted with the product of a comparatively short period of time. No other nation on the face of the globe has undergone the rapidity of population growth experienced by the United States since the year 1830. At that time, the national population stood at nearly 13,000,000. One hundred and twenty years later, it totaled 154,233,000 — a gain of more than 140,000,000.

This vast increase in population resulted in an intensive urbanization, the clustering together of people in cities. Thus in 1870 only 23.1 per cent of the native white population was urban, while in 1950 this proportion had risen to 64 per cent.[1] In the year 1880, there were but 76 cities having a population of 25,000 or more; in 1950, that number had increased to 481.[2]

Basic Origins

American cities were of routine origin. The early American settlers, pioneering a new world, clustered together in small groups for purposes of self-protection. The first cities were founded as governmental centers. Later came the westward push, and with it the necessity for strategic locations. The selection process followed the then immutable law of transportation convenience. New cities sprang up along waterways or at the intersection of transportation arteries. This was natural and necessary. Water

---

[1] Source, Bureau of the Census.
[2] *Ibid.*

routes (and later railroads) carried the commerce and communications of the nation. Purely as a matter of self-preservation, cities were compelled to locate along the lines of communication where fuel and food — the principal necessities of life — might be obtained.

While the causal origin of the city was the advantages so bountifully supplied by nature, the techniques of a modern civilization have, to some extent, made it independent of the natural advantages that helped to create it. This is particularly true in respect to the development of communications and transportation. Consider, for example, the degree to which the situs of cities is affected by the advent of radio, teletype, air mail, and television. Consider also the extent to which developments in the field of transportation influence that same situation. Bus and motor truck lines crosshatch the map of the nation, and the airplane has already affected the national distribution of our urban centers and even the local pattern and plan of our cities.

Yet, the basic natural advantages that spawned the American city still influence the pattern of its growth and will continue to do so. Research and experiment in engineering and technology should continue to amplify and magnify the value of those original advantages. Thus, the development of the St. Lawrence waterway will enhance the natural values of the cities that lie along its course. Improvements in transportation — in the forwarding processes of goods, commodities, and materials — will increase the productive economy of our commercial, trading, and manufacturing centers. Because the original city pattern continues to exert its influence on the population growth and prosperity of the city, the historical background conditions the appraisal problem.

The Population Curve

Analysis of the population trend in the city is more important than analysis of the national trend. As we get closer to the core of the data program, population trends become increasingly significant. The city is the immediate legal and social entity that surrounds the neighborhood and the specific property. Its growth presages a demand for housing. Demand influences values.

In the past, those engaged in the valuation of real estate have leaned, with good reason, on population growth as a reliable indicator of the trend of values. Whether they can exercise the same degree of reliance for future value estimates is not certain. It has been shown that the rate of national population increase declined steadily until the period 1940-1950 when the trend was reversed. Local trends (in cities) will reflect national trends, except for the shuttling back and forth of segments of the population between cities and farms.

The industrial revolution brought about an exodus of ruralites to the cities. This migratory movement has been arrested in the past only by periodic cessation of employment and lack of economic opportunity in the urban areas. Since 1930, however, there has been a steady movement from the farms to cities and villages. It is these shifts in population, as well as national growth trends, that challenge the interest of the valuator of real estate. As long as the city holds out cultural, social, and economic advantages over the hinterland or near-by cities, it will continue to draw and attract new residents.

The Economic Pattern

As cities grew, they took on formative characteristics expressing their economic nature. Today, we may classify most of the large cities of the country into one of several types based on their functional variation. These have been conveniently arranged by Weimer and Hoyt as follows:

1. Commercial cities (to include farming centers), such as cities located on and along oceans, lakes and rivers; also rail terminals
2. Industrial cities, devoted to the manufacture and processing of commodities
3. Extractive-industry cities: mining, lumbering, fishing
4. Political cities, where the major income source arises from salaries paid to governmental workers
5. Recreational and health cities
6. Educational cities.[3]

To understand clearly the economic nature of the city and the sources from which it draws its sustenance is to be able to interpret these data into an opinion of the city's growth and economic prosperity. "As a people we have not yet learned to evaluate these things which are the basic causes of city growth and values," says

---

[3] Arthur Martin Weimer and Homer Hoyt, *Principles of Urban Real Estate* (New York, The Ronald Press Company, 1939), Ch. II, p. 31.

Dr. Clark.[4] This is undoubtedly so, for the history of valuation practice proves that many of those engaged in it are more concerned with the development of mathematical techniques than with the basic economic factors that incessantly tip the value equilibrium either up or down.

The fact that Detroit is an industrial city with a major percentage of its workers employed in the automotive (or allied) industries is important in any analysis of the economic scene. The fact that New Orleans is (in point of dollar volume of tonnage passing through it) the second largest port in the United States is important as an index to the future level of real estate values. The fact that Miami is a large resort center with a tremendous influx of winter visitors all bent on recreation and pleasure is important in analyzing the future level of realty values as predicated on the present specialized economy of that city.

It is not an overstatement to say that a thoroughgoing knowledge of the basal economy of cities on the part of those engaged in the valuation of real estate might have avoided, in the past, losses running into the millions. There is the example of the mining center that once contained a population four times its present size, with a downtown retail area three streets in width and six blocks in depth. Today, this area has shrunk to a mere handful of stores clustered along one street, and its population to a few thousands. What happened to bring this about? The mineral resources on which the city lived are still in the earth surrounding it, but after twenty-five years of continuous operation, mining operations must now be carried on at such a depth as to make current operations unprofitable. Competing industries located in other mining centers can lay the raw materials on top of the ground at prices cheaper than in the city under discussion. The resultant effect on the realty market for homes in this community has been disastrous. Many other similar instances could be quoted where inadequate analysis and study of the city's economic pattern have resulted in costly mistakes.

Economic Trends

A comparative study of the trends of industrial production, pay rolls, and employment levels tells us where the city is going eco-

---

[4] Horace F. Clark, *Appraising the Home* (New York, Prentice-Hall, Inc.. 1930).

nomically. These indices point to prosperous or unprosperous conditions; they index fluctuations in the curve of real estate values. Ample local statistical data recording these inclinations are available, and they should be a part of the information plant of the appraiser. In the large industrial city, any sloughing off in industrial production means a consequent lessening of employment, diminution of consumer income, and a general worsening of the real estate market. Conversely, increased production means a rise in employment levels, increased pay rolls, and a demand for housing.

This leads to a discussion of that type of community one writer has defined as the "insensate industrial town." [5] In this category might be listed a number of large cities in which one half or more of all consumer incomes derives from manufacturing.[6] In that situation, where most family incomes arise from one type of employment, the values of real estate will be found to be delicately poised, awaiting sharp and sympathetic reaction to the supply or demand for the commodities produced by the particular kind of manufacture. Conversely, real estate values will be well stabilized in those communities where consumer incomes derive from a combination of sources—such as trade and commerce, as well as manufacturing.

Further refinement of this principle directs attention to the diversification of industry and employment as a stabilizer of realty values. History shows that the fluctuations in the curve of values of real property will be less in communities whose economic background discloses a number of different industries.

In the "one-industry" city, we find a highly volatile economy resulting from a concentration of workers in one type of manufacture. When the demand for this commodity slacks off (as in the large automotive center, for example), employment ceases and pay rolls diminish, resulting in: (1) an exodus of workers to other cities in search of employment; and/or (2) a "doubling-up" of families—that is, double-family occupancy of a single-family residential unit. These conditions produce an oversupply of housing, with a consequent reduction in rental and sales prices.

In the city possessing a diversified industrial background, there is more stability. All of the economic eggs are not in one basket.

---

[5] Lewis Mumford, *Culture of Cities* (New York, Harcourt, Brace and Company, Inc., 1938), Ch. III.
[6] Weimer and Hoyt, *op. cit.*, p. 46.

Employment hazard is spread over many types of manufacture. There are more *kinds* of factories with fewer employees per factory. Reductions in employment in one industry may be absorbed, in part at least, by other industries, with the result that the migratory movement of workers and their families is arrested. And even though such absorption fails to take place, the shutting down of one industry does not disrupt the economic whole to the extent felt in the "one-industry" city. Rentals and values may decline temporarily, but the fluctuations in the curve will be less abrupt and less extensive.

The economic trend of the city reflects its desirability as a place in which to live, as an attractive place in which to earn a livelihood. The extent of this book, dealing as it does with the processes by which real estate is valued, does not permit a detailed exploration of the data appertaining to the city as an economic and social entity. The subject presents a wide field of study in itself. The student of real estate values should explore this field in considerable detail in order to supplement his understanding of the causal factors that underlie real estate values.[7]

The Ethnological Pattern

The large American city represents an agglomeration of people of many races and national backgrounds. This is so because of the volume of immigration from abroad, which gave stimulus to the national growth prior to the promulgation of laws setting up sharply reduced quotas.

As a consequence, the social complexion of the large city reveals a number of groupings that are usually demarcated as racial or national neighborhoods. No one phase of the valuation problem is quite so interesting as this, because of the effect produced on real estate values by the movement of these groups within the city structure.

Primarily the native-born whites, by comparison in number with any individual ethnical group, represent the mass market for housing. They dominate the situation; they are the typical purchasers of homes. Minority groups are usually unable to pay the

---

[7] See: Richard Theodore Ely and G. S. Wehrwein, *Land Economics* (New York, The Macmillan Company, 1940); Herbert Benjamin Dorau and A. G. Hinman, *Urban Land Economics* (New York, The Macmillan Company, 1930); and Richard U. Ratcliff, *Urban Land Economics* (New York, McGraw-Hill Book Co., 1949).

price that new housing commands and are most often found in occupancy of the older structures.

As a rule, the minority groups are poorly housed and many pay a higher cost per room for housing than the cost of comparable shelter for other groups. The reason for this increased cost arises from the limited availability of space.

The minority groups, because of low family income, usually must utilize accommodations discarded by the most recent owners of housing originally built for the majority. The supply of low-cost housing units is usually far below the demand thereby setting up within the body social stresses that demand relief. Relief comes in the form of an overflow movement. The low-cost housing district bursts its confines and overflows into the near-by better class district, which, in turn, is already on the wane because of the proximity of the poorer district.

The point of emphasis is that the movement is one of economic compulsion and not one of deliberate invasion of the majority by a minority group, whose members invade a new (to them) district only when overcrowding has become intolerable and when the housing units in the invaded district have been brought down, through a supercession of declining usages, to a cost level commensurate with the ability of the lower-income group to pay the price.

From this we may generalize that, in the city that houses a large percentage of people of foreign birth, or their children, or that contains a substantial minority percentage of people of races other than white, residential real estate values in the older districts bordering those at present inhabited by the minority peoples will exist in a state of threatened status quo.

The racial and ethnical traits of city population are an important phase of valuation study. The well-equipped appraisal laboratory will contain a map of the city showing the location of these groups and tracing the history and direction of their movement.

The Geographical Pattern

A study of the geographical pattern of the city supplies an understanding of its ability to grow in certain directions. City growth follows the line of least physical resistance. It tends toward the free and open ends, and away from the dead ends. These dead ends are barriers, either legal or physiographical, that inhibit the extensory mechanism of the city. The legal barriers take the form of abutting city, county, state, or national boundaries. The physical barriers are rivers and other bodies of water, mountains, swamps, or lowlands, and other such impediments that discourage physical expansion. A city with physical outlet to the four points of the compass has the opportunity for future prosperity, provided the surrounding land is usable. Conversely, a city that is entirely encompassed by another and larger city and that has consumed all the usable land within it, has reached its zenith in point of horizontal expansion.[8]

Governmental Policies

The average American, challenged on the issue, will declare with great gusto that his is the best governed country on earth, a statement which, while true, may not mean that he is the subject of good government. This implies no intention to negate a statement made previously — that the upkeep cost of citizenship in the United States is nominal in proportion to the benefits thereof. It is, however, the intention to assert that homeownership in this country is a luxury! And it is a luxury to be enjoyed by a minority of American families.

Ownership, in the true sense of the word, means a condition that is absolute. When we say that a large percentage of the families in the United States own their own homes, we have reference, for the most part, to a conditional form of ownership. It is a kind of "if-as-and-when" wealth.[9] As one writer puts it:

Your present wealth as you regard it should be — for unconfused observation and reasoning — divided into two categories. First, there are those things which you may be said truly to own, in that you can dispose of them in any way that suits your fancy. In the second category, there would be the forms of wealth which you may own, and no doubt in the future will, *if* a large number of persons, corporations and States fulfill promises that have been made to you directly or indirectly.[10]

In the case of privately owned real estate, the totality of ownership by the individual is always conditioned on the implied prom-

---

[8] Detroit and Boston are each examples of the complete encirclement of one city by another.

[9] Harry Scherman, *The Promises Men Live By* (New York, Random House, Inc., 1938).

[10] *Ibid.*

ise of the city and state to assess taxes on a basis compatible with the ability of the owner to pay. This promise has not been kept in most instances. Local governments, in an effort to meet the ever-mounting costs of government, threaten to throttle the goose that for years has been a first-class producer of golden eggs in the form of tax money.

Why the owners of real estate should bear the lion's share of governmental upkeep is unknown, except that present systems of taxation evolve from a policy of *laissez faire* on the part of the taxing body, that it is easier to continue the present system than to change it, or that it is simpler to tax real property than personal because the latter is so hard to find.

No one factor in the present scene offers so great a threat to the security of real estate investment (and a home is an investment in good living) as the one of real property taxes. Examples are many where assessed values in aged residential districts exceed values in the market place. Situations are reported where tax levies absorb as much as 30 to 40 per cent of the annual gross rent of urban properties.

The governmental policy of the city, particularly with regard to taxation, connotes the desirability of the municipality as a place in which to own a home. A desirable city is one that is well governed. No city is well governed that continues to discourage home-ownership by disregarding the principle of fair and equitable taxation of real property.

Transportation

A casual study of the growth characteristics of any large city will reveal the important part played by public transportation in the development of the urban economy. Cities may grow to a certain stage with only ordinary facilities for the travel of its citizens from one location within it to another. But there comes a time when the amount of time consumed in transit between these localities borders on being a nuisance. The reaction is hedonistic; the pleasure or profit of getting to the destination is outweighed by the personal inconvenience sustained.

Inadequate transportation system plainly retard city growth. When the outer fringe of the megalopolis has become so far distant from the downtown section as to make shopping a drudge — a sort of Cook's Tour in the matter of travel time — the principal retail center will soon lose its appeal. This sets in motion the forces of decentralization — of retail as well as residential districts. The resultant effect is a number of smaller shopping centers or large regional centers (characterized by branches of the principal downtown stores) located along main arterial routes of transportation at a considerable distance from the downtown section.

These same forces actuate the movement of the city dweller to the suburb. Because of the inhibitory travel time involved (either because of the heavy congestion of surface transportation or because of the lack of sufficient facilities) in going toward that area which houses the shops and offices of the city, life in the city ceases to be attractive as compared to conditions in the near-by suburb, which is served by steam or electric trains or by fast, through buses.

Notwithstanding that there are approximately 50,000,000 automobiles privately licensed, we will require a form of public transport that will move a mass of people within the city between points of social interest and economic necessity.

Public Utilities

Homeowners and renters will be attracted to a city that offers adequate public utility service at a fair cost. The services of telephone and gas and electric power are an important part of the mechanism of housing. Today, electricity washes the clothes, cleans the rugs, irons the shirts, heats the homes, refrigerates and cooks the food, makes the ice, winds the clocks, curls the hair, plays the music, reports the news, provides visual entertainment and shaves the face of the nation. So does gas in lesser degree.

The cost of these services has direct relation to homeownership appeal. Proof of this is shown in those instances where the population "pull" of the suburb as opposed to the city is negated by the increased cost of suburban utilities.[11] It is frequently found, for example, that the cost of telephone service just over the boundary line of the metropolis is more than it is within it. Instances are found also where the cost of power and gas is more outside the metropolis than inside its boundaries, where the same service is offered by a different and competing company.

---

[11] The expressed philosophy of the average suburbanite, however, is that, while it costs more to live in the suburb, the benefits derived are worth more.

The extent to which the motivating energy of household equipment is dependent on public utilities makes their adequacy and cost an important factor in the analysis of the city as an ideal housing center.

Climate

The climatic conditions of the city exert powerful influences upon its desirability as a place of residence. With some exceptions, the most noticeable growth in the past has occurred in those centers where there are no extremes of temperature and where meteorological conditions are not disturbed by violent departure from normal. The frequent and seasonal occurrence of winds and hurricanes, protracted periods of fog and rains, as well as excessive heat and cold, are not features calculated to encourage a constant and steady growth of new population. Health, winter, or summer resort cities, while enjoying a seasonal prosperity, present the spectacle of widely fluctuating consumer incomes between seasons.

Moreover, the city that offers specific climatic advantages in the form of relief from winter cold or summer heat will ordinarily have a population ceiling limited to the number of permanent residents who can live for twelve months of the year off the economic sustenance furnished by the transient population during a few months of the year.

But this rule, like many others emanating from the study of urban land economics, is characterized by notable exceptions. New York and Chicago, for example, possess no outstanding climatic advantages; they are hot in summer and cold in winter. Their prosperous growth is undoubtedly due to the motivating force of their genesis. The natural advantage of location along transportation routes was paramount, in the process of origin, to all other considerations, including that of climate.

Recreational and Cultural Facilities

The city is a place in which to live. Good living, as we construe it, includes ample facilities for recreation and culture. There must be opportunity for play as well as work. Public parks and their accessibility, playgrounds for children, public golf courses, beaches and swimming pools, community centers, stadia where sports and games may be held — all these contribute to social stability and to the enjoyment of an urban existence.

There must be sufficient opportunity for cultural advancement within the city. Good schools, churches of the principal religious denominations, art centers and public libraries — these contribute to educational growth and culture. They are an important complement to the social pattern of the metropolis.

The Age Analysis of Neighborhoods

No other facet of our urbiculture is so in need of intimate analysis as the history of the movement of residential neighborhoods and the trend of present influences that impel such movement. In most of our large urban areas, the high- and low-water marks of the old residential districts are still easily discernible. They are distinguishable by the remaining architectural types that connote neighborhood age.

The life stage of the neighborhood has an important bearing on the present appraisal problem. Neighborhoods at varying degrees of age present varying degrees of mortgage risk and owner-occupancy appeal. The neighborhood past midlife in which the various structures have undergone a succession of uses and ownerships exhibits risks that are not apparent in the new district characterized by new structures and a high percentage of owner occupancy. For that reason, lenders of mortgage funds look with some suspicion upon a neighborhood that has passed the peak of desirability of ownership. The age of the structures makes long-term lending hazardous. Furthermore, the impending infringement of retail, industrial, or commercial uses, or the infiltration of minority groups, accelerates the obsolescence of neighborhoods and decreases the volume of homeownership appeal.

A study of the ever-changing social status of neighborhoods is a fundamental necessity of the appraisal process. The necessary records in the form of maps to show classes of occupancy, use, and the comparative desirability of owner occupancy should be available as part of the general data appertaining to the problem.

Retail District Trends

The growth of cities has been characterized in the past by the locational pattern of its various economic functions. At the core is found the downtown shopping or retail area, located at the point where the main lines of city transportation converge. In the past, two principal influences have operated to maintain the uni-nucleated pattern of retail areas: (1) shopper convenience compelled location of the retail district at the city center, at the point of downtown terminus of street railway and bus lines; and (2) the method of commodity transport (rail and water) compelled the location of department stores and specialty shops at points of convenience to freight receiving centers.

The use of automotive transport, both for passengers and commodities, has changed all this. It has assisted the escape of the central retail district from the downtown area to a series of smaller subcenters located in the outlying sections, usually at the point where arterial highways intersect. The shopper has become independent of the street railway and bus systems because of his ability to provide his own transportation. He has become disinclined to drive his automobile into the central business area because of traffic congestion and parking difficulty, which are far less of a problem in the outlying subcenter.[12]

The retailer no longer has to depend on his nearness to railheads or freight forwarding terminals. The long-lived pneumatic tire with which motor trucks are now equipped and the giant freight trailer have revolutionized marketing practice. The manufactured product is crated and loaded into trucks at the factory, transported directly to the point of customer distribution, unloaded and placed on the shelves of the merchant. The movement and handling of railway freight is sluggish by comparison, as anyone will testify who has ever tried over a period of days to locate a "lost" car of merchandise.

Automotive freight transport has had a reducing effect on the cost of merchandising in three ways:

1. *In the time consumed in transit.* Truck routes are through routes. There is an absence of the delays that ensue in rail traffic where it is necessary to remake a train because of the change of routing at the terminus of one rail system and the commencement of another.

2. *In the timing of shipments.* The timing of shipments can be more precise. No longer is it necessary to order in carload lots far in advance of consumption needs, with the consequent necessity of maintaining large inventories and freezing capital therein.

---

[12] This has literally forced some of the larger department stores into the construction and operation of multi-level shopper-parking facilities. Examples: The Hecht Company in Washington, D.C., and the J. L. Hudson Company, Detroit.

3. *In the reduction in handling costs.* Under a system of exclusive rail transport, shipments of commodities were unloaded at the railhead and then reloaded for delivery by dray or truck to the outlying retail center. Today, the automotive freight car picks up the goods at the factory and lays them down at the store, regardless of its location within or without the city center. Excessive handling is eliminated.

From all this, we may generalize that future retail operations within the city differ from those of the past. Heretofore, the underlying motive of the successful retailer was to bring the people to the markets. Now the markets are being taken to the people.

How will this affect land values in the downtown district? The answer appears to be obvious. The continued and inevitable decentralization of the downtown shopping area and its reconstruction in the nuclei of shopping centers serving outlying areas in or outside of the city cannot help but affect adversely land values in the present 100 per cent "hot-spot" area.

What is the significance of the changing retail scene as it affects the valuation of single-family dwellings?

1. It minimizes the locational importance of residential districts in relation to the downtown shopping area.

2. It emphasizes the necessity for convenience of travel to the retail subcenter.

3. With the development of the outlying retail district, with a full complement of all retail types, to include places of amusement, the old catch phrase of the realtor, "only thirty minutes to downtown," will continue to mean less and less.

The Locational Trends of Industry

In its original aspects, industry within the city was characterized by certain rules of situs compulsion.

Assuming the assurance of an adequate supply of labor, the following rules applied:

1. There was the necessity for locating its plant near the termini of rail or water transport.

2. It required the proximity of volume public transportation in order to facilitate the going and coming of its employees.

3. It required convenience of access to the focal point of communication systems — mail and telegraph.

All this implied that the industrial plant required a location within the city which was central and that its location, once established, was permanently fixed and immobile.

But the scene changes. Revolutionized methods of transportation have affected industrial production to as great an extent almost as retailing. While heavy manufacture may still require a location that facilitates the receipt of raw materials by rail or water,[13] the shipment of manufactured products is carried on to a large extent by automotive trucks. (Bulk and size of the product seem to make little difference, as witness the volume of auto-truck transport of new passenger automobiles from factory to dealer.)

The proximity and adequacy of street railways and buses as a means of transporting employees have given way to private automobile transportation. The American factory worker goes to work in his own car or in one owned by a fellow worker, to whom he pays his share of the transportation cost. Around the large industrial plant are vast parking areas, packed with motorcars, which, though of doubtful vintage, still provide the means of getting to and from the factory. Thus, the means of public transportation are no longer as important an influence on compulsory plant location as they were once.

Our system of communications has been speeded up. The long-distance telephone places the manufacturer in immediate contact with his far-flung operations, at home or abroad. The downtown telegraph office and its nearness to the plant, along with the uniformed messenger boy, are no longer an indispensable adjunct to the central location of the industrial plant. The teletype machine set up in the plant office provides instantaneous two-way communication with the four corners of the nation, wherever there is a receiving instrument.

Industry picks up its incoming and delivers its outgoing mail to the post office with its own mail truck. Where once the wheels of industrial progress waited on the postman, industry now performs a part of its own mail services. Under these conditions, it matters little whether the plant is located close to the central post office or out in the suburbs; its letter, written at the plant located

---

[13] There is, however, an observable tendency on the part of the heavy-goods industry to forego the locational convenience of inbound transport in favor of a site closer to the source of consumption of its products.

in the Midwestern city this morning will, via the medium of air mail, be read in New York or San Francisco tomorrow.

These observations compel the assertion that industrial locations within the city are no longer fixed by what were once compulsory factors.

The past tendency of heavy manufacturing to occupy central locations has been reversed. Industrial uses are found in bands running outward from the center along transportation lines or river valleys, or in groupings at the outskirts where land is cheaper, taxes lower and transportation facilities available in belt lines or truck routes.[14]

From a condition of immobility there has developed a condition of mobility. Industry, although established in one location over a period of years, can and does move.[15] In fact, it may be claimed that any factory centrally located within the city and subject, *ipso facto*, to the current tax liability, may find it convenient one day to seek the hinterland, where land costs are cheaper, taxes lower, and labor unrest comparatively absent. Its decision to do this will pivot largely on its ability to liquidate its present investment in land and buildings without loss.

The significance of this trend toward industrial decentralization warns against the too-oft expressed willingness of the appraiser to view industry as a predictor of realty values. The assumption frequently is made that, because certain industries within the city are in course of expansion, with consequent increase of personnel and pay rolls, the curve of values will ascend in economic sympathy. This is true only in so far as industry can be considered as permanent and fixed in its locations. Observation shows that this is not the case. Already the periphery of our large cities is dotted with small plants engaged in light manufacturing. Their location is a symbol of the freedom with which modern industry may pick and choose its situs, as a result of changes in methods of transportation and the improved rapidity of communications.

Land-use Control by Local Government

The laws affecting the uses to which land may be put — namely, zoning ordinances — require study and analysis. The question as

---

[14] Richard U. Ratcliff, *The Problem of Retail Site Selection* (Ann Arbor, University of Michigan Press, 1939).

[15] In 1928, the Ford Motor Company picked up its equipment of machinery, along with some 80,000 employees, and moved from the city of Highland Park, Michigan, to the Detroit suburb of River Rouge.

to whether zoning is a good or bad influence on realty values has not been fully resolved. As in many other situations, the intent of the law is good. The method of its administration, however, is something else again. The intent of a well-constructed zoning ordinance is to protect land uses presently established by custom and to regulate the character of future uses. None will deny that zoning as a principle of town planning implies a stabilizing influence on realty values. Yet, instances are known where the administration of such laws has had an opposite effect, due in every case to the ineptitude of the enforcing body to recognize and understand basic principles. Thus, it has been claimed that certain cities would have been better off without a zoning ordinance, because of the laxity of the enforcing officials and their willingness to change the classifications of districts established by the law without due justification. Generally, however, it may be claimed that, while zoning may adversely affect the interests of a few, it will accomplish the greatest good to the greatest number, provided there is an intelligent administration of the use regulations of property as defined by the zoning ordinance. Since zoning limits the uses to which property may be put, and since use is a concomitant of value, these data must be examined in connection with the property to be valued.

Attitude toward Governmental Housing

The attitude of the local government toward participation in the slum-clearance and low-cost housing programs of the Federal Government will, of course, influence our analysis of the city in which the valuation problem lies. These programs require the co-operation of the local government. The nature of this problem has already been discussed. The extent of participation by the local government will measure the seriousness of the problem as it affects the general question of local housing.

Welfare and Relief

Widespread conditions of unemployment in the past have developed a new index to the economic prosperity of cities. These are the figures that reflect the number of families receiving relief in the form of cash, food, fuel, or shelter allowances from the local government. A careful study of this curve should be made in comparison with the figures that reflect the comparative volume of employment. These figures should also be studied in connection with the cost of relief as related to the general financial position of the municipality and its ability to make such expenditures within its income.

Conclusions

"The city in its complete sense, then, is a geographic plexus, an economic organization, an institutional process, a theater of social action and an esthetic symbol of collective unity." [16] Because of the complexity of its organism, the interpretative influences now at work toward change cannot be easily read and diagnosed. We know from the signs about us that the urban metropolis is "in a state of constant flux, growing or shrinking in response to economic forces and ever readjusting its component parts in reacting to internal stresses." [17] The ability to read these signs and to interpret their future effect on the present scene is the essence of the appraisal problem. It is of no great moment that the appraiser shall have demonstrated his efficiency to appraise a particular property. It is of considerable moment that he know the causal factors that underlie value. These causes are discernible in the dynamics of city growth, of which he must perforce be a student. A knowledge of why and how the city grew, and a thorough understanding of its present political, social, and economic trends, will enable him to understand why real estate values exist and the trend of future real estate prosperity.

---

[16] Mumford, *op. cit.*, p. 480.
[17] Ratcliff, *op. cit.*, p. 2.

CHAPTER 8

Analyzing the Neighborhood

What is a neighborhood? According to Webster's *New International Dictionary,* a neighborhood is "a district or section with reference to the character of its inhabitants." As is the case, however, with words that, through usage in a particular field, become a part of its terminology, "neighborhood" for appraisal purposes has been defined within narrower limits.

The American Institute of Real Estate Appraisers says, ". . . neighborhoods rise from the desires of people having comparable interests, related traditions or similar social and financial standing. . . . A neighborhood is a segment within a larger unit, the community. It is shaped and molded by social, economic and civic factors." [1]

The student of the urban scene will observe that a neighborhood is a clustering of people in certain districts where the inhabitants have a sameness of income level, of racial and national traits, and (to a lesser degree) of religious affiliations. The fact that the housing they occupy is similar is an effect produced by the economic levels of the inhabitant families. The volume and character of the shelter they can afford is dictated by their income. Incomes define and classify the social strata. These strata have been arranged and classified in the order of comparative incomes:

1. Senior executives
2. Junior executives
3. Foremen and chief clerks
4. Skilled mechanics and office workers
5. Semiskilled mechanics and lower-grade clerks
6. Laborers

[1] *The Appraisal of Real Estate,* 1951.

It is admitted that, in any given neighborhood, there will be found a wide spread between a few high and low incomes. In general, however, the mass of the inhabitants will approach the average; the majority will lie in about the same income bracket. This supports the sociological truth that contentment of living is present in greater abundance in that circumstance where the inhabitants of a particular district have the same level of income, social attributes, ethnics, culture, and education. Where this ideal situation is observed in the structure of a neighborhood, there will also be found, as its product, a marked stability of realty values.

Thus we may think of the neighborhood as an integrated social and economic entity enfolding the property to be appraised and exerting its influences upon it. As the property is the heart of the problem, so is the neighborhood the pericardium which surrounds and protects it. The response of the property to influences and forces that generate in the neighborhood is quick — even more so than to those originating in the city proper. As an example, the influx of a large body of foreigners or people of lower living standards into the city will not affect the neighborhood unless, of course, the neighborhood is itself entered. But let one of these families move into the neighborhood, and the deteriorating response is almost instantaneous. Or, as another example, let the city erect a large garbage disposal plant in the outskirts. The neighborhood far removed will feel no effect. But let the city erect such a plant — even at the linear boundary of a well-stabilized neighborhood — and all the forces of blight are turned loose upon the surrounding area.

The Barometer of Economic Quality

Economic quality, the investment rating of the neighborhood in which the property lies, is the first thing that should claim the appraiser's attention.

Some years ago, we were asked by a friend to look at a lot which he intended to buy and upon which he intended to build a house. The lot was in a high-class residential district. We accompanied him to the site, walked over the land, and then asked him what he wanted to know. His question was, "Is it worth the $2,500 I am asked to pay for it?" Our reply was disappointing, perhaps. We told him we did not know and could not answer his question until he could tell us who lived in the block (which was about 50 per cent built up) on either side of the street. This statement perplexed him, but we went on to explain that he was buying this lot ostensibly for the purpose of building a home in which he intended to reside for the rest of his life; therefore, what he was buying was not merely a piece of land or a building, but an environment in terms of the people with whom he was to live and associate in the years to come.

He had to satisfy himself that these people were approximately at his economic level, that they held about the same cultural interests, and that they were of his race and preferably of his religion, in order to assure himself that his interests and living habits and those of his neighbors would be parallel. We told him that once he had the answers to these questions we could tell him whether or not this was the lot he wanted to buy and that comparing the price asked with prices of other lots in the neighborhood was a very simple thing he himself could do.

He was more than a little annoyed by our opinion and asked rather tartly if he was expected to go up and down the street ringing doorbells and asking the neighbors the questions we had suggested. We replied that he did not need to do it himself. He could ask the real estate broker who was trying to sell him the lot to prepare a map showing the lots on either side of the street, both vacant and improved, and to inform him concerning the people who lived in these houses, since this was part of the service the broker was supposed to render in return for his commission. To make a good story out of it, he bought the lot, built a fine home on it, and is very happy and contented there today.

People make value. The point illustrated by this anecdote is one that every experienced and skillful appraiser knows — people make value! All an appraiser does is to observe, analyze, and record the phenomena of the market place and to catalogue that information, either documentarily or in his head (preferably the former), so that when he is engaged in an appraisal operation he can apply these recordings to the instant problem. In so doing the appraiser is able to arrive at an answer based upon a comparison with the data he has accumulated.

It should always be remembered that real estate values are made by people, evolve out of the behavior of people in the mass operating within the real estate economy, and are indicated by the wealth-getting and wealth-spending habits of people. "Wealth" in this case means material objects of their desire, and, in the particular, it means real estate or homes. Whatever people do in the mass in their desire to acquire housing is an indication of value in the market place. This is what the appraiser records. This is why it is said that people, not appraisers, make value — a good thought to keep in mind as an aid to the proper humility necessary in our profession.

That values are made by people is evidenced by the analysis of any residential neighborhood in the United States today where the history of the rise and decline of the neighborhood is known. Every instance will show that values rose, values maintained an equilibrium, or values fell because of the behavior, the traits, the living habits, and the backgrounds of the people who lived in the neighborhood. So the first phase of our operation is an attempt to calibrate the investment quality of the area under study.

Renters vs. owners. Investment quality is best ascertained by the simple expedient of learning the per centum of owners to renters in the particular area.

This is not to decry the social status of the tenant whose ability to pay rent creates values in investment real estate. It is simply to say (and no one will deny this fact who has been either an owner or tenant or both) that in an owner-occupied home the standards of upkeep, of maintenance, of pride of ownership are obviously greater than in the tenant-occupied dwelling.

It is pride of ownership that tends to point up and to register the investment rating of a neighborhood. If there are any further doubts on this point, go into a neighborhood twenty-five or thirty years old and find out what the terms are concerning the purchase of a house as compared to those in a new neighborhood (barring, of course, any government restrictions on credit which might be in effect). You will find that in the old neighborhood the down payment is higher and tenure of mortgage or purchase contract, as the case may be, is far shorter than they are in the newer neighborhood. This is because owners and lenders know that this older neighborhood, now approaching midlife or slightly past it, is a hazardous proposition and any investments made in it must be well secured by large down payments and quick "payouts."

The downward trend of neighborhoods. History and fact bear out this statement: From the time a neighborhood comes into being as a newly platted subdivision, the structures built within it begin to wear out. They wear out physically and functionally, the latter because of the development of new inventions in the field of building materials and equipment. Designs wear out also to such a degree that no matter what expenditure may be made to modernize the building, it will probably exceed whatever additional capital value may be created.

This leads to the inevitable course of events — the coming in of lower income groups or the beginning of what we may call hyper-intensive uses, namely, commercial, industrial, or otherwise, any one of which gives the neighborhood a push downward and depreciates its residential investment quality.

Again, pessimistic as this may sound, history will bear out the fact that, barring such situations as a war-time economy which may not permit owners to pick and choose freely the location of their habitation because of the shortage of homes, the trend of a residential neighborhood is, generally speaking, almost always down.

The Physical Aspects

Whether or not a particular neighborhood exhibits appeal to the homeowner will depend upon its topographical characteristics. Flat or rolling surfaces have their attractiveness for people of particular income levels and for particular kinds of houses. What we propose to talk about here and in later chapters is low-cost housing, inasmuch as this represents the mass of our problem.

In confining our discussion to the low-cost house ($12,500 to $15,000), we find that the builder is usually interested in flat land surfaces. Flat surfaces do not present any of the problems common to rolling ground, and consequently will easily accommodate buildings without having to relate their placement to the contours of the land. Obviously, where we have rolling terrain, nonstandard and expensive construction problems are involved. In the mass production of houses at a price level of $12,500-$15,000, the aim is a house that can be built with the utmost economy and priced at the lowest possible figure in order to attract the great mass of purchasers of small homes.

In the low-cost housing neighborhood there should be some features of *natural beauty*, such as woods, streams, ravines, and hill-

sides. Usually they command a premium over the usual flat surfaced area. But on the whole, the new, small home is usually
built in an area where the builder can procure lots at a minimum
of cost; natural beauties, such as shrubbery and trees, must come
later as new, man-made cultural improvements.

Subsoil conditions are important in studying the topographical
factors involved in the analysis of the neighborhood because we
know that the variable conditions affecting the soil underneath
the ground have much to do with construction costs. For example,
in New York City where there is an outcropping of rock at the
surface, construction problems are involved and expensive. Again,
in and around Detroit, Michigan, a belt of quicksand, running
from Lake St. Clair on the north to Lake Erie on the south, presents
considerable construction difficulty with a consequent heavy cost
for foundations.

Our ideal neighborhood should be able to grow in all radial
directions and not be stopped by *natural barriers* such as mountains, hills, or rivers which might impede its geometric development. While they may add much in the way of scenic beauty,
they may prohibit the gradual and flexible expansion of the
residential neighborhood.

Our ideal neighborhood ought to be characterized by *good
drainage*. We know that mass building operations are not conducted where we have such conditions as low swampy ground.
As a rule the density of settlement tends toward the "fast" land
or the high ground which is free from the risk of inundation and
which has perhaps more value in point of vista and outlook.

The neighborhood area. Let us have in mind again our definition of a neighborhood as "a district or section with reference to
the character of its inhabitants." The word "character" means the
economic and social as well as the moral qualities of the neighborhood's inhabitants.

Furthermore, we must not confuse the definition of neighborhood with size, since the size of a neighborhood does not in any
way affect the definition. What we should have in mind is the
homogeneity of the people who live within the area. It may well
be that a neighborhood thus considered could be one containing
as few as fifty houses, and conversely, it might be one as big as
Levittown, Long Island, New York, containing thousands of
houses

Of course, the size of the neighborhood adds protection from these deteriorating influences that tend to cause neighborhood decay. We know, from a study of neighborhoods in large urban centers throughout the country, that when hyperintensive land uses, such as commercial or manufacturing, or infiltration of an antipathetic minority group, or other deteriorating influences begin to gnaw at the edge, it will not be long until direct access will be had to the very core of the neighborhood itself. It is a well-established principle that a large neighborhood is an economically safer neighborhood over a longer period of time than a small neighborhood. From this we may assume that the large neighborhood possesses the advantage of extra insulation over the small one. The *location* of the neighborhood should be qualified as to whether it provides easy access to the principal points of social and economic interest that may lie outside of the neighborhood itself. As a matter of fact, it is a basic principle of city planning that good neighborhoods usually lie across the directional path of the city's growth. "Neighborhoods not in the path of a city's growth usually lack marketability and tend to deteriorate," says the Federal Housing Administration in its Underwriting Manual. We know too that a great many mistakes in the planning of neighborhoods back in the 1920's were made because this principle was flagrantly violated.

The Pattern of Land Utilization

The appraiser must be conversant with land uses because he is (whether he knows it or not) a student of land economics. Land economics is a study of the uses which grow out of land; that is, real estate, and the values that result therefrom. These uses, of course, are both public and private. Public uses include parking areas, streets, alleys, city parks, and buildings housing the government of the city itself. Private uses are those of the residents of the community — those occupying the single-family homes, the apartments, and the stores and factories that serve the community.

In any intelligent neighborhood study, it is necessary to know what these relationships are. In other words, the uses should be tabulated and classified. We made many mistakes back in the 1920's because of the desire to plat a great preponderance of our property into what was called "business frontage," overlooking entirely the fact that there is a definitely known ratio between the number of families and the number of stores within a community; that a certain number of families can support only a certain number of stores. A study of these tabulations will prevent mistakes in the overplatting of certain types of land uses and will avert a repetition of the errors of the 1920's.

Zoning and its controls. Within the last twenty years we have seen the practice of zoning invoked in most of our large cities. The appraiser must recognize that zoning laws and regulations tend to define and to an extent limit the uses to which property may be put. Zoning also tends to create a stabilized valuation equilibrium. It does so because there exist, as a matter of law and record, the uses to which particular parcels of land can be put. These legal restrictions on use limit the income of investment property and thereby limit its price in the market place. Our difficulties have resulted from the fact that currently we have tried to apply zoning principles to cities already grown and in which the use-pattern has been permitted to evolve without the benefit of intelligent city planning. However, because zoning controls land use, which is a connotation of land value, and because zoning tends to assist the stabilization of real estate values, a study of zoning laws and regulations is all-important.

Restrictions on the land are a necessary part of the valuation study because, again, they limit land uses and also define land uses. This is equally true of local building codes and ordinances covering fire protection and sanitation.

The street pattern. Any attractive neighborhood must be laid out with a street pattern adequate to serve the inhabitants. There must be convenient access from the neighborhood itself to the major streets within the general area. The point to remember is that it is not always mandatory that the good neighborhood be served with wide boulevarded streets. As a matter of fact, there is a general tendency today, in town planning, to limit access to the main highways because automobile traffic has brought with it the hazards of high speeds. There is an observable tendency in town planning to lay out new subdivisions in blind courts, or what we might call cul-de-sacs, for the prime reason that planners attempt to discourage automobile traffic through a residential neighborhood. However, it is necessary for the central streets within the neighborhood to give access to the main arteries that will speed the neighborhood resident from his home to points outside the neighborhood he must reach as a matter of economic or social necessity.

Public transportation. Despite the fact that there are approximately 50,000,000 cars registered in the United States, we still continue to depend on public transportation. Every family cannot afford to own an automobile or may not be able to acquire one in times of shortages. There must be such public transportation as street cars or buses or subways, which will carry the neighborhood resident where he wishes to go. These services must be adequate, and the fares must be reasonable. It is well known that certain suburban areas have not been developed as fast as they might because public transportation is difficult and costly. On the other hand, some of the largest housing developments in this country (thirty miles south of Chicago on the Illinois Central Railroad, for example) have been successfully located at considerable distance from the metropolis, because the homeowner can get to the city proper in a short time and with a minimum of cost.

Despite the fact that every American family may hope to own an automobile, the bus is here to stay, as witness the new streamlined vehicles which are practically noiseless (compare them with the old square-wheeled antiques!), and which are equipped for quick acceleration and quick stopping. The point is that no new residential neighborhood has much hope of real estate prosperity unless there is adequate public transportation in at least either the form of street cars or buses.

Retail facilities. There must be, and town planners have long since recognized the need of, a well-balanced and well-diversified assortment of retail stores accessible to a majority of the residential neighborhood's inhabitants. Shopping habits of the past ten years have undergone a drastic change. Time was when people called the neighborhood grocer by telephone and had him deliver the family's groceries to the back door. Today, large supermarkets have sprung up in every city in the country. All sorts of automobiles, from the old jalopy to the streamlined Cadillac, cover huge parking lots outside the markets, awaiting the owner who carries his own groceries out of the store and home in his own car. This change in retail merchandising has been brought about by the advent of the larger grocery chains whose pricing policies enable the customer to buy at much lower prices than he formerly paid his independent grocer. Therefore, we require in any ideal neighborhood an assortment of retail services. We need food stores in the form of supermarkets and the whole galaxy of retail services which clothe, feed, and service the American family.

In passing, we must remember that the neighborhood retail area does not have to be located right within the neighborhood itself. As a matter of fact it usually is well beyond walking distance from, and probably on the fringe of, the new area. This simply indicates that the American family shops by automobile and a mile or so is not a deterring factor. As a matter of fact, in many new residential areas being developed today with $12,500 to $15,000 houses, the shopping area is as far as two miles distant. This does not discourage the prospective home purchaser because in most cases he has an automobile (or he shops jointly with his neighbor who does have one), and when he shops he buys enough supplies to last for several days, a week, or longer.

Parking facilities at the retail center are all-important. Platting practice today is to provide at least three square feet of parking space for each square foot of retail sales space. Real estate operators have discovered that the large supermarket is not interested in any location where there is no provision for parking space offering a ratio of three to one.

Recreational opportunity. A good neighborhood has convenient to it plenty of parks and playgrounds. It is observed that in the platting of large garden-type apartments the planners have wisely confined their land use of buildings to not more than thirty per cent of the available area. (FHA's permitted density: twenty units per net acre.) This recognizes the necessity for providing such facilities as playgrounds and wading pools for the use and recreation of the children. In addition, however, the attractiveness of any good neighborhood is enhanced by such near-by facilities as public golf courses, tennis courts, and the closeness of lakes and beaches which provide recreational facilities to the American family. Furthermore, in speaking of recreation let us remember the motion picture theater which exerts its influence on neighborhood desirability, as a form of low-cost entertainment. At one time its presence within or close to the ideal residential neighborhood was mandatory. Whether or not this will remain true with the advent of television is not yet known.

Public utility services. These are important, as they add to the attractiveness of the ideal residential neighborhood. The family must have gas, electricity, and telephone service; the supply must be ample and the cost reasonable. In other words, the cost must certainly be within the reach of the neighborhood inhabitant. As technological invention continues to progress, gas and electricity will, more and more, assume greater importance in the labor-saving devices within a home. Their cost and their availability are important to the prospective home purchaser in any neighborhood.

The Social Structure

No intelligent appraisal of a parcel of residential real estate can be made unless the appraiser knows something about the inhabitants of the neighborhood.

The skilled appraisal technician, viewing for the first time the neighborhood in which the property lies, will ask himself these questions:

"Who lives here? Who are these people? Where do they work? How much money do they make per month? Where do they go to church?"

This kind of interrogation indicates a clear understanding of the fundamental problem involved because, as we have said, values are made by people.

In studying the history of the inhabitants of the neighborhood, we must recognize the kind of nation in which we live. We are a thoroughly mixed-up lot of many races, religious creeds, and national backgrounds. The United States has long been known as the melting pot of the world. We have been able, by virtue of our system of government and our opportunity for providing a better way of life for people from other lands, to attract people from all over the world to this great country of ours where they may find that opportunity — and usually do.

In the valuation study, an overloading of any particular national or racial group within a neighborhood will be evidenced by certain backgrounds, family traits, and social customs. These particular group characteristics, in large measure, go back to the habits of their ancestors in the country from which they came. The housing standards of such groups are frequently indicative of these habits. So it is important for us to know the percentage of these various national or racial groups within a neighborhood. Any up-to-date information plant should contain a map of the city within which the appraiser operates showing the ethnic (racial) distribution of these groups within the city structure. This is important for a number of reasons. In addition to pointing out the demanded standard of housing of these particular ethnic groups, it will also demonstrate their geographical and directional housing trend within the city.

Family attitudes. In the ideal neighborhood there must be, first of all, a respectful attitude toward the law of the land, a willingness to support the laws of our country, particularly as they refer to property rights. What happens to residential neighborhoods in some of our large cities where this is not the case, can readily be seen. We can also see what happens when unlawful use of property, such as vice, arises in the neighborhood. There is conclusive recorded evidence that when property is used unlawfully in any neighborhood, the respectable and law-abiding citizens start moving out, and the desirability of the neighborhood as a place to live and raise one's children begins to wane.

There must also be a proper attiude toward and an appreciation of homeownership. This is easily observed in any neighborhood by simply cruising up and down the streets in an automobile, noting the condition of lawns, shrubbery, and plantings. The appearance of the house itself — is it well painted and well maintained — is further proof of pride of ownership. Homeowners are customarily regarded as good moral risks for the lender of mortgage funds. For the same reason, they are good neighbors for the prospective home purchaser who wishes to buy or build a home in the neighborhood. Also, since these people have exhibited a standard of civic consciousness by the way they keep up their homes, the prospective purchaser is assured that his investment in this neighborhood will be well protected.

We have spoken before about the percentage of owners in a given neighborhood as an index to its economic stability. This is also an index to its social stability. It is generally conceded that the moment the number of owners begins to decline in a particular neighborhood, the renters who replace them have lower income levels and, consequently, lower social standards.

The family size. The student appraiser should study the ratios on family size established by census figures. We know fairly well from these what the average family size is for the nation and for different cities. The important factor here in a consideration of

family size is that the size of the family usually indicates the size
of the house they occupy. This means that the average size of a
family in a neighborhood will in most instances give the appraiser
a good idea of the average size of the houses in that neighborhood.
We know that a family composed of more than four persons will
ordinarily require a three-bedroom house, whereas a lesser number can be housed in a two-bedroom building. We know further
that the family usually grows in size and that a new neighborhood
consisting of two-bedroom houses is usually occupied by newly
married couples. But as the size of the family increases and the
children begin to grow up, more sleeping space is required. If
that cannot be had within the present structure, the inhabitants
will move to another neighborhood where their needs can be met.

Study of school enrollments. The Federal census of 1950 contains more information on housing than any prior census, but
unfortunately, the Government is able to do this study only once
every ten years. Therefore, we need current figures that will
indicate what neighborhood growth is from year to year. This
can ordinarily be found from a study of the school enrollments in a
district. If we know, for example, how large the average family is
in the district, the school enrollment published every year for
that particular district, will give some information as to the trend
of population growth in the neighborhood.

The Economic Structure

It has been mentioned that the first phase in the neighborhood
study is to determine who lives within the neighborhood and what
their economic and social characteristics are. Annual income of
the American family has long been recognized as a reliable cri-
terion of housing demand. Therefore, in applying his professional
microscope to the neighborhood, the appraiser should know something about the occupational characteristics of its inhabitants.
Classifying these characteristics will usually reveal the salaries
and wages paid in each category which, in turn, will give him the
monthly income per family. Since we have reliable indicia as to
the share of its monthly income a family can pay for shelter, we
are able to estimate the probable value level of the houses within
the particular neighborhood under study.

The importance of family income as an index to shelter cost is
based on well-seasoned economic statistics. Economists have

figured that the monthly shelter cost per family should not exceed 25 to 30 per cent of a monthly income. On the same basis, it has been indicated that the purchase price of a home should not exceed two-and-one-half times the family annual income. Of course, this latter index is apt to be markedly distorted when applied to the ratio of monthly expenditures of family income necessary to take care of mortgage debt service, including not only payment of principal and interest, but taxes and insurance as well. Furthermore, the Veterans Administration housing loan program has tended to reduce the economists' idea of the permissible monthly dollar outlay per family, so that it may no longer be said, with finality, that the average family must be limited in its purchase of a home to a price equivalent to two-and-one-half times its family income.

As a matter of fact, the recent market has clearly indicated that home purchasers, particularly in the $12,500 to $15,000 class, are not so much concerned with the price of the home itself as with the share of their monthly income which must be paid to take care of debt service items. This appears to be sound reasoning. After all, what the family can really afford to pay is controlled not so much by the over-all price of the house as by the portion of the monthly pay check which must be earmarked for the cost of shelter. Furthermore, to assume that the average family is not able to buy a home because the price is too high does not mean very much. In purchasing a house, most young couples start out with the optimistic idea that they are buying a home in which to live the rest of their lives, but it just does not happen that way. It may be recalled that in a national survey made in the late 'twenties to determine the tenure of homeownership it was discovered that the average purchaser in the large metropolises who was buying a new home for the first time lived in it for an average of little more than seven and a half years. This was particularly true of the large industrial centers. Therefore, what concerns the family and what concerns the appraiser, as an index to housing values, is the monthly payment the family can afford to pay for housing and its ratio, percentagewise, to the family's monthly pay check.

The study of income stability. In his analysis of family income, the appraiser should give close attention to the stability and permanence of that income. We have already mentioned, "the insensate industrial town," which is dominated by a single industry manufacturing a product with purely seasonal appeal. In these situations the real estate economy is highly volatile, and the curve of real estate activity in such a city will show abrupt peaks and valleys. This is due, of course, to the fact that the industrial payrolls in these cities are irregular. This is a situation that may properly be called the "feast and famine" cycle.

The most favorable situation is one in which the annual family income is entirely stable or in which the breadwinner is a salaried employee (instead of a worker on a piecework basis or in a seasonal occupation). Under these circumstances it is found that the valuation equilibrium will be tilted but slightly pro or con. If the family has a stable income, it can plan ahead; it knows how much money it has to work with, and it knows, consequently, how much money it can afford to spend for a home.

This stability of income is a reliable index to builders. The operational pattern of realtors and mortgage lenders is cut to the monthly income pattern of purchasers. The up-to-date information plant of the alert appraiser will contain year-round employment statistics that he has compiled and can study as indicators of what will happen in the real estate market, barring any abrupt distortion of the economy.

Real estate market study. It is generally agreed that in times of increased market activity, it does not take a great deal of skill to be an appraiser; when there are plenty of transactions occurring in the market place it is simple for anyone — he need not be an appraiser — to compare prices and, on the assumption that truly comparable properties are being compared, to determine, to some extent at least, the value of the property in which he is interested. However, there is one catch in this process. Sometimes, the appraisal tyro will discover that he has been comparing lemons with an apple.

Also it must be remembered that the appraisal process is a thing which is a fixed part of our real estate economy at all times, in all seasons, and in all phases of the real estate cycle. Properties are appraised not only during times of good market conditions, but also at times when there is no market. Therefore, the way of the apprentice in this field at times when there is no market for real estate (and there definitely was such a time between the years 1930 and 1935) is apt to be fraught with a great deal of hazard.

Sales and rental market index. It is essential, however, that the real estate appraiser have at all times, practically at his finger tips, a knowledge of existing market conditions, particularly the supply and demand factors and the ratio of supply to demand. For example, the best all-round index to market conditions is not sales, as some people believe, but rentals. There are times during the market cycle when there are no sales, but there is seldom, if ever, a time when properties are not being rented. Therefore, the appraiser's study of the market should include a study of vacancies, and his information plant should in time record the comparative vacancy percentages over a number of years. This matter of establishing a rental index is not a difficult undertaking. A simple method is to take the advertising columns of the Sunday newspaper and, where rentals are quoted for particular sections of the city, to copy these rentals, list them, and average the rents. This, while not developing a finite conclusion, will show the trend of rentals in any given community over a given period of time.

It is necessary, of course, to explore all available market data. The number of properties being offered for sale in the market place and the transfers reported are significant factors. In some cities this is not difficult to obtain because there are certain agencies, either public or private, that report these transactions. If the data obtained over a period of time from the reports of sales and offerings in a particular district are graphed, they should reflect information that is bound to be a valuable indication of the direction and trend of the real estate market.

The appraiser should know something about *building permits* and keep records of the trend in the number of permits issued for new houses. Building permits are one definite base upon which to erect a prediction as to what will be the trend of the market.

He should keep abreast of the trend of mortgage lending policy. For years we have made it a point to check periodically with the larger insurance companies as to their current policies. The same thing applies to FHA. Since these mortgage lenders are large bulk operators, they are intensely alert to the situation and sometimes recognize more quickly than other people in the business straws blowing in the wind.

The foreclosure index. The alert appraiser will be cognizant at all times of the trend of foreclosures in the particular district he has under examination. This curve is studied closely by real estate economists. It is the subject of a very interesting chart put out by one firm.[2] The rise and fall in the number of foreclosures is the weather vane which tells the appraiser the trend of housing demand at a particular moment. Any sharp rise in the foreclosure curve will denote one of a number of things. For example:

1. That, because of lack of employment and consequent depletion of family income, the homeowners in the area are not able to keep up their mortgage payments. This, of course, will result in large forfeitures of property and a mass movement from the neighborhood brought about by the lowering of the social standards which in turn is brought about by the influx of renters whom the mortgagees will put in the houses, assuming that economic conditions are such that there is no sales market.

2. That the ratio between family income and the cost of home-ownership is disproportionate, brought about by either abnormal debt service payments or high taxes.

3. That the appraisal on which the mortgage was originally based was excessive — that it was padded — and that some time thereafter the borrower, realizing that the amount of money he owed on his house exceeded the value of the property, willfully defaulted in his mortgage payments and moved out of the district.

The thing to be noted is that a high foreclosure curve at any time, in any city or any neighborhood, is the red light to the appraiser calling his attention to conditions that indicate a falling market.

The tax situation. There is a hackneyed phrase to the effect that "it isn't the initial cost; it's the upkeep" — and so it is with housing. We have just recently passed through a cycle in which homeowners have been able to purchase homes with lower down payments than ever before in the history of our country. Some people, and particularly some real estate economists, believe that down payments, particularly to veterans, were scaled too low. This lack of equity in a property is always a risk to the mortgage investor because the occupant or the mortgagor can at any time step out of the property and lose practically nothing; or whatever he does lose, can be charged off to rent. The recent volume market

---

2 Real Estate Analyst Inc. (Roy Wenczlick), St. Louis, Mo.

has seen us giving little attention to the amount of the down payment. Consequently, the original payment involved in the purchase of a house has constituted no bar to mass homeownership. It is the upkeep that makes it tough, and the largest part of that upkeep is taxes.

The tax load must receive careful scrutiny from the appraiser on the grounds that this is a charge against homeownership. If that charge is inequitable or abnormal, he will be dealing with a neighborhood which lacks appeal to the homeowner.

Also, with particular reference to new subdivisions, scrutiny should be made of the potential expense involved in special assessments. These may be for the paving of new streets, sewers, and other improvements. Here again, if these special assessments are disproportionate to the value of the improvement, the neighborhood will lose prestige and lack appeal to the average home buyer.

The retail facilities. Although, as has been stated previously, the American family of average income owns its own automobile, it is still necessary to have a well-stabilized retail center as an integral part of the well-stabilized residential neighborhood. Retail facilities must be available. They must provide a profitable business opportunity for the retailer; otherwise, he will not remain in the location. It is generally agreed that the chain stores have had a stabilizing effect on residential neighborhoods because as a rule chain operators will not go into a neighborhood until they have carried out an intensive market research program. They know before they start — before they make any investment in land or building — that the business potential is there — that there are sufficient customers to justify the investment in the building which they either lease or build. Therefore, it may be taken as a reliable sign in any residential neighborhood where we see the chain stores well established, particularly the supermarkets, that there is stability both of residential occupancy and of retail operation.

Furthermore, as a rule, when the chain store operator comes into a district he stays. Consequently, the people who live in such a neighborhood are almost definitely assured of permanent retail services. It can be claimed, therefore, that chain store operations lend stability to real estate values in particular neighborhoods; that they tend to prevent the shifting of the occupants from one neighborhood to another; that perhaps they stimulate neighborhood growth. Certainly, they make a general contribution toward the stability of property values.

Neighborhood Mortality

The mortality of a residential neighborhood is just as solid a fact as the mortality of man. Any student of urban land economics knows this. Any analysis of neighborhood patterns within any large city will disclose the truth of this statement. For example, there is always the district just outside the downtown or central business area which represents the oldest residential section. Here the uses for residential purposes have long since expired. Beyond this are other districts not so old but where there is already evidence of decay. Then, located at some distance from the downtown section, are the well-established areas, not quite so old, where sales are few and far between but where it is still possible to obtain mortgage loans, although not from routine bulk sources and not at valuations and at interest rates which represent the mass of the mortgage lending operation in newer housing.

The reason for this is that the mortgage lender, having learned a good many lessons from the depression of the 'thirties, has now begun to look askance at the neighborhood which is past midlife and which is on the way down. He knows that there are plenty of hazards to the safe investment of his capital manifest in the current scene. He knows that the risk is too great. He foresees the encroachment of declining uses and the possible infiltration of racial or national groups foreign to the major group which once occupied this entire area. He sees that this once desirable residential neighborhood is rapidly coming to the end of the use cycle to which it was originally dedicated.

It is practically impossible to measure the life span of a neighborhood because the forces of decay act with greater or lesser impact and with greater or lesser speed in different neighborhoods in different cities. However, the quantum of economic and social stability is the measure of how long the neighborhood can withstand the attacks of obsolescence. There is always, of course, in the life of every neighborhood a point of peak desirability. In the opinion of this writer, that peak moment arrives just prior to the time when the original owners begin to sell and move out. Ordinarily, this is a gradual movement developing slowly as present owners find the neighborhood no longer offers maximum desirability and as the first renters begin to appear, supplanting the owners. Of course, on the other hand, obsolescence arising from social causes may attack so fast as to catch the owners entirely unprepared and off balance. In such circumstances, the situation becomes practically an epidemic and the entire district may expire before the owners have a chance to salvage their investments.

It is rather difficult to measure with a "slip-stick" or any other device the economic age of a particular neighborhood. The student of valuation practice can only compare the neighborhood under appraisal with those other neighborhoods with which he has had experience and attempt to determine how much of its life-path has been traveled. All neighborhoods exhibit some symptoms of social decay, except the one that has been newly platted, where the houses are all new, and there is no tenant occupancy. Aside from these exceptions there can always be detected the sign of some downward trend, barely perceptible though it may be. It is these signs for which the appraiser must look. He must be always on the alert to detect the one type of depreciation — the ravaging force — which again is the genesis of the axiom "more houses are torn down than fall down."

Summary

In summarizing this discussion about neighborhoods, let us emphasize that the study of the neighborhood is far more important than the study of the physical property itself. We have said before that values are not made by physical things; the fact that the house may have cost a certain sum of money is no index to its value in the market place. The problem is the attempt to determine what the house is worth because of the things that are going on in the market place and because of the social and economic habits of the people in the area surrounding the property under appraisal. Again let us state (and this is repetitious but it should be repeated time and time and time again) *people make values.* They make values by virtue of what they do in the pursuit of homeownership and in the acquiring of real estate by virtue the prices or rents they pay and the standards of maintenance they apply to their particular homes. They make or unmake values within a neighborhood because of the shifting characteristics of the homeowners, the moving out and the moving in.

Thus, as was stated at the outset, the neighborhood is the all-important entity in the valuation study because it is indeed the "peritoneum" which surrounds the particularly vital object of the valuation study. Once that social membrane becomes infected, there is no hope for any subject which lies within it, namely, the real estate which is under appraisal.

We may conclude this discussion, therefore, by posing one question the answer to which will enable us to diagnose the economic and social characteristics of a neighborhood: What is an ideal neighborhood? The answer might run as follows:

1. It is a clustering together of people in which there is a congenial and well-balanced society; satisfaction, contentment, comfort, and asociation with persons of similar social characteristics.

2. It is a district that provides the services of convenient and pleasant living.

3. It is a district that portrays a rational and well-balanced economy of housing.

4. It is one that provides freedom from the hazards of the weather, from the hazards of transportation, from the hazards of ill health.

5. It is one that must exhibit to the fullest possible degree the amenities of homeownership.

Posed in simpler terms the question for the appraiser to ask himself may be: Is this the kind of neighborhood in which I should like to buy or build a home and where I should like to live and raise my children for the next ten (fifteen, twenty) years?

If not, why not?

CHAPTER 9

Analyzing the Property

The appraiser is a man of many parts; he must combine in his professional background a knowledge of many subjects, such as economics, engineering, sociology, and particularly, law. It is, of course, necessary for the appraiser to know the nature of the different estates in property because they, to an extent, control and indicate relative marketability. We shall not, however, engage here in a lengthy discussion of real property law, although an indication of the need for this knowledge is the fact that most of the major colleges and universities in the country include as fundamental to any study of the real estate economy a complete course in real estate law.

In order to keep the discussion simple, we shall assume that we are dealing with an estate in fee simple, which is legally defined as "an estate or ownership of real estate vested in the owner, and his heirs forever, generally, absolutely and simply, without mentioning what heirs, but leaving that to his own pleasure, or to the disposition of the law."

Since we are concerned with the single-family home, we shall assume that the appraiser's object is to find market value; that the market value does indeed exist; and that there are no leases in effect or other encumbrances which might impair the free marketability of the title. (The valuation of real estate in which the title is less than absolute, such as a life estate, leased fee, or leasehold estate, is more fully covered in texts dealing with the valuation of investment properties.) We shall also assume that there are no problems of encroachments or other factors which affect the property lines, on the grounds that the appraiser is not a surveyor and cannot be expected to determine property lines with the engineering exactitude of a surveyor.

In brief, we shall assume that nothing is present in the problem that would in any way impair the title and that consequently the title is marketable.

Building Diagnosis

In Chapter 8 we examined the neighborhood surrounding the property. We shall now proceed to examine the jewel within the setting. But before doing so, we ought to utter a word of caution. The most difficult thing the appraiser has to do, particularly in appraising single-family homes, is to rid himself of all personal prejudice and look at the problem through the eyes of the market place. The ideal appraisal operation (if such there be) would be characterized by this level of judgment, though few appraisers are able to exhibit a perfect sense of tolerance in viewing the appraisal problem. There can be no sound valuation of real property under any circumstances unless the appraiser is qualified to look at the problem entirely apart from his personal likes and dislikes, to view it, in other words, through the eyes of home purchasers.

We cannot repeat too often: values are not created by appraisers; they are created by the people who live in the homes of the nation. To say this another way, value is not represented by the quantity of brick, lumber, mortar, or other materials within a structure; values are determined by the buying habits and the social traits of people. The country's universities and colleges have recognized this in their real estate courses, most of which include economics and sociology.

Economics is at the root of our problem, as the appraisal process is essentially a venture in the field of land economics. Land economics is a study of the uses that grow out of land when viewed as property. Any study of the uses necessarily implies a study of the values.

In order to make clear the need for an open-minded approach to our problem, let us look at the latest edition of Levitt & Sons single-family homes, appearing on the facing page.[1] This is being built in a vast new development in Bucks County, Pennsylvania. The typical occupant of a "conventional" (old-fashioned?) house will not be enchanted with the exterior design, particularly the

---

[1] At Levittown, Pennsylvania.

THE "LEVITTOWNER," LEVITT AND SONS, NEW YORK. (*Courtesy William W. Thomas*)

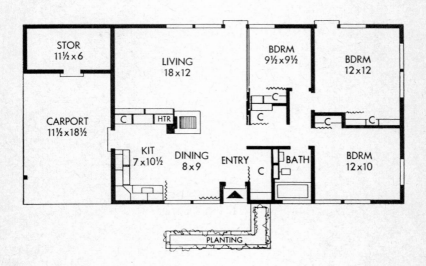

low-pitched roof. This is largely because he envisages this dwelling in his own neighborhood of "conventional" houses; he forgets that once it is placed in a neighborhood where it will be surrounded by its own kind, his objections to the looks will disappear.

Now let us turn the page and look at the floor plan. Here is the compact house. The layout of the rooms and services though unusual is amazingly simple and efficient.

Note the smart plan of opening the whole living room area as one big room without any sacrifice of privacy. Note also that every part of the house is immediately available from the front entrance without having to pass through any other part. The living room can be made larger by rolling back the wall (a sliding panel) which separates it from the adjoining spare bedroom. Thus the living area meets the needs of the expanding or shrinking family — from two bedrooms to three bedrooms and back to two bedrooms. The dining area can be shut off from the street and the kitchen by sliding basswood screens. These same basswood curtains are utilized as closet doors, making the closet available for its full width. The fireplace is open on three sides, and is situated in the center of the house.

This design recognizes a fact that has long been ignored in house planning in this country; namely, the house is a machine for living. The reader may not like the terminology, but that is exactly what it is and what it should be. Too long have we placed undue emphasis on exterior design and neglected the functional aspects of the interior. We wanted the outside of our homes to look nice in the eyes of our neighbors and to passers-by; as a consequence, we were willing to forfeit part of the structure's ability to function as an apparatus for convenient living. We developed large areas of waste space (in the attic for example), all sacrificed toward building a structure that had a pleasing exterior design.

What the appraiser should give attention to in the valuation of single-family homes is not so much what the house looks like on the outside (so long as it conforms to its neighbors), but how it functions as a facility for serving the daily needs of the family that lives within it. The appraiser of single-family homes must keep himself thoroughly attuned to the desires, attitudes, and housing habits of the American people in order to record faithfully what goes on in the market place. He must resist reactionary tendencies; he must be prepared to accept new departures in housing design. He may think the Levitt home is radical, but he cannot escape the fact that thousands of people have bought it and live in it —and like it! Because 150 years ago we built a house by the process (for example) of throwing wet plaster on green lumber to form a partition, it does not follow that the same method should be used today. To do so serves only to bring into sharp focus the comparative dearth of technological progress in the field of house building.

The Principle of Conformity

We said above that there should be no objection to exterior designs so long as they conform to those of the surrounding houses. This touches upon an important principle of valuation called the *Principle of Conformity,* which propounds that values will be stabilized in a neighborhood where the houses have a sameness of design (design meaning exterior style, construction materials, floor plan, and equipment within the structure); conversely, where this sameness does not exist, the value of the incongruous dwelling will not be equivalent to its cost, nor will it command a price level proportionate to the other houses that surround it.

The house is an integral part of the neighborhood. The factors of design and utility serve to indicate the income levels of the people in the neighborhood and indicate the class of housing the particular group can afford. The prospective home seeker is naturally attracted to a neighborhood where he knows the bulk of the housing is within the limits of his purse and adequate to the needs of his size family. Therefore the neighborhood that is comprised mainly of conformable housing will naturally attract the mass of the market. That is to say, conformable housing in a particular neighborhood attracts purchasers in volume. Conversely, since the mass purchaser is shopping in the particular neighborhood because he has been told, or knows by personal inspection, that the houses there are within his income range, the nonconformable house finds a market solely by chance. If a home seeker stumbles on the incongruous house by accident, he may buy it, but the chances are greater that he will buy one of the conformable houses.

Let us illustrate this principle by example. Let us imagine a $30,000 house in a neighborhood where the great bulk of the

houses is in the $15,000 range. Our prospective purchaser shop-
ping in the neighborhood is attracted there because he feels that
he can afford a $15,000 dwelling. Seeing the $30,000 dwelling, he
may be interested, and he may even be so foolish as to stretch his
budget in order to buy it. But when he does this, he immediately
classifies himself as an isolated purchaser. He does not represent
the mass of purchasers for homes in this particular neighborhood.

The second example is the reverse of the above — a $15,000
house in a $30,000 neighborhood. The market here represents
purchasers who want and can afford $30,000 homes. A typical
purchaser, looking for a $30,000 home, sees the $15,000 item, and
notwithstanding that it is the cheapest house in the block, he
decides that maybe it is so cute he ought to buy it. Again, let us
remember that his action typifies the special buyer and the special
marketing circumstance. He is not the mass purchaser for homes
in the $30,000 neighborhood.

Someone has rightly said that optimum value will be achieved
in a property that offers the most utility to the greatest possible
number of people. This statement emphasizes the basis on which
any large group of buyers pegs the market: it approves a market
price for conformable housing and disregards the price paid for
nonconformable housing as being nonindicative of neighborhood
value levels.

The principle of conformity does not concern uniform price
level alone, but covers sameness of design, placement on the lot,
and exterior appearance as well. There are many examples of
houses that were the subject of faddish planning, and that fail
to conform in exterior appearance, placement on the lot, or interior floor plan to the mass of other residences in the neighborhood. We do not mean exact standardization. We are not
talking about houses so alike on the exterior that a man coming
home late at night, slightly befogged, might fail to recognize his
own residence. What is meant is simply that conformable housing promotes stability of values, that where we depart from this
conformable norm we are bound to generate a depreciation of
public interest which, in turn, will be reflected in lower values.

The Principle of Balanced Utility

Another important principle with which the appraiser is concerned is the *Principle of Balanced Utility*. He must remember
that the home, as the place in which the family lives, must serve

efficiently the purposes and functions of family life. It must serve the purposes and functions of a family of particular size. Certain rooms have certain uses. Ordinarily, the living room is the gathering place for the family to talk, read, watch television, play canasta, or entertain guests; the bedrooms provide sleeping space; in the dining room are served the meals prepared in the family kitchen.[2]

Obviously the rooms which get the largest amount of use should be the largest size. In a three bedroom home, this refers particularly to the living room and the master bedroom. The principle of balanced utility dictates a rational space balance between room functions and room uses, between waste space and finished space, and between rooms of minimum use and rooms of maximum use; where this rational balance does not exist, the functional inadequacy will result in a loss in value.

The floor plan. A good floor plan ought to display three fundamental characteristics: (1) convenient routing into and out of the building; (2) convenient interior means of getting to and from rooms of related use; and (3) ample light and air. With regard to point 2, the kitchen, where the family meals are prepared, should be accessible to the dining alcove or breakfast nook; bedrooms should be located near bathrooms; halls should afford convenient entry to the rooms they serve. In wise planning point 3 would be evidenced by intelligent window treatment, assuring plenty of sunlight and cross ventilation, particularly in bedrooms. The floor plan should take full advantage of local climatic conditions. Where there are varying winds in summer, for example, the openings — doors and windows — should be so arranged as to take full advantage of them.

Placement. The principle of balanced utility also seeks intelligent placement of the building on the lot. Setback lines, elevations above street level, location of walks and driveways are all important indexes to the functional adequacy of the dwelling.

We are assuming in this discussion that the small house is being sold to a family, let us say, of four. We must therefore

---

[2] The recent trend in small housing is to eliminate the dining room, a step approved by the author. We have for long claimed that the dining room is the most expensive part of a small dwelling, considering the minimum use to which it is put. The trend today in the $15,000 house is to provide a small dinette, or dining area, off the living room in recognition of the fact that it does not pay to put money into construction of a larger room that is so little used.

apply the principle of balanced utility to the services within the dwelling that will be demanded by the head of this family unit and his spouse. What are the important features the lady of the house looks for in the new home she and her husband are about to purchase? The author's observation over a period of years in real estate brokerage and mortgage lending is that her paramount wishes and desires are as follows:

1. There must be ample closet space for linens and other articles as well as seasonal storage of clothes.

2. The kitchen must be well planned, for here the lady of the household spends a large portion of her time. The modern kitchen has become small and compact. Architects and house planners have recognized that the services incident to the operation of the kitchen, particularly in preparing a meal, must be arranged so as to flow around the operator, thus cutting down the number of steps and the physical effort necessary in the preparation of family meals. This calls for a room with very few openings and plenty of wall space; the ideal kitchen today is U-shaped or L-shaped. This flow of services should be from left to right, as a natural directional habit. However, there are still many examples of so-called modern kitchens where the reverse is true in whole or in part. Ordinarily, in preparing a meal, the first step is to remove the food from the refrigerator which ought to be the first unit on the left-hand side as we enter the kitchen. The food is then prepared and cooked, and the kitchen cleaned up. The location of kitchen equipment should correspond to this routine.

3. The design of the rooms must accommodate a pleasing and intelligent placement of furniture. The housewife demands sufficient wall space in the living room so that she may place the family furniture in a pleasing arrangement. She wants to know how her furniture will fit. As a matter of fact, the first thing she does is to visualize just what the layout of the furniture will be.

And what does the "head of the household" demand?

1. The heating equipment must be efficient because the small-home purchaser is usually his own janitor. He is, therefore, naturally concerned with the efficiency of the heating unit, for whether it is hand fired or automatically fired, he knows it will be his responsibility.

2. The bathroom must have good lighting, so that he can get

his morning shave without difficulty, ample room for bath linens, and an overhead shower that works, a shower that will not freeze him or boil him but will temper the water to his demand.[3]

The principle of balanced utility further relates to a rational and economical plan for the heating, plumbing, and electrical equipment. Statistics are readily available showing the normal proportionate cost of these installations in a small one-family home. An overexpenditure or an underexpenditure for these units in portion to the total cost of the dwelling will create a loss in value. This applies to insufficient lighting, lighting fixtures, or electrical outlets; to undersized or oversized heating plants; and to inadequate plumbing equipment (for example, one bathroom in a dwelling with five bedrooms).

Appraisal of Construction Quality

We come now to a most important part of the appraisal process, an examination into the quality of construction and the standards of workmanship in the structure.

There is a wide range between good and poor residential construction. Poor construction usually arises from economic conditions at the time the structure is built. A lowering of quality standards may result from an unusual demand for housing at a particular moment or a stampede for shelter in times of housing shortage. Construction difficulties arise during periods in which the Government imposes restrictions on what may be termed "conventional building materials" or during war time when it is necessary to use relatively unskilled workers because of a great shortage of labor and a shift of skilled construction people from the residential construction field to war industries.

Since the bulk of appraisal operations concerns the small home, we cannot make a comparison between an architecturally planned and supervised dwelling and one that is not, because in the low-cost dwelling the services of an architect are seldom employed. Where an architect is employed, construction quality need not bother the appraiser too much because the assumption can be made that the architect supervised the materials and craftsman-

---

[3] And, why not more divided bathrooms, where the only extra expense would be one additional lavatory, one short partition, and a door separating the two compartments, thus making possible the simultaneous and private use of both units by different members of the family?

ship that went into the building, thereby providing a reasonable assurance of good construction. Where the small dwelling is involved, however, the appraiser must depend upon his examination of the building at the time of appraisal.

We should make a distinction here between a building financed with an FHA insured mortgage and one that is not. In the former case the appraiser is, to a degree, assured of good construction quality, because FHA inspection practice is designed to assure compliance with its construction standards, which are by no means low. (To digress for a moment, the appraiser should keep in his library a copy of the FHA Underwriting Manual, which is a good appraisal text and also has much other information that will help him.) The FHA compliance program calls for at least three inspections. The first may be made when the excavation is completed, before the footings and foundations have gone in, or alternatively when the foundation walls are complete and ready for back fill. This enables the inspector to determine the quality of the footings and their ability to bear the load of the structure and to ascertain whether or not provision has been made for proper drainage, both inside and outside the foundation wall. The second compliance inspection to determine whether FHA construction standards are being met is made when the building is inclosed, though the structural members can still be seen, and the roughing-in for heating, plumbing, and electrical work has been done. The third inspection is made when all the work has been completed and the building is ready for occupancy. These inspections tend at least to assure the appraiser that FHA's construction standards have been met in the new dwelling.

In the old dwelling the appraiser's problem is more difficult, for here he has to depend largely upon deductive reasoning in order to determine construction quality. If an FHA mortgage existed on the property, the appraiser will again have some assurance as to construction quality. Otherwise, he must base his opinion on his inspection of those parts of the building which, as a rule, display the characteristics of cheap or good workmanship. The appraiser cannot see the frame of the finished building, or the studding, or the construction of the outer walls, but he can see the exterior of the building, he can see the basement, if there is one, and he can see the attic. Any one of these, or perhaps all, will provide the evidence of good or poor construction.

In the basement, close inspection should be made of the quality of lumber used for joist construction. Good or poor quality lumber is easily discernible. Most residential appraisers know the different grades of lumber, or at least the difference between clear lumber and lumber that is filled with knots. He ought to observe the size of the joists, and how they are supported. (A good appraisal habit, in walking through the first floor of a home, is to try to "spring" the floor; if it gives at any particular point, you may conclude that the structural strength is insufficient to carry the floor load adequately.) He ought to observe the size of the beams, and whether they are of wood or steel. He should examine the subfloor construction; the basement should be checked for signs of seepage to make sure it is damp-proof; the quality of the masonry in the outer walls should come under close scrutiny. (An old trick of the author's was always to carry a good-sized spike in his kit, so that he could scratch the masonry joints and determine the quality of the mortar used.) Any evidences of settling in any part of the substructure would be an indication of insufficient footings. A number of other places in the basement will indicate whether or not a good job was done when the building was built. (Of course one good way to make a determination is to investigate the builder and find out his reputation in the community, particularly with those who have bought and now occupy houses he built.)

If he can get at the attic he ought to inspect the rough lumber used for studding, the roof rafters and the roof boards, and the sufficiency of support of the roof load. In the attic he will also be able to determine whether or not the building is properly insulated. (No small home today may be considered well built, unless there is insulation at least underneath the attic floor so as to protect the occupants from excessive heat during summer and heat loss and discomfort during cold weather.)

As he goes through the building, the appraiser should examine the proper framing of door and window openings to be sure they have been well fitted and sealed. He should try all the doors to see that they fit properly and are not sprung. It is well also to take a look at the wooden trim around the openings, looking for nail splits, as an example of poor craftsmanship. He should look for openings between the wood-finished flooring and the shoe (or round moulding) which trims the joint between the walls and the floor; a loose fit may denote the use of green lumber. He ought to take a look at the kitchen cabinet work to discover whether it was built from good lumber or from scraps which accumulated on the job. Throughout this inspection process the appraiser proceeds upon the theory that if poor construction shows up in one place, it exists in others.

These are but a few of the points that bear watching. There are many others, but space will not permit their inclusion. But, again, if the appraiser has any doubt as to the quality of construction of a building, he may inquire among clients and builders' organizations; these will usually disclose the builder's professional status. It is gratifying to know that, although the house building business is "small business" in terms of the number of units built per builder, the poor builders do not last very long. The public, in recent years, has become quite alert regarding house construction, although they occasionally buy without the thorough inspection that is required. It may safely be said that small house construction, with the last decade particularly, has shown a marked improvement in quality.

Diagnosis of the Site

Let us turn now to a diagnosis of the site. We shall not attempt any valuation of land; our aim is an investigation into the services offered a building by the particular home site on which it stands. Does the land provide utilitarian services adequate to the type of building upon it? In answering this question, the appraiser must try to measure the use capacity of the land. As stated earlier, he is concerned, specifically with the physical factors of the particular lot.

Let us start by discussing the attractiveness of flat land as against rolling home sites.

The flat-surface lot appears to offer maximum utility for the low-cost house. The construction problem is simple, thereby eliminating the problem of abnormal construction cost. The question of what is desirable in a home site is answered by the appraiser's knowledge of the kind of people who live in the particular neighborhood, what they require and what they demand. It ought to be noted also, that the principle of conformity applies here as fittingly as it did in our discussion of the building.

In talking about these physical factors, let us remember that *soil conditions* merit considerable analysis, even in the low-cost home. The low-cost home is enhanced by the beauties of nature, flowers, shrubs, and a good-looking lawn. All this requires good soil. *Subsoil conditions* are equally important. Presence of rock, quicksand, or other soil that increases the construction problem adds to the cost of the dwelling.

The *size* must be sufficient to frame the building attractively. We have talked about placement before. The aim here is an attractive appearance. Thus, the lot must not be overcrowded and must be of sufficient width to frame the building attractively. If the garage is attached, ample room must be allowed for the driveway. To avoid having the buildings appear to lie closely against one another, *width* is important. So is *depth* to a degree, and while lot depth in low-cost housing may vary from as little as 80 to 150 feet, the norm is usually around 100 to 125 feet.

The *shape* of the lot is important. In the past the high cost of residential land in urban areas has been responsible for the grid-iron pattern of lot arrangement, (although this type of town planning goes back to the Middle Ages). But, in the lush days of the 'twenties, the subdivider, who was seldom a developer in the true sense, had, as his objective, the development of the maximum number of lots per acre. (Again FHA has exerted a control on this type of operation and has made certain demands with regard to adequate lot sizes before approving commitments for insured mortgages.) This gridiron pattern of lot arrangement in the past has made for rather monotonous building operations. It was claimed, of course, that the economics of construction prevented any departure from this dull alignment of row upon row of lots, all of the same dimensions and the same geometric design. The square house was the most economical to build, and the rectangular lot was adjudged most adaptable to the square house. Odd-shaped lots presented problems of design, and the small builder could not afford to attempt more attractive land planning because of lack of capital. However, the large builders, within the last decade, have departed entirely from the gridiron plan of lot arrangement.

The appraiser, ought too, to consider the *orientation* of the lot; that is, the position of the lot in relation to the points of the compass, as this may have considerable bearing on its desirability. We are referring now to the winds of favored temperature, either summer or winter, and the desirability of directional exposure. Or, it may be that the prevailing winds are undesirable, as in northern climates where the winters are severe and where the desirable exposure is toward the south.

The *direction* in which the lot faces should be related to the floor plan of the dwelling. In some sections of the country it is desirable to have the living room at the front of the house, in others at the rear. For example, in Alexandria, Virginia, in a section located on a high ridge, the new housing built in the last decade has, for the most part, located the living room at the rear of the dwelling, thus taking full advantage of the view across the Potomac River toward the national capital.

It is often found that lots on one side of a street are far more desirable than those on the opposite side, purely because of the directional exposure, meaning that in one case the exposure is favorable and in the other objectionable. Thus, in the example cited above, the lots on the side of the street facing the Potomac River are far more desirable and hence more valuable than those on the opposite side where the view is blocked by the houses having the more favorable outlook. Vista is important in house planning, offering to the homeowner advantages which make life in a particular location more enjoyable.

The appraiser must remember also that prevailing winds sometimes carry disagreeable odors or the smoke of near-by factories and that these conditions may affect the desirability of a home site because they affect proper ventilation. What he should seek are the aspects of intelligent planning that take all possible advantage of outlook, light, air, and such natural comforts of occupancy as the lot may afford the building.

Drainage is an important factor. The ideal residential lot must be well drained with enough elevation above street level to assure the discharge of surplus water caused by storms and sufficient "fall" to enable sewage and waste water from within the building to pass through the lateral sewer lines to the main sewer in the street without difficulty.

Let the appraiser give attention also to other improvements besides the residential building, such as landscaping, fences, driveways, and sidewalks. Let him remember, too, trees which assist in beautifying the home site and which provide shade during the warmth of summer. Trees add value to a lot; the average small house purchaser will pay more for a lot having trees than for one without.

The appraiser must also analyze some of the *legal aspects* of his problem, because as we know, restrictions of various kinds limit use of property. These restrictions are of two kinds: (1) those imposed by law, and (2) those running with the deed to the land. The first instance usually includes zoning ordinances, the second, restricted covenants, which are occasionally imposed by written recorded agreement by the owners of the restricted area.

In examining these factors, a check should be made of the *use classifications* in the block. The author assumes that every appraiser knows that zoning is an important matter; that every appraiser's library should have a copy of the zoning law; that one of the first things he must do is to check the zoning classifications to see that they permit present usage.[4]

There is also the matter of private or unrecorded agreements affecting the property. These usually consist of an easement or a grant to a public utility to cross over or under the land either with power or pipelines; to the municipality or other political subdivision of government for the passage of sewage facilities; or to abutting owners for the use of mutual driveways. Any of these easements granted by the present or former owner operates as a restriction on the free and unimpeded use of the land. As we have said before, what we are studying here is uses which grow out of land when viewed as property. Where these uses are limited, value is affected.

We have stated that the appraiser is not responsible for any certification of the *validity of title*. This responsibility belongs to the lawyer. The appraiser has a right to assume that the title is marketable unless he has been informed to the contrary, but where an encroachment of which he has not previously been made aware is plainly visible to him in his inspection of the property, that fact should be reported and a survey probably asked for. Usually in a problem of this kind, where an encroachment exists, value is affected by the amount necessary to cure it, either by its removal or by satisfying the party whose land is encroached upon by paying damages, or optionally, by purchasing additional abutting land to cure the difficulty.

There are *related factors* which should also be checked, par-

---

4 Occasionally it will be found that they do not.

ticularly the location of the lot within the block. The near-by neighborhood may have certain influences that are either objectionable or advantageous. The proximity to these influences will affect the desirability of the particular lot under investigation. Also not to be forgotten is the matter of egress or means of getting from the particular location to the main traffic artery or to the other points of social, economic, or cultural interests with which the family is concerned.

Much of what has been said about application of the principle of conformity and the principle of balanced utility to a diagnosis of the building applies equally well to the analysis of the lot upon which the building stands.

CHAPTER 10

Estimating Building Costs

Irrationally held truths may be more harmful than reasoned errors.
THOMAS HUXLEY

In our outline of the data program in Chapter 4, certain data are called for relative to the costs of buildings. The purpose of these data is to form a base on which to prepare the appraisal problem for treatment by the cost approach to value. In the use of this approach, an estimate is made of the reproduction cost, new — at today's prices for labor and material — of the property under appraisal. From the resultant figure, a deduction is made to compensate for items of decreased desirability (depreciation), and to this remainder is added the land value as found by comparison with other similar lands. The product of this operation is called "an estimate of value by the cost approach."

The first step in the process, therefore, is the estimate of today's reproduction cost, new. By the "reproduction cost, new," of a residential building, we mean the cost of exact duplication *in today's market,* with the same or closely related materials. By "today's market," we mean the labor and material prices that exist at the time of appraisal. Sometimes, in the appraisal of old dwellings, we find materials (such as walnut and mahogany, for example) that are out of use. The definition implies that, in the use of the method, we should contemplate the use of modern materials that are closely related in price to obsolete materials. The method always presumes to duplicate the building at today's costs, regardless of its age. The appraiser is not concerned with its original cost at the time it was built. The appraisal is being made as of today; therefore, today's cost must be used.

This requirement places the appraiser in the temporary role of cost estimator. Is he competent to do this work? The answer is that he must be. A necessary part of his educational background requires that he be able to estimate costs. He may be called upon to make an appraisal of a property where the building has not yet been built — that is, from plans and specifications. Often commitments for mortgage loans must be made before construction starts. These must be based on valuations of the to-be-completed building and the land.

It is the purpose of this chapter to discuss methods of estimating. It is not the intention to detail the technique of cost estimation as it is done by the builder or the architect, for estimating is a study in itself.[1] It is the intention to explore the precepts underlying five principal methods, and to recommend three of these methods as being dependable to the point of practical accuracy and, therefore, of value to the appraiser.

The Quantity Survey Method

The quantity survey is a detailed inventory of all the materials and labor that go into the finished building. This method of cost estimation is sometimes called the "construction breakdown" or a "take-off" of the construction job. It is the method commonly used by architects, builders, and contractors. As a first step in the process, the quantity of each class of materials and equipment is listed from the plans and specifications. The cost of these quantities is then computed. To this is added the estimated cost of the labor for each of the building trades necessary to process these materials into the building. Addition is made for the contractor's profit and overhead, and the result is the estimated cost of the building.

While this is an exact estimation method, it is not to be inferred that it will always produce optimum cost, because of the variations that will develop in any bidding operation where a group of contractors is asked to bid on the same set of plans and specifications; but it is the precise and detailed method of arriving at cost.

In the appraisal of a property yet to be built from plans and specifications, this method (or one of the two described in fol-

---

[1] The appraiser should be conversant with one or more of the many texts on estimating, such as: Gilbert Townsend, J. R. Dalzell, and James McKinney, *Estimating for the Building Trades* (Chicago, American Technical Society, 1938); FHA, *Underwriting Manual*, Revised 1947, Part II, Sec. 8; Construction Cost Data.

lowing paragraphs) must be used, provided a reasonably exact figure of cost is desired. In the appraisal of the used house constructed some time prior to the appraisal, some difficulty may be encountered in its use. The plans and specifications may be no longer available, or the materials originally used may be obsolete or no longer obtainable. But a more important objection is that proficiency in the use of the method requires almost daily contact with the labor and material markets. The time involved in a quantity survey of the original building cost in each appraisal job is hardly justified by its importance to the valuation process.

The Unit-in-place Method

This method is a mathematical compression of the quantity survey. It short-cuts the process. It is used with considerable accuracy by builders and contractors, especially in cases where the types of buildings involved are duplicative. Thus, the contractor who specializes in a particular type of building has no difficulty in estimating by this method because his original estimate derives from a quantity survey, and deviations from the base specifications can easily be computed by applying the differential of cost represented by those items that differ from the base specifications. As an example, assume that the builder in question specializes in a particular type of house that contains a heating plant costing (in place) $400, and that he is asked to bid on a house where the heating plant is to cost $600. If all other specifications are the same, it is simple for him to add an extra $200 to his base estimates for the typical dwelling in which he specializes and computes his cost accordingly. Other departures from his base specifications, plus or minus, are computed in the same way — that is, by the plus or minus differences in cost of the unit-in-place in the building.

This method, which is also precise (since it stems from the quantity survey), still involves considerable time and detail. It again places the appraiser (if he uses it) in the role of quantity surveyor or professional estimator. The appraisal process cannot give time to this detailed procedure. The appraiser is called upon in his work to play many roles. He must be city planner, sociologist, economist, engineer, builder, mathematician, architect, realtor, researchers, statistician, and a good many other things. He has dire need, therefore, of a method of computing costs by a shorter method that will produce reasonable accuracy.

How accurate must the cost figure be? The desideratum of the appraisal process, it has been stated, is value. The cost of the new building added to the land cost will not produce value unless the highest and best use of the land has been obtained and unless there is complete absence of any factor of decreased desirability. This is not to gainsay the advisability of accurate cost estimation in the case of the new structure; it is to emphasize a fundamental appraisal axiom; that, although the new structure may have been estimated to its finite cubic inch, the result may *not* index value.

In the case of the used house, costs need be determined only to the point of practical accuracy. Why is this so? For two reasons: (1) cost is not an exact correspondent of value; and (2) the generally nonprecise character of the appraisal process mitigates against the discovery of an accurate figure of value.

To exemplify this principle further, let us assume that we have under appraisal a residential building that has lived one half of its economic life. Mathematically, it has depreciated 50 per cent. If the original cost, new, had been computed in error at $10,000, instead of $10,200, the resultant error is $200 less 50 per cent, the amount of estimated depreciation. The net error, therefore, is $200 less 50 per cent, or $100. The appraiser has not yet been born who could estimate the value of any property, regardless of the value bracket into which it may fall, within limits of $100. The resultant net error, therefore, is negligible in influencing the final valuation figure.

The appraisal process requires a method of cost estimation that short-cuts the quantity survey and the unit-in-place method and gives results within the realm of practical precision.

The Cost per Cubic Foot Method

The cost per cubic foot method meets the requirements of the appraisal process. A product of the quantity survey and unit-in-place methods, it establishes a cost per cubic foot for the subject building and multiplies that unit cost by the number of cubic feet within the subject building to arrive at a figure of cost.

The opinion persists in many quarters that "cube costs," as they are popularly called, are the result of the appraiser's ability as a "guesstimator." It may be true that some appraisers guess at the cube cost of the building they have under appraisal, just as some appraisers guess at the value. The sound appraisal technician, however, knows that cube costs are basic statistical data that have their origin in the quantity survey and/or the unit-in-place method described above; that they actually represent the true construction costs of the building; and that, when used correctly they lead the appraiser toward a definite conclusion as to the dollar cost of the subject building.

The method of compilation. Considerable data on the cost of buildings per cubic foot are a necessary part of the appraiser's information plant. Obviously, each separate appraisal study cannot wait on the individual analysis of its cost per cubic foot arising from a quantity survey. There must be at hand a cost manual furnishing the cube costs of many sample or "bench-mark" buildings to which the subject building may be related with the object of determining its cost by the cubic foot method.

The buildings to be used as bench marks or base types should represent the character average with which the mass of the appraisal operation has to deal. Thus the appraiser who specializes in small residential properties that accommodate themselves to mortgages of $10,000 or less will assemble a cube cost catalogue of base-type buildings that fall in this bracket; the appraiser who specializes in retail stores, for example will assemble a collection of base types that fit this kind of problem.

The buildings selected should represent the average of construction quality and the average of utility. There is no point in compiling cube cost information on nonstandard types because of limited appraisal use.

When these base types representing the bulk appraisal problem have been selected, advice should be sought from at least three contractors. Care should be taken to see that the contractors are reliable and that the prices quoted do not reflect any undue desire to "shoot" at a low or a high figure. It is a well-known fact that any group of bids on a given construction project will (where there is no evidence of collusion among the bidders) develop some spread between the high and low figure. This may reflect inaccurate figuring by the estimators; again, it may reflect their willingness or unwillingness to secure the job. The abnormally low bid may also involve the ability of the contractor to buy at bulk prices, just as the abnormally high bid may indicate the high bidder's inability to do the same. The appraiser's objective is the *average* construction cost. Assurance that the bids reflect averages will often require the assistance of an expert estimator, as well as a check of the bids against comparable buildings currently being offered for sale in the market.

Derivation of the unit cost per cubic foot. After compilation of total costs representing, in the opinion of the appraiser, the average cost of the base-type buildings, the cubic volume in feet of the several types is found, and this volume divided into the total cost of each building to determine the volume cost per cubic foot. The number of cubic feet within a building is the number of cubic feet actually displaced by it.[2]

Restrictions on arbitrary use. While cost data offer the appraiser a precise mathematical process by which to start the valuation analysis, there are restrictions on their use with which we must be familiar in order to avoid error.

1. The base-type buildings must represent the average of construction quality. They must not be too expensive or too cheap. In appraisal work, we deal with value as it is determined by the great mass of purchasers seeking the average in price level. Thus our studies, as represented by these sample properties, must reflect the average type of building, the average level of price, the average standard of quality of workmanship and materials.

2. The cost per cubic foot of residential buildings will vary with their size, but usually in inverse ratio. Thus, if a house containing 28,000 cubic feet works out at 70 cents per cubic foot, the same house of the same specifications containing only 23,000 cubic feet will probably show a cost of 75 cents per cubic foot. This is because there are certain fixed charges applicable to the two buildings that nominal changes in size will not affect. Charges for sewer and water installation, heating system, bath, kitchen, and electrical fixtures may be equal in both instances; they may serve both houses equally well. The cost of these items may be, and frequently is, the same; hence the over-all cost of the larger building is not affected by the cost of these items, while the cost per cubic foot of the smaller is — and upward.

This principle, it should be remembered, operates only within reasonable limits of variability. It cannot be assumed that, be-

---

[2] Method of computing the cubical content of a building is shown in the Appendix, page 266.

cause a building containing 20,000 cubic feet costs 75 cents per cube, it will, if it contains 200,000 cubic feet, cost zero.

The base-type buildings selected for these studies should represent the average in cubic volume, thus avoiding the necessity of attempting to relate cube costs of the building being appraised to a base type of radically disproportionate cubical content.

Additions to, or deductions from, the skeleton specifications of each base type must be adjusted in the cost per cubic foot. Thus if the skeleton specification for the base type calls for gravity hot air heating, costing approximately $500, and if the building under appraisal contains a plant of a cost of $800, the increase in the unit cost is the difference or $300; in a building containing 20,000 cubic feet, the cost per cubic foot would be affected by the prorata difference, or $0.015 per cubic foot ($300 divided by 20,000 cubic feet).

If there are other extras not listed in the skeleton specifications, their cost must be in ratio to the total cubical volume, and the rate per cubic foot adjusted therefrom.

Irregularity of design must be accounted for in the cube cost. The correlation of a building of nonstandard design to a base-type building of standard or average design will produce erroneous calculations unless the differential in the cost factor is taken into account.

The plus or minus perimeter of the walls as it varies from the base type must be accounted for in the unit cost. For example, a building 40 by 40 feet contains 1,600 square feet; so does a building 80 by 20. Yet, in the first building, we have 160 lineal feet of wall (40 plus 40 plus 40 plus 40); while in the second, we have 200 lineal feet (80 plus 80 plus 20 plus 20). If, in this case, the unit cost per cubic foot were on the basis of a sample building of the dimensions 40 by 40, the cost indexes thus developed could not be applied with the hope of accuracy to the 80 by 20 building because of the excessive cost of wall construction involved in the latter.

The same principle must be applied to problems of subnormal or abnormal design. Where the base-type building provides, for example, for six rooms and the property under appraisal contains eight (with no increase in cubical content), the appraiser must allow for the cost of extra partitions, doors, and so forth. Again, where the base-type costs are predicated on the standard type of attic and the building under appraisal, while corresponding in every other detail to the base type is found to contain finished attic rooms, the appraiser must adjust the cost per cube to allow for the increased cost of construction.

All nonstandard features of design must be carefully weighed in respect to their effect on the cube cost relationship between the subject property and the base type with which it is compared. Large bays, dormers, and offsets in the walls that vary from the standard design must be given their proper cost allowance.

The Square Foot Method

The square foot method derives from the same source as the cubic foot method; that is, from the quantity survey or construction breakdown. It is similar to the cubic foot method except that it is based on the *usable* number of square feet within the building, meaning the livable space. It has the same advantages and disadvantages as the cubic foot method.

The Wenzlick Method

The contention that the cubic foot and square foot methods of estimating the reproduction cost of buildings overlook the variable of the length of the perimeter walls is entirely valid and if they are used without regard for this variable the result may be serious error. In order to overcome this difficulty, the Roy Wenzlick Company of St. Louis has developed a new method of estimating reproduction cost by breaking apart the component parts of the structure into two categories: (1) the cost of the exterior walls, and (2) all other costs to include the interior of the structure and the service and accessory items. These costs are graphed according to ground area and perimeter in Figure 3 which follows. The building involved reflects costs in the city of St. Louis as of 1952 (if this graph is used in actual practice, allowance must be made for the difference in costs between St. Louis and other cities in the country, as well as for differences in the type of construction involved in different areas) and is a one-story brick veneer residence with full basement of average construction, with foundation of concrete block or walls, exterior walls of four-inch brick veneer, interior walls of three coats of plastering over rock lath or metal lath, asphalt shingle roof, oak floors, one tile bathroom, forced warm air heating with blower and automatic humidifier, natural fireplace with chimney, and four inches of insulation on the ceiling and in the exterior walls.

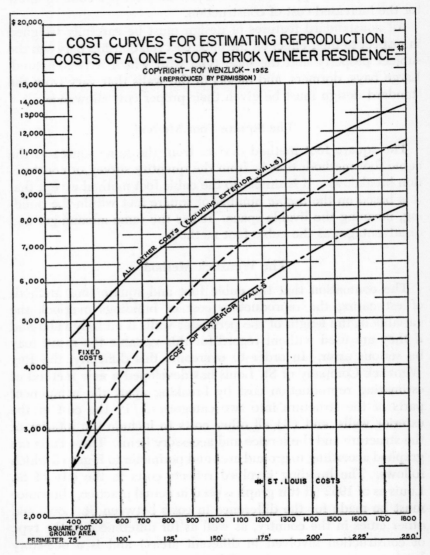

Figure 3.

Applying the cost curve to two typical dwellings, let us imagine a residential building, which we shall call Building A, of the dimensions 40 feet by 30 feet containing 1,200 square feet and with the perimeter measuring 140 feet. By reference to the curve as shown in Figure 3, it will be shown that the cost of the exterior walls is approximately $4,800 and all other costs are $9,750, or a total of $14,550. As a second example, let us consider Building B, (a ranch-type dwelling) with a center section and two wings containing 1,200 square feet of floor area but with a wall perimeter of 182 feet (one wing 25 by 16, a second wing 20 by 25, a center section 20 by 15). Again reference to the graph in Figure 3 shows that the cost of the exterior walls for this dwelling is $6,150; all other costs $9,750; total cost, $15,900. It will be seen that this method immediately takes up the slack involved in the additional cost of exterior walls. The technique appears to be entirely valid for houses up to 1,500 square feet of floor area; beyond that the cost of extras must be added. These extras would involve better materials, better grade of finish, and additional plumbing fixtures, such as additional bath and/or lavatory. It is obvious, of course, that in any house of super size, costing upwards of $25,000, the quality of construction would approach that of high-class and high-priced residential properties. The additional cost would lie, as stated, in the materials, the equipment, and the heavier supporting materials and framing.

This method, while entirely new, seems for the first time to provide the appraiser with a tool for the short-cut estimating of reproduction cost of residential buildings which is as nearly foolproof as anything devised up to this time.

The contractor's profit. The contractor's profit is a part of the direct construction cost and is always included in the cost study of the individual building. This is usually estimated at approximately 10 per cent.

Architect's fees. Where the building under study has been the subject of architectural treatment, it is customary to add these fees (approximately 6 per cent) to the construction cost. This is presumed to cover preliminary sketches, working drawings, and supervision during construction.

Reconditioning Costs

The efficient appraisal of used housing requires that the appraiser be competent to estimate reconditioning costs. The usual problem concerns the need for bringing items of deferred maintenance up to par. In fact, each appraisal of a used house is

really two appraisals in one, for the result should reveal the value
"as is" and the value "as reconditioned." This treatment discloses
the extent to which the reconditioning expenditure may be recaptured and, in many cases, the increment of value resulting from
rehabilitation. As an illustration, the appraisal may show a value
of $10,000 "as is." Reconditioning costs are estimated at $1,500,
upon the expenditure of which it is found that the property will
have a value of $12,500. In the process of reconditioning, it is
calculated that there will have been created an increment in
value of $1,000, the estimated value over and above the "as is"
value plus the actual cost of the reconditioning.

"Eye" value. Sometimes the nature of the reconditioning is
designed to appeal to the eye. Painting and decorating programs,
modernization of outmoded kitchens and bathrooms, or the
modern treatment of an antiquated facade will create "eye value."
Not only is the reconditioning expenditure recaptured, but,
further, value is enhanced because of the added attractiveness
resulting from the reconditioning. The reverse of this is exemplified in the expenditure of $500 for installation of new sewer and
water services because of the inadequacy or failure of those
originally installed. In this case, no "eye value" results; the
installed items represent normal purchaser expectancy.

Reconditioning cost estimation. Reconditioning costs are estimated by the unit-in-place method. The new roof is estimated to
cost $15.00 per square of shingles, meaning the installed cost.
Exterior painting is estimated at $0.70 per square yard, meaning
the applied cost. The new heating plant is estimated at $800,
meaning the installed cost. Thus, it is necessary that the appraiser's information plant be equipped with up-to-date schedules
of reconditioning costs, for in the appraisal of the used house, the
estimated cost of rehabilitation is an essential part of the appraisal
problem.

Reconditioning costs are always higher than new work of the
same type. This is due to the difficulty of discovering concealed
damage. Repairs to foundations, floors, porches, and those parts
of the building possessing structural affinity for the load-bearing
members are always estimated with a liberal factor of safety; the
contractor does not know what may be disclosed by those conditions that cannot be seen and estimated. Furthermore, the
ordinary reconditioning job on the used house is small in dollars.

This occasions a larger percentum profit to the contractor than in the case of new work, particularly in those states where the law requires the contractor to carry public liability and compensation insurance.

In conclusion, the estimate of building costs is a skillful and helpful tool in the hands of the appraiser equipped with the necessary factual data with which to apply it. The "short-cut" methods (cubic foot, square foot or Wenzlick) are convenient and accurate means of applying to the appraisal problem the measurement of the original cost. As in all work, the tools are not an end in themselves; they are only the means to an end. Paint and brushes do not create fine landscapes. These are the product of the technique of the artist — the sum total of his experience, his knowledge, his skill. The value of the technique of building cost estimating lies in the ability of the appraiser to apply it with a skill born of accumulated knowledge and a judgment nurtured by experience.

CHAPTER 11

The Theory of Depreciation

So fleet the works of men,
Back to their earth again,
Ancient and holy things
Fade like a dream.

CHARLES KINGSLEY

In all used dwellings and in many new ones that are subjected to appraisal, certain conditions make for decreased desirability. In the old house (and we may think of a house as beginning to be "old" from the time construction is finished), the reason for the existence of these conditions is obvious: Age has taken its toll; the supersession of new designs, new materials, new construction methods, and new equipment have emphasized the unattractiveness of the older building; it lacks functional sufficiency as compared with the house built according to current standards.

This lack of desirability is reflected in the quantity of value that the mass market places on the property. It compares the property under observation with the ideal property of the same type; where it fails to measure up to the ideal, the market discounts the price paid in an amount compensatory for this lack of desirablity. This discountable factor is known as "depreciation." "Depreciation," says the American Institute of Real Estate Appraisers, "is a loss in capital value."[1]

The word "depreciation," in general usage, denotes a wearing out as a result of age. But here again is a word that, through particular use in valuation practice, is given a specialized definition. As part of the vernacular of the appraiser, it is not always a correlative of, or a synonym for, "age." It is rather synonymous with loss in value, which loss may or may not result from age.

---

[1] American Institute of Real Estate Appraisers, *Appraisal Terminology and Handbook* (Chicago, American Institute of Real Estate Appraisers, 1950).

HOME OF JAMES WHITCOMB RILEY IN INDIANAPOLIS, INDIANA. BUILT IN 1872.
(*Courtesy H. Lieber Company*)

HOME IN LOS ANGELES, CALIFORNIA. BUILT IN 1940. RICHARD J. NEUTRA, ARCHITECT.
(*Courtesy Luckhaus Studio*)

HOME BUILT IN DETROIT — 1926.

HOME BUILT IN WASHINGTON, D. C. — 1952.

(Keyes, Smith, Satterlee and Lethbridge, Architects.) *(Lautman photo)*

"More houses are torn down than fall down," is another way of saying that structural decrepitude alone is the least of the causes that bring about a loss in value. The proud mansions of yesteryear still stand in their original locations. Physically, they may be sound; functionally, however, they are inadequate. The inventive genius of man as manifested by improvements in design, planning, and equipment has made them obsolete. Social change in the neighborhood has made them undesirable as places in which to live. The point is that age alone is not solely responsible for their loss of esteem in the mind of the home buyer. Far more important is the change wrought by progress in the arts and by the lowered social level of a worn-out residential district.

The age of the structure has, of course, nothing to do with depreciation found in the new dwelling completed yesterday. Here, because of some mistake in planning, design, or economic unsuitability (such as an overimprovement or underimprovement of the land), depreciation was inherent in the plan itself and was brought into being when the completed dwelling was placed on the market, where the purchasing public, disregarding the *costs* involved, placed a price on it that reflected the penalty arising from depreciation. Thus we see that, while age tends to develop one form of depreciation, it is one of the less important forms. As a matter of fact, residential buildings that are well maintained tend to exist in perpetuity. Dr. Clark[2] cites the example of a residential building in Ruedesheim, Germany, which has been continuously occupied for more than 1,300 years. And in our own country houses surrounding Lexington Green, at present tenanted and well maintained, were there and occupied when Captain Parker and his Minutemen made their historic stand in the year 1775.

To create a clearer understanding of the valuation problem and achieve greater precision in estimation, let us subdivide depreciation into three classifications: (1) physical deterioration; (2) functional obsolescence; and (3) economic obsolescence.

Physical Deterioration

"Physical deterioration" is defined as loss in value arising from:

1. Structural decrepitude

---

[2] Horace F. Clark, *Appraising the Home* (New York, Prentice-Hall, Inc., 1930).

2. Wear and tear
3. Action of the elements
4. Disintegration through use

This is a type of depreciation that arises from two causes: (1) wearing out of the parts of the structure, and (2) lack of proper maintenance. As was stated above, a well-maintained residential structure will have an indeterminate physical life. It is the cumulative effect of deferred maintenance that accelerates depreciation. The roof of the building wears out and begins to leak; if the condition is not cured, structural failures will result, in the form of rotted roof boards, rafters, and plaster. What was originally a minor repair that could have been made at the cost of a few dollars may result in a major repair program costing many hundreds of dollars.

Physical decay may result from rot occasioned by dampness or lack of ventilation. Damp-rot is frequently observable in exterior wood surfaces that have not been painted at definite periodic intervals. Worn-off paint exposes the bare wood to the action of the elements, with the consequent breakdown of the resistive surfaces.

In some sections, the lack of proper termite protection causes heavy damage to the load-bearing members and the undersurfaces of buildings.

The metal parts of the building, especially those exposed to the weather, give rise to a form of decay occasioned by rust. Roof flashings and the gutters and conductors that carry rain water are subject to corrosion unless given frequent protective treatment with paint.[3] The undermining of foundations by floods in those areas subject to inundation causes severe physical damage.

The chemical properties of water sometimes have the effect of shortening the life of heating and plumbing equipment. The diminished efficiency of this equipment as a result of corrosion accelerates depreciation.

A primary cause of decay in the physical structure lies in cheap construction. Insufficient footings, improper framing, poor masonry, cheap lumber, second-grade equipment, and poor workmanship all speed the early physical failure of the building. In every building, physical decay will accrue with the years. In

---

[3] Unless constructed of copper, which is found only in the more expensive buildings.

a building characterized by cheap materials and shoddy workmanship, it will accrue faster.

Functional Obsolescence

The second classification of depreciation is "functional obsolescence." This type of depreciation, like physical deterioration, is intrinsic in character. It arises from sources that lie within the structure. It is defined as loss in value arising from:

1. Superadequacy and inadequacy
2. Antique design
3. Eccentric design
4. Outmoded equipment
5. Lack of utilitarian convenience compared to an up-to-date building

Superadequacy and inadequacy. These two items connote violations of the principle of balanced utility, discussed in Chapter 9. (They should not be confused with the underimprovement and overimprovement of the land discussed below under "Economic obsolescence.") By "superadequate" is meant those items within the property that are surplus utility and that are out of economic balance with the whole. In a building costing $12,000 a heating and cooling plant priced at $4,000 is superadequate, on the grounds that a heating plant costing $1,000 would be sufficient to satisfy the demands of the typical purchaser.

By "inadequate" is meant those items within the property that are utility deficits and out of economic balance. A good example of this type of functional deficiency is the building in which the clothes closets are of insufficient size to serve the bedrooms or in which there are five bedrooms and only one bathroom.

Antique design. The word "design" here designates the type of architecture, the construction materials, and the floor plan of the building. Improvements in housing styles are progressive as new and more efficient designs are developed. Functional obsolescence accumulates as design becomes outmoded through the public acceptance of newer and more modern architecture, plans, and materials.

An example of the extent to which changes in the use of building materials causes an accrual of functional obsolescence is found in the widespread use of insulation, extending down into the bracket of buildings costing under $10,000.

The heat loss in an uninsulated building, as compared with one that has been subjected to modern insulation treatment,[4] can be accurately measured.[5] Lack of insulation, therefore, is a functional deficiency that carries with it the liability of increased heating costs, the possibility of decreased efficiency or breakdown of the heating unit because of overfiring, and the discomfort that results from living in a building that is not as weatherproof as it could be.

The conservation of heat within the building during the winter season is but one of the benefits of insulation. It serves also to keep out the rays of the sun and thus makes the inside of the building more comfortable during the heat of summer.

Into this same category of functional obsolescence falls the old-style building with extra high ceilings and extra thick walls. The high ceilings make for abnormal heating costs above and beyond what should be necessary. Thick walls are unnecessary in these days of specialized insulation treatment.[6]

Eccentric design. Departure from the norm carries with it the value penalty that must ensue. Freakish architecture, faddish planning, and nonstandard materials and workmanship belong in this category. An artist built his house for his own use and devoted more than half of the first-floor area to a skylighted studio. This special-purpose planning was satisfactory to him while he kept the house for his own use, but it carried a heavy penalty of obsolescence when he offered the house for sale in the market place.

Outmoded equipment. Inadequate or obsolete equipment is a cause of functional obsolescence. The modern system of heating calls for filtered, clean, or washed air and a proper system equipped with mechanical devices for forcing the air through all of the rooms of the building. An alternative is "radiant" heat-

---

[4] This means something more than the ordinary tarred building paper sometimes used over wood sheathing. By "modern insulation treatment" is meant the use of any of the many fibrous insulating boards or mineral wool batts that baffle heat rays or foil surfaces that refract them.

[5] The appraiser should be familiar with formulas developed by the American Society of Heating and Ventilating Engineers for the measurement of B.T.U. loss and heating efficiency.

[6] Recent trends in prefabricated housing reveal wall construction of five-ply laminated wood less than one inch thick.

ing in which heat is radiated from a series of pipes usually imbedded in the floors of the structure. In any event, good construction practice requires that even in the low-cost houses (below $12,000), modern systems of heating reflect the demand of the mass market. As a consequence, the old-style gravity systems, as well as steam and hot water, with old-style "loop" radiators, are obsolete. The same is true of old-style bath, plumbing, and lighting equipment. Insufficient electrical outlets also belong in this same classification.

Lack of utilitarian convenience, compared to an up-to-date building. In Chapter 9 the layout of the modern kitchen was described. The old-style kitchen with its multifarious openings, lack of wall space, and scattering of the service units over a large floor area calls for the application of functional obsolescence.

Special conditions of climate require special functional services within the building. In the northern climes, storm sashes are standard equipment; in the extreme south (New Orleans, for example), few modern houses are built without the installation of a ventilator fan situated in the attic, which provides a forced circulation of air during the months of abnormal heat.

Relation of functional adequacy to neighborhood standards. In his observation of the items of functional deficiency existing within the structure, the appraiser is sometimes prone to relate the quantum thereof to the present neighborhood standard. For example, in the review of many appraisal reports on used houses, the author has noted the complete absence of any deduction from the cost, new, to cover functional obsolescence. This is usually explained by the appraiser on the grounds that, while the floor plan and the equipment of the subject building are indeed obsolete, the buildings themselves — because of their age — do not deserve, nor would the inhabitants appreciate, modern housing and equipment.

Any such hypothesis as this is fallacious. The question confronting the appraiser is not what the inhabitants of the neighborhood want or would appreciate. Nor is it a question of what the occupants merit in the way of modernization, nor of the economic soundness of any such program, nor of neighboring standards. Rather, are we concerned with the question: If these same houses were being constructed new today, would the finished structures involve the same architecture, materials, floor plan, heating, plumbing, and lighting equipment, and kitchen layout as exists in them now? If the answer is no, then functional obsolescence is present in the structures, and the necessary allowances must be made for it.

The quantum of functional obsolescence is not made less or more because of the acceptance of it by those who occupy outmoded housing. It becomes less or more in direct ratio to the progressive development of house building techniques. Thus, if the style and efficiency of present systems of heating remain constant over a long period of years, little functional obsolescence will arise from this source. But if tomorrow a new device is invented having one fourth the bulk of the present one and with a higher degree of heating efficiency, obsolescence of those systems now in use will accelerate rapidly.[7]

Functional obsolescence can be arrested completely only when science and invention cease to exist. If the reader accepts the definition quoted above, which stipulates that this form of depreciation is made manifest by comparison "with efficiency in a modern building," then it must be acknowledged that functional obsolescence exists in some form in every used house and may exist in any new structure that violates the principle of balanced utility.

Summarizing, we may conclude that any lack of utilitarian convenience, compared with what may be expected in a modern building, is chargeable to functional obsolescence.

Economic Obsolescence

Economic obsolescence, the third classification of depreciation, is defined as loss in value arising from lack of demand and usually attributed to:

1. Oversupply
2. Changes in the character of use
3. Legislative enactments
4. Proximity to nuisances
5. Infiltration of inharmonious people
6. Underimprovement or overimprovement of land

The nature of this type of depreciation differs from those previously discussed. The first two, physical deterioration and func-

---

[7] Example: forced warm-air systems versus "radiant" heating.

tional obsolescence, are intrinsic in character. Economic obsolescence is extrinsic, for it arises from forces outside of the property. And while physical deterioration and functional obsolescence are to some extent curable, through repair and modernization, this type is well nigh incurable.

Oversupply. Oversupply is the disruption of the balance between supply and demand. In building booms, when production has proceeded far beyond the ability of the market to absorb the surplus of units, demand subsides and, in fact, may disappear altogether, thus loading the market with an oversupply of housing. Or, the workers may elect to follow a large industry that is responsible for a major share of family income in a community and that has decided to move to another, distant location; this, too, has the effect of throwing into the market a surplus of housing. Any condition that results in surfeiting the market, with the consequent depressing of values, is classified as "economic obsolescence."

Changes in the character of use. This form of economic obsolescence arises from transition of uses in districts and neighborhoods. As the uses to which the buildings were originally dedicated begin to change and the social quality of the neighborhood begins to decline, the district loses its appeal for the mass of prospective home purchasers, with resultant loss in value of the properties. Economic obsolescence and neighborhood decadence are synonymous. The gradual decline of occupancy quality, the supersession of gradually declining uses, the transition from single-family occupancy to multifamily occupancy, the change from residential to retail, commercial, or industrial uses, the encroachment of inharmonious racial or national groups — all these bring with them a decrease in owner-occupancy appeal and a loss in value. The market for these properties, instead of appealing to the great mass of home purchasers, becomes more and more constricted, until finally it ceases to exist altogether.

Legislative enactments. Under this heading should be considered zoning and other forms of legislation that inhibit the optimum use of real property. It has been previously stated that zoning acts to stabilize values, but in some instances, zoning may well have operated to depress values, in which event the property could be charged with this type of depreciation. Condemnation actions by the local unit of government may also be considered under this caption. Economic obsolescence has accrued in any number of situations as the result of the construction of super-highways, changes in grade, and the relocation of streets and highways.

Proximity to nuisances. Locations close to railroads, factories, coalyards, lumberyards, gas stations, and stores; exposure to smoke, odors, noise, schools; resorts, amusement parks, theaters, and car lines — all these affect the degree to which the property will be attractive to a large number of purchasers.

Infiltration of inharmonious people. The encroachment of an antipathetic racial or national group brings with it, first, the threat and, ultimately, the effect of decreased values. The reason for these movements was discussed in Chapter 7 in connection with the ethnological pattern of cities. In every large city housing a proportion of foreign-born or people of races other than white, this situation must be reckoned with. The evolution of economic obsolescence does not await the actual penetration of a neighborhood. It exists as soon as the threat is visible and known. Tracing the movement of one of these groups toward a heretofore unaffected residential district, it will be noted that, as the movement gets progressively nearer, values in the area become progressively less. Some time after actual penetration they find their new and lowered level.[8]

Overimprovement. A common cause of economic obsolescence is overimprovement. This is exemplified in the case of a building costing $20,000 constructed on a lot valued at $2,000, in a neighborhood where the bulk of the housing is in the $10,000 value bracket (land and building included). This form of depreciation is present because the property fails in its appeal to the typical buyer. The mass market, in this instance, is represented by the $10,000 purchaser. Eventually, a purchaser will be found who, although unwilling to pay a sum commensurate with the replacement cost of the property, will pay a sum slightly in excess of the price level established by the bulk housing in the neighborhood. The principle affirmed, then, is that, while value in the market place will not in any case be equivalent to cost, it will be a figure somewhat higher than the bulk housing price level. Restriction

---

[8] This is certainly true as regards "value"; it is conversely true as regards "price" owing to the operations of the speculator whose presence on the scene is synonymous with the impending change to use by a lower income-level group.

of marketability to the typical purchaser (that is, in the above example, the $10,000 purchaser) makes for decreased value.

Underimprovement. A cause of economic obsolescence almost as common and less understood by appraisers is underimprovement. This is the antithesis of the foregoing example. The contention is frequently made that underimprovement is not as serious as overimprovement. Is this a fact? Careful analysis of the situation will furnish an answer.

1. Let us assume that the lots in a $20,000 neighborhood bear an established value ratio to the buildings on which they stand, and let us assume further that that ratio is 5 to 1 — namely, that the buildings had an original construction cost of approximately $16,650 and that the demand price of the lots is approximately $3,350. Since the lot offers a volume of services compatible with a $16,650 building, the effect of placing on it a building costing less than $16,650 is to bring about a depletion of the warrantable value (that is, utility) of the land. Stated differently: If the lots in this neighborhood have a value of $3,350, based on their adaptability to and serviceability for $16,650 buildings, thus developing a total value of approximately $20,000, a lot servicing a building of substantially lower cost will not have a warrantable value of $3,350. It will have a value less than that figure. Depletion of utility brings with it depletion of value.

2. The underimproved property, like the overimproved property, will not attract the mass market. The typical purchaser is the occasional purchaser. Buyers of homes should know that to purchase the smallest house in the neighborhood is more of a gamble than an investment; it involves more of a hazard than the purchase of the conformable house. And if they do not know it at the time of purchase, it will be brought home to them with startling force when the time comes to sell it.

3. The underimproved property has the effect of depreciating neighborhood values, particularly those of the abutting properties. Thus a $10,000 building that is sandwiched between two properties valued at $20,000 will decrease desirability of the properties surrounding it. The situation exemplifies the old fable of the one rotten apple among all the good ones; the effect is to make, not the bad apple good, but the good apples bad.

It may be concluded that underimprovement exhibits a factor

of economic obsolescence in the sense at least of depleted land values, and because of the consequent restricted marketability, the land may not be worth its cost as of the date construction is finished.

Economic obsolescence is a ravaging force. It is the most ravaging of all the forces of depreciation. It is the basis of the axiom that "more houses are torn down than fall down." Physical deterioration can in part be cured by proper maintenance and replacements. Functional obsolescence can be cured at least to the extent of modernizing the design and equipment within the building from time to time. But there is no cure for economic obsolescence, because it has its origin in social rather than in physical sources.

CHAPTER 12

The Estimate of Depreciation

Continual dropping wears away a stone.
LUCRETIUS

The examination of any appraisal report in which the appraiser has attempted to detail depreciation method will provoke ample ground for argument. Likewise, the testimony of expert witnesses covering this phase of the appraisal process will give rise to sharp dispute. Why is this so? Answer is found in the analysis of the methods used to calculate depreciation. Bonbright speaks of the "inherent difficulties of measurement — difficulties of which no experts have yet found satisfactory solutions." [1] Measurement of depreciation is indeed difficult because of the various techniques used in commercial appraisal to estimate it, many of which serve to confuse rather than to elucidate.

There are many methods of estimating depreciation, especially in the general field of valuation practice. In this chapter we shall discuss two, both of which have particular relation to the valuation of single-family dwellings; we shall recommend one.

The Theoretical Method

The theoretical method attempts to calculate depreciation by the process of simple mathematics. It originates from tables that are supposed to show the average *economic* lives of buildings of various types of construction and use. The most popular of these tables is published by the United States Treasury, Department of Internal Revenue (known as "Bulletin F," 1946) to use in fixing proper charge-offs of depreciation for income tax purposes. In

---
[1] James C. Bonbright, *The Valuation of Property* (New York, McGraw-Hill Book Company, 1937).

this survey, several thousand buildings were studied and classified according to construction types and character of use; from these statistics, an optimum use life was estimated.[2]

As an example of this method, we may assume that a building had an original cost at the time of construction of $20,000 and that, as of the appraisal date, it was 25 years of age. Reference to the table indicated shows that the building has an optimum use life of 50 years. Since it has lived 25 years, or half of its useful (that is, economic) life, the method teaches that the accrued depreciation is 50 per cent of the original cost, or $10,000, and that the building at the time of appraisal is "worth" the remaining $10,000.

The "effective" age. A variation of the method requires the appraiser to estimate the "effective" age of the building. In doing so, he is expected first to classify the building according to the table mentioned and then to estimate the expected use life that the building will have from the date of the appraisal. This estimate is subtracted from the "ideal" age, according to the table, and the result is said to be the effective age. This result is then multiplied by the proper percentum figure, as shown by the table, to arrive at the depreciation to be charged. The method is demonstrated in the following example:

1. Average economic life of the structure as per depreciation table .... 50 years
2. Appraiser's estimate of the remaining economic life (minus) .... 35 years
3. Effective age as per the appraiser's estimate .... 15 years
4. Indicated depreciation rate per annum as per Item 1 .... 2%
5. Effective age 15 years x 2% per year equals total depreciation 30%
6. Assumed construction cost new $20,000
7. Cost, new, $20,000 x 30% equals total dollar amount of depreciation .... $ 6,000

In this process, it will be noted that the appraiser is asked to predict, on the basis of what has already passed, the quantum of building cost which will continue to live and the extent of its life. An ability to do this with accuracy would lie well within the arts of legerdemain. We have many elements in the appraisal process that rest on rather thin ice, but none quite so thin as this.

If this method of building ages multiplied by percentums has

---

[2] See Appendix, page 269.

any validity at all (and the author questions whether it has), it is the recognition of its use by at least one agency of the Government. But against that one advantage lie many disadvantages. For example:

1. Any table of expected building lives must necessarily be based on averages. This is another vain attempt to reduce the commodity of real estate to the basis of exact similiarity, which it does not and cannot possess.

2. Life tables make the fallacious assumption of identical construction practice — the use of the same quality of labor and materials in all buildings that may come under study.

3. The faulty assumption is made that all buildings decline in value at an equal percentum rate per annum. This discounts the great variable arising from the qualitative differences in programs of maintenance carried out by one owner as compared to another.

4. The assumption is made that the building lives expire at the same percentum amount per annum. Experience proves, however, that the depreciation curve is not a straight line; rather, it is an irregular curve, rising slowly in the early years and more precipitately in the later years.

Despite the apparent approval of the method by the Department of Internal Revenue, it is not so well thought of in other quarters. Listen to the language of the United State Supreme Court: "The testimony of competent valuation engineers who examined the property and made estimates in respect of its condition is to be preferred to mere calculations made on averages and assumed probability." [3]

And, says the American Institute of Real Estate Appraisers, "In estimating accrued depreciation the age-life concept is an oversimplification of the problem of depreciation. . . . it is clear that any age-life method of estimating accrued (past) depreciation assuming as it does that depreciation of building value causes loss of value in equal yearly amounts has very definite hazards." [4]

The method itself is purely theoretical. Furthermore, it places the user in an indefensible position, because the depreciation charges made cannot be justified on a factual basis. Any reader who has had experience as an expert witness and who has been

---

[3] McCardle v. Indianapolis Water Co., 272 U.S. 400, 416, 47 S.Ct. 144, 71, L.Ed. 316 (1926).

[4] AIREA, *op. cit.*

asked in cross examination, "How did you determine that the accrued depreciation in this case amounted to X per cent?" will agree with the foregoing statement. As far as commercial appraisal is concerned, it is thoroughly unreliable. It may have its proper place in accounting practice, where it is the desire to measure the remaining *cost* of a capital asset at a particular time of life. But in the appraisal of real property, the desideratum is value; this is the end product, and it cannot be accomplished solely by mathematics which is the basis of the theoretical method. This is a device for window-dressing the appraisal report. If it were a logical method, the percentum taken could be justified by something other than the appraiser's mere unsupported declaration, "This is my opinion, based on my observation and my experience."

Most appraisers use it to lend strength to their findings, and not as a device to estimate value. Questioned on the point, the average appraiser will admit that his estimate of depreciation is an after-product of his estimate of value. Thus the replacement cost, new, is ascertained, value today is estimated, and the differential is called depreciation of all kinds. There remains only the necessity of dividing the depreciation into the physical, functional, and economic classifications and dropping it into these particular slots where it can be made to look reasonable. Is it any wonder then that the estimate of depreciation is confusing, not only to the reader of the appraisal report, but to the maker as well?

Because this technique is widely used by many appraisers, who apparently consider it the simplest and easiest, and because it is the basis of practically all the confusion and argument surrounding depreciation estimating as a phase of the appraisal process, more space has been devoted to it than is warranted by its worth as a valuation tool.[5] And while this book is designed to present proper methods of appraisal, a clear understanding of depreciation techniques necessitates an analysis of devices that have considerable popularity but that, upon searching investigation, are found to be spurious tools.

The Quantity Survey Method

The quantity survey method, which in the opinion of the author is sounder than any other used in the appraisal of residential

---

[5] Let's face it, men; this is the lazy appraiser's way of estimating depreciation.

properties, is based upon the observed deficiencies inherent in the structure and, where curable, the measurement of the curative cost. Its use removes most of the guesswork involved in any estimate of depreciation by the theoretical method.

The framework of this technique was first explored by the late Victor Free, M.A.I., of Cleveland, and discussed by him in the *Appraisal Journal*.[6] The writer subsequently attempted to amplify it and to remove some of the objections to its use that he considered ambigiuous. It is presented here as a tried and tested method of depreciation that has been used in the field with authenticated result.[7]

The approach. The approach to the measurement process necessitates breaking apart the items of physical deterioration and functional obsolescence into two subclassifications, called "curable" and "incurable." This is done for two reasons: (1) to facilitate the ease and accuracy of measurement; and (2) to discover the dollar amount of the recapturable items — namely, the physical curable and the functional curable. The allocation of these curable items assists in estimating the amount of money that must be expended, through repair and modernization, to correct certain physical and functional deficiencies. "Physical deterioration" and "functional obsolescence" are now redefined for the purposes of this technique.

Physical deterioration, curable. This is defined as "that amount of money necessary to restore the structure to physical parity; the cost of the repairs necessary to preserve and maintain tenancy (in the case of rental properties) or to develop optimum marketability." It is the cost of restoring items of deferred maintenance and to assure the stoppage of further structural decrepitude.

Physical deterioration, incurable. This is defined as "the appraiser's estimate of the loss incurred through the wearing out of nonreplaceable items." It refers to concealed wear and tear — the decay of structural and load-bearing members that cannot be restored except by an almost complete dismantling of the building. It may also be defined as the loss existing in items the restoration

---

6 Issues of January and April, 1939.

7 The author first taught this technique in the Appraisal Institute's case-study course at Yale University in 1940, after it had been tested on more than 300 appraisals of single-family homes and the results subjected to thorough clinical analysis. Since that time he has used it continuously not alone in the appraisal of residential property but on investment properties as well, including apartments, stores, office buildings, and industrial plants.

of which would fail to satisfy the law of profitable contribution.

Of all the items to be explored in this process of estimating depreciation, this is the only one that can be accused of depending to some extent on theory. Obviously, the estimate must correlate age. It cannot arise from any other source because the appraiser cannot see the bone structure of the building. The accuracy of this estimate, therefore, is stigmatized by the purely theoretical premise on which it is based. But this is by no means fatal, for, as will be shown in the schedules that follow and as can be proved by actual practice in the field, the incurable physical deterioration in any used residential structure will usually represent but a small percentage of the total depreciation estimate.[8]

Functional obsolescence, curable. This is defined as "that expenditure necessary to modernize the design of the building and its equipment so as to restore or create optimum functional adequacy." These expenditures must recapture their cost; they must satisfy the law of profitable contribution; otherwise the functional inutility is not curable. Examples of operations that do effect such recapture are found in the modernization of kitchens and bathrooms, heating plants and electrical equipment, the rearrangement of floor plans, the modern treatment of antique exteriors, and so forth.

Functional obsolescence, incurable. This is defined as "that loss in value arising from lowered rental income resulting from functional deficiencies that cannot be cured economically because they fail to satisfy the law of profitable contribution." For example, the second-floor plan of a residence is found to be functionally inadequate, but to rearrange it will involve relocating to downstairs partitions in order to support the load of the newly located second-floor partitions. The cost of this operation is found to exceed the amount of additional value that may be created. The functional obsolescence is said in this case to be "incurable."

Other examples would be a house in which the first-floor ceilings are twelve feet high or one in which the first-floor level is abnormally high. In either of these examples, the defect will not admit of economic cure, and as a consequence, the buildings will be written down by prospective buyers or tenants to the extent that

---

[8] Except, of course, in the case of those buildings that have been the victims of disaster—such as flood, fire, earthquake, and hurricane—and also those that have been the subject of vandalism.

they fail to conform to the ideal house. That differential is the key to the amount of incurable functional obsolescence that is present within the structure.

Economic obsolescence. This is redefined for the purpose of the quantity survey method as "the capitalized value of the rental loss *attributable to the building* because of the decreased desirability of the neighborhood." This method of calculation is divided into the following steps:

1. The existing rental value (actual, in the case of tenant-occupied property and hypothetical in the case of owner-occupied property) is estimated.

2. The rental value obtainable in the ideal neighborhood, where the depreciatory influences now at work in the subject neighborhood do not exist, is estimated.

3. The dollar difference between items 1 and 2 is computed.

4. The amount of item 3 is capitalized at the rate prevalent in the ideal neighborhood to establish the capitalized value of the rental loss attributable *to the property* (that is, land and building).[9]

5. The ratio of land to building value in the ideal neighborhood having been determined, that ratio is applied to the result found in item 4 to compute the amount of economic obsolescence attributable to the subject building.

Toward a clearer understanding of the quantity survey method, let us examine a sample problem.

The sample problem. We have under appraisal a brick-veneer, two-story, six-room residence approximately fifteen years of age. The neighborhood has become subjected to buyer disfavor because of a near-by disagreeable influence, in the form, let us say, of an amusement park where midget auto races are held nightly. Because of this nuisance, the neighborhood has become comparatively undesirable, resulting in the downward trend of sales and rental prices. The cost approach is invoked, with its usual three mathematical sequences, as follows:

1. The cost of the building new is estimated.

2. The depreciation is estimated and deducted therefrom.

3. To the result of step 2, the land value (based on the today's demand price) is added.

---

[9] In order to use this method, there must be a clear understanding of the relation between income and value, as discussed in Chapter 15.

The resultant total is the estimate of value via the cost approach.

This sample problem is concerned only with step 2, the estimate of depreciation. It is assumed that a careful inspection of the property and the neighborhood has been made, from which the following quantity survey of depreciation originates:

Schedule I
Estimate of Physical Deterioration

A. Physical, curable

New roof, exterior painting, new gutters and conductors, new tin deck over sunporch, new porch rails, tuck-pointing of masonry, floor refinishing, plaster repairs and redecorating... $1,250

B. Physical, incurable

Based on inspection and estimated physical life; "bone structure" only exclusive of finishings and equipment
1. Actual age .... 15 years
2. Effective age after reconditioning .... 10 years
3. Remaining economic life after reconditioning .... 30 years
4. Normal life expectancy — similar new building .... 40 years
5. Cost new; present building $18,000
6. Proportionate cost, "bone structure" @ 30% .... $ 5,400
7. Estimated physical deterioration — "bone structure"
   (Item 4 above divided by Item 2)
   $\left(\text{ or } \dfrac{10}{40} \right) = 25\%$ p.d.
8. Thus $5,400, Item 6, × 25% $1,350

Total physical deterioration $2,600

Schedule II
Estimate of Functional Obsolescence

A. Functional, curable

1. Modernization of kitchen, to include new linoleum floor; new two-compartment sink; new counters with Formica surfaces and splash; new chromium fittings; new cupboards and hardware; and relocation of partitions and doors to provide necessary wall space .... $ 900
2. Modernization of bathroom, to include new chromium fittings; new medicine cabinets; new toilet tank and seat; and new linoleum floors and walls 450
3. Modernization of electrical equipment to include new fixtures throughout, plus installation of extra wall plugs and door chimes 175
4. Insulation of second-floor ceiling 90

$ 1,615

B. Functional, incurable (based on estimate of rental loss arising from superadequacy of second-floor hall; small bedrooms because of waste hall space; small bedroom closets; remote location of bathroom)

$10.00 per month, the rental loss, capitalized @ 12% per annum
(the observable rate) or $\dfrac{\$10 \times 12 \times 100}{12}$ .... $ 1,000

Total functional obsolescence .... $ 2,615

Schedule III
Estimate of Economic Obsolescence

A. Estimated monthly rental of subject property if located in the ideal
    neighborhood (after curing physical and functional deficiencies, as
    per Schedules IA and IIA) .... $ 150
B. Present monthly rental value (after curing physical and functional
    deficiencies, as per Schedules IA and IIA) .... $ 125
C. Estimated rental loss (A minus B) .... $ 25
D. Yearly rental loss ($25 × 12 months) .... $ 300
E. Capitalization rate applicable to properties in the ideal neighborhood
    (i.e., the ratio of the per annum rent to market value) 10%
F. Capitalized rental loss ($300 ÷ 10 × 100) .... $ 3,000
G. Percentum ratio of land to building value in the ideal neighborhood,
    buildings 85%, land 15%.
H. Rental loss imputable to the subject building in the present neigh-
    borhood 85%
I. Capitalized rental loss (item F above) × 85% equals J.
J. Estimated economic obsolescence .... $ 2,550

Note in Schedule IIB that functional obsolescence, incurable is
reflected in the rental loss that occurs because of these incurable
deficiencies. The presumption — and usually the fact — is that
with these deficiencies absent the property would rent for $10.00
per month more. Note also that this loss is capitalized at 12 per
cent per annum (or by the use of a monthly multiplier of 100)
as indicating the ratio between rents and sales prices in the neighborhood under present conditions, namely, the nuisance that now
exists.

In Schedule III above, it is important to note that economic
obsolescence is a form of depreciation that affects both land and
building. The economic loss is reflected in the rents or the differential between the rental value of the subject property and the
rental value of the same property properly environed and minus
its surrounding objectionable influences. The rents arise from the
property, and not the building alone. Thus, if economic obsolescence is to be measured in terms of rental loss, the result furnishes
an amount of depreciation that is attributable to the land as well
as to the structure. The method detailed in the above schedule
allocates that portion of it which is attributable to the building
by establishing the ratio of land to building values in the ideal
neighborhood.

In item F of the above schedule, the capitalized rental loss is computed at $3,000. This, it should be observed, is the total of economic obsolescence arising from rental loss attributable *to the property*. In order to accommodate this computation to the mathematical sequences of the cost approach (as detailed in the definition of the sample problem), it is now necessary to abstract out of the total economic obsolescence attributable to the whole property ($3,000) that share of it which is attributable to the building.

The reason for this is obvious. Since the land value (which is to be added to the depreciated value of the building as the final step in the cost approach) is based on today's demand prices, such prices reflect the present decreased desirability of the land because of the objectionable features that have created a lack of optimum demand. The demand price, therefore, reflects the quantum of economic obsolescence that has already accrued in the land.

Thus, if the abstraction process detailed in items G, H, and I above were not carried out, it would mean that the economic obsolescence attachable to the land would have been twice charged against the property: once in the item of $3,000, and once more in the present demand price. The mathematics used in items G, H, I, and J, on the other hand, makes the clear-cut implication that the subject lot, if located in an environment where the present nuisance did not exist, would be worth (at least) $450 more than the present-day demand price in this area — that is, $3,000 (item F), the total economic obsolescence existing in the property, less $2,550 (item J), the amount chargeable to the building.

Note also that the rental loss because of the undesirable conditions in the neighborhood is capitalized at 10 per cent (or with a monthly multiplier of 120) as contrasted to the rate of 12 per cent used in Schedule IIB above. This difference recognizes the added degree of risk to investment capital in the neighborhood involved as compared to the "ideal" neighborhood devoid of this same element of risk.

Reconcilement of Schedule III. It is desirable to emphasize at this point that this technique for the quantitative analysis of economic obsolescence cannot be used unless the "ideal" neighborhood and the "ideal" rate exist in fact rather than in fancy.

It is not enough that the appraiser imagine the existence of some district in which the subject nuisance is absent. In fact, the entire method is fraught with distastrous consequences unless it can be shown that the building, if imaginably transported to a district free from the objectionable features in the subject district, will command an increased rental and that the capitalization rate is justified by the record.

Furthermore, the mechanics itemized in Schedule III are subject to reconcilement. The rental comparison, actual and ideal (items A and B), reflects the commandable rent in the subject and ideal district after having cured all the physical and functional deficiencies itemized in Schedules IA and IIA. Thus the assumption is made that if the property were ideally located the only remaining charges for depreciation would be those itemized in Schedules IB and IIB, or the incurable items. Economic obsolescence as computed in Schedule III would disappear because of the absence of the amusement park and the auto race track.

As a first step in the reconcilement of these estimates, let us assume that the subject building can be reproduced new for $18,000, and that similar lots can be purchased for $2,700 (see Chapter 13, page 162). On the assumption that this property was located in the ideal neighborhood, that the building was still 15 years of age, and that physical deterioration and functional obsolescence, incurable (as detailed in Schedule IB and IIB), were still present in the structure, the procedural steps of the cost approach to value would be itemized as on page 151.

1. Cost, new (main building and attached garage)		$18,000
2. Less depreciation:		
a. Physical, incurable, from Schedule IB	1,350	
b. Functional, incurable, from Schedule IIB	1,000	$ 2,350
3. Depreciated reproduction cost of building and garage		$15,650
4. Land value (based on demand price in the subject location, $2,700) *plus* the recapture of economic obsolescence in the ideal location, as implied by the difference between items F and J of Schedule III or $2,700 + $450, or land value		$ 3,150
Value via the cost approach in "ideal" location (called)........		$18,800

This is the first step in the process of reconcilement. These figures indicate that, if value in the ideal location were indexed by cost less depreciation, plus a land value devoid of economic obsolescence, such value would approximate $18,800.

The second step is one that exerts a control on the use of the entire method. Referring now to items A and E of Schedule III, we find the implied assertion that the subject property, if given proper social environment with the abatement of the neighborhood nuisance outlined in the definition of the problem, would command a rental of $150 per month, or $1,800 per year; that amount, it is claimed (as per item E), is equivalent to 10 per cent of the value of the property. The capitalized value of the property, therefore, in the ideal location is $18,000 (1800 divided by 10 multiplied by 100). This figure approximates the value via the cost approach in the "ideal" location, as found above.

From this process of reconcilement, the following rules governing the use of this method evolve:

1. The actual rental and the ideal rental used to compute economic obsolescence as a percentum of capital loss must reflect the cure (or the absence) of physical deterioration and functional obsolescence.

2. The ideal rental and the ideal capitalization rate must reflect situations known to the appraiser.

3. The value found by capitalization of the "ideal" rent at the "ideal" rate should approximate the value found by estimating the cost, new, deducting therefrom physical deterioration and functional obsolescence, incurable, and adding thereto the land value for the "ideal" location.

Schedule IV
Recapitulation of Depreciation Estimates [10]

Physical deterioration, from Schedule I	$2,600
Functional obsolescence, from Schedule II	2,615
Economic obsolescence, from Schedule III	2,550
TOTAL DEPRECIATION ESTIMATE	$7,765

Advantages of the quantity survey method. Analysis of the depreciation itemized in the foregoing schedules will disclose the absence of nebulous theory in estimating the quantum of decreased desirability. No computations are used that are correlatives of building age, except in the one item of physical deterioration, incurable. Every other item is supportable by plausible and logical conclusions.

---

[10] Note "Specimen Estimate of Value via the Cost Approach," in Chapter 13, in which the total depreciation estimate shown in Schedule IV appears in proper mathematical sequence.

Physical deterioration and functional obsolescence, *curable*, are estimated from a quantity survey of the cost of correction that can be accurately estimated.

Functional obsolescence, *incurable*, is computed as an item of decreased rental value in the market place arising from the penalty of a structural functional deficiency that is economically and physically noncorrective. The reasoning in the sample problem itemized above implies that, although every other item of decreased desirability was brought up to parity with the ideal building, this item of incurable functional deficiency would still lead to a loss in rental value.

Economic obsolescence is computed by this method as a dollar loss of capital value, and not as a percentum of cost.

Finally, the method and the computations made arise from observation, and not from empirical assumptions the validity of which have not been authenticated in practice.

The field of use. The quantity survey method of estimating depreciation is generally applicable to all types of depreciation as defined in Chapter 11, with the exception of economic obsolescence arising from oversupply. In this category may fall the sudden collapse of the real estate market at a time when the program of house construction in a certain community has achieved considerable momentum. If the collapse is city- or nation-wide, as it is likely to be at such times, there is no "ideal" neighborhood that we can use to measure the differential of rental loss and to capitalize therefrom the dollar loss in value that develops. In this situation, the measurement of economic obsolescence must evolve from the estimate of replacement cost, less physical deterioration and functional obsolescence, compared to what buyers are willing to pay. Of course, in the case of utter collapse, there may be no buyers. But there always will be plenty of offerings establishing the upper limit of value.

CHAPTER 13

The Cost Approach to Value

Labour alone, therefore . . . is the ultimate and real standard. . . .
ADAM SMITH

The cost approach to value is the first of the master tools of the appraisal process introduced to the reader in Chapter 3.

In this chapter we shall discuss the mechanics of this approach to value, and explore its advantages and limitations. Actually, we are already well along in this discussion because of what has gone before. Chapter 10, dealing with building cost estimates, and Chapters 11 and 12, dealing with depreciation, pave the way for a formal discussion of the cost approach. The estimates of building cost and depreciation are respectively steps one and two of this method.

Cost: The Objective Theory of Value

The cost approach is not a convenient theory recently conceived to assist the process of commercial appraisal. It has its roots deep in the lore of classical economies. In 1775, Adam Smith, "the father of economics," in the following words excerpted from his *Wealth of Nations,* laid the foundation of the philosophy which teaches that cost is a concomitant of value:

Labor alone, therefore, never varying in its own value, is alone the ultimate and real standard by which the value of all commodities can at all times and places be estimated and compared.

This idea was enthusiastically espoused by Henry Charles Carey, first of the American school of economists, who, in his *Principles of Political Economy,* published in 1837, contended that labor was the sole cause of value. Thus, there developed

158

down through the years the "cost of production" school of economics, which teaches that value is expressed in the thing, or the good itself and is measured by the quantity of the labor — that is, the cost — to bring it into being. This is known in economics as the "objective theory of value," with which the cost approach is complexioned. It differs from the subjective theory, which teaches that value exists and has its being in the mind of the individual who desires the thing and that the intensity of his desires indexes the price paid and therefore the value, irrespective of the cost involved in its production.

To accept literally the dicta of Smith and Carey and apply it to the valuation of real estate would mean that the cost of real property in all cases would be the measure of its value. The absurdity of this reasoning is exemplified by the purely imaginary case of a 30-story hotel built in the middle of the Great Sahara Desert. Its cost might approximate several million dollars; its value might well be zero. Or, assume that a new automobile was purchased 10 years ago at a cost of $3,000, driven from the salesroom to the garage of the owner, jacked up, and left there until today. Can it be said that its cost is equivalent to its present value? Value and cost *may* be synonymous at a particular moment in time, but in the case of real property only those properties that represent the highest and best use of the land at the date and hour when construction is completed may be said to synchronize cost and value. Thereafter, the accrual of economic obsolescence, which bears no relation to the cost of production, will effectually distort any relationship between the two.

This forces the admission that the cost approach in real estate appraising is not the pure cost of production as is thought by economists. Rather, it is a system of starting with the cost of the property as a base and gradually working toward a conclusion of value, doctoring the process the while with items of depreciation, some of which are related to cost (physical deterioration and functional obsolescence, curable) and others to value in the market place (functional obsolescence, incurable, and economic obsolescence).

But synthetic as the process is, viewed from the standpoint of the economist, it has its place in the valuation process, for, as will be shown in a later discussion of market and income approaches, it provides under all market conditions a firmer base of logic than the market approach and just as firm a base as the income approach.

The Principle of Substitution

The reliability of the cost approach rests on the trite economic principle that a thing cannot be worth more than its cost of replacement. This is known as the "theory of substitution." This theory propounds that value cannot exist above the cost necessary to replace the thing that possesses value, provided the substitution can be made conveniently and without delay. Applied to the commodity of real estate, this means that value cannot exist above the necessary cost involved in the purchase of a property similar to the one to be duplicated, or the purchase of a similar lot and erection of a similar building on it.

This illustrates the principal advantage of the use of the cost approach: it fixes the upper limit of value. The property may bring more in the market than its cost of reproduction, but it cannot be worth more. Scarcity of supply and exorbitant demand may cause it to command a higher price for a certain period, but the cost of reproduction will be the value ceiling.

The example that aptly illustrates this point is found in a large Midwestern city during the boom period of the 1920's. Mortgage funds for the financing of homes were scarce, owing to the competition offered by investment opportunity in stocks and bonds of municipal corporations and high call-money rates. Mortgages were uniformly limited to 60 per cent of appraised value. The demand for housing was running far ahead of the available supply. To relieve this situation, junior financing appeared in the form of the land contract in which the vendor's equity, over and above the first mortgage, found a ready discount market at rates as high as 35 per cent. Thus the operative builder, having sold at $10,000 a residential property that carried a first mortgage of $6,000, immediately proceeded to sell his equity of $4,000 ($10,000 minus $6,000) to a land-contract equity purchaser at a price of $2,600 net, or $4,000 less 35 per cent. Thousands of such sales were made.

In the above case, value was $8,600, or the reproduction cost of the properties. Market price, because of trick financing, had ascended to $10,000, but based on the theory of substitution, the value ceiling remained at the level of the replaceable cost.

Examples are also found in many of our large cities where infiltration of an old (and practically worn-out) residential district by a minority racial or national group is taking place. A speculator buys up these old properties at figures approximating their intrinsic value, boosts the price fifty per cent or more over the value figure, sells the property to the present occupant or the incoming family and obtains a second mortgage which he later discounts at any obtainable rate (sometimes as much as fifty per cent). The sales prices in these instances may be as high as $12,000; value is probably $7,500 to $8,000. Here reproduction cost may be said to represent the upper limit of value.[1]

Relevant Items

The items properly comprising the production cost of a single-family residential property are as follows:

1. The demand price paid for the land.
2. The cost of the main building, to include the cost of the appurtenances to the main building — garage, driveway, fencing, sidewalks, sodding or seeding, shrubbery, grading and filling, retaining walls and sewer, water and gas lines.
3. The cost of professional services in the construction of the improvement — architect and contractor.

Sales commissions. One item not relevant to the cost of the property is the commission paid to the real estate broker. Some appraisers include this as a part of the cost. Assuming that the appraisal process deals with the general problem, it seems improper to include this item, because it is not incurred in every instance in which property is appraised. The sales commission is a fee paid to a broker for his services in selling the property; it is not a part of the cost of producing the building or the property.

---

[1] If reproduction cost can be accurately estimated. In this situation the buildings are usually upwards of 50-60 years of age and, because of architectural style, materials, floor plan, and equipment, are not, in fact, reproducible. The difficulty in establishing accurate reproduction cost is therefore obvious. In fact this poses the question as to whether the cost approach in this type of appraisal problem is indeed a dependable tool. Perhaps an analysis of the financing — the percentum of the amount loaned to value (as indicated by lending policy in the area) of the first and second mortgages, the discount rate of the second mortgage, and the amount of equtiy payment will develop more conclusive evidence of value than the cost approach.

Mechanics of the Approach

The progressive steps in the cost approach are as follows:

1. An estimate is made of the reproduction cost, new, of the building and its appurtenances, based on today's labor and material prices (usually by the method of estimating the cost per cubic foot, as described in Chapter 10).

2. From this amount is deducted the estimated amount of depreciation (as discussed in Chapter 12). This result is called the "depreciated reproduction cost of the improvement."

3. To the figure found in step 2 is added the land value as found by comparison with other lands offering like services. The result is an estimate of value via the cost approach, as shown in the following schedule:

Specimen Estimate of Value Via the Cost Approach

1. Estimated reproduction cost, new (main building and appurtenances) $18,000
2. Less depreciation (from Schedule IV, Chapter 12)   7,765

3. Depreciated reproduction cost of main building and appurtenances 10,235
4. Plus land value found by comparison 2,700

5. Estimate of value via the cost approach (called).. $12,935

Accuracy of the Method

The cost approach is a reasonably accurate tool in the hands of an appraiser who understands its underlying principles. Assuming those principles are understood, he must also have information as to building costs that is accurate, knowledge of land values that is ample, and foolproof skill in handling depreciation estimates. And here we discover the Achilles heel in the cost method — namely, the ability to estimate depreciation accurately. If depreciation estimates were carefully made by the quantity survey method (described in Chapter 12), estimates of value via the cost approach could be relied upon with greater dependability. Unfortunately, however, too many appraisers prefer to use the theoretical method and to estimate depreciation by the simple expedient of concluding that, because a building is of a certain age, it necessarily must have depreciated a corresponding amount. The method is easy to use and simple of explanation, provided one does not inquire into the reasons behind the estimates. During an active market, many who employ appraisers are disposed to be intolerant of appraisal methods they consider "too technical." [2]

Since, therefore, age-percentum computations are still used in the measurement of depreciation, it must be assumed that estimates of value that involve the use of this technique are of questionable merit. This gives rise to the axiom that the estimate of value via the cost approach is no more reliable than is the estimate of depreciation.

Treatment of Amenities

The cost approach as a legitimate method of estimating value has been attacked on the ground that it fails to reflect the amenities of homeownership. This might be true were the cost approach a pure cost of production estimate. But it is not. The estimate of the reproduction cost of the building and its appurtenances is but the first step in the process. As the process develops, cost becomes adulterated with depreciation. Certain types of depreciation reflect the amenities, or rather the lack of them — for example, incurable functional obsolescence and economic obsolescence. Where the former is represented by an ill-arranged floor plan that cannot be corrected, value will be affected to the extent that this defect fails to provide the optimum quantity of convenient living. And where the latter arises from objectionable influences at work in the neighborhood, value will be affected by the extent to which the amenities are deficient as compared to the ideal neighborhood. Thus the cost approach does reflect the amenities.

Dependent Character of the Method

It should be observed that the cost approach is but one of the tools of the appraisal process. The market and income approaches

---

[2] Singularly enough, the appraisal process is never so completely ignored as during those periods when it is most needed—namely, in times of real estate prosperity and building booms. At such times, and especially in a highly competitive mortgage market, with lenders engaged in hectic bidding for money outlets, the appraisal process is looked upon as a barely tolerable nuisance. But let the other extreme of the market cycle arrive, and the holders of real estate securities purchased or loaned upon during the high-price era are suddenly all in a dither to know what their real estate is actually worth, whereat there is loud demand for the expert appraiser and the holy promise that never again will appraised values be ignored in favor of a fictitious price level. Of course, the promise is kept inviolate—until the next boom occurs.

are equally important. Because the nature of the appraisal process is not precise, all of the tools must be used. To rely on the cost approach alone is to risk imperfection in the process. A house of sorts may be built with a saw and a hammer; a better and more durable edifice will have received the additional benefit of plumb line, plane, and level.

Moreover, the cost approach cannot stand alone in the completed estimate; it must depend to some extent on the checks and balances exerted by the others. Along the route lies the possibility of error. For example, the estimate of the cost, new, may have been incorrectly computed; depreciation estimates may have been too small or too large; the land may have been erroneously valued. Any of these may lead to serious error in the final result. Detection of error comes by comparing the estimate of value by the cost approach with estimates by the market and income approaches. If the former is badly out of line with the latter, reinvestigation is called for, and the various steps of the process are rechecked to locate the error. (This is the process of correlation described in Chapter 3.) Therein lies the value to the entire appraisal process of the three approaches and the operative efficiency of their combined usage: each may be checked against the other, and resultant errors discovered.

The cost approach requires a higher order of training and ability than either of the other methods. Thus, the appraiser must be skilled in a greater number of individualized technical operations.

1. He must be a capable estimator; he must be familiar with building costs and construction practices.

2. He must be able to estimate competently the cost of reconditioning and modernization in order to calculate the items of curable deterioration and obsolescence.

3. He must know land values, for in the use of this method (unlike the market and income approaches) land values are estimated as a separate item in the process.

4. He must be able to estimate accurately depreciation of all kinds.

CHAPTER 14

The Market Approach to Value

The approach to value by the means of examining the market place is a search for the "just" price.

To students of economics, this term is familiar. The philosophers of the Middle Ages, dabbling in economics, recognized it; Thomas Aquinas referred to the "just" price as emanating from an ideal concept of human relationships.[1] But the "just" price, according to the writers of this time, still had its origins in the cost of production theory. This is the objective theory of value, as discussed in the preceding chapter.

An opposite value theory was developed by the Austrian school of economists, who followed Adam Smith and his contemporaries. The teachings of this school have been recorded by Alexander Gray as follows:

Firstly, as against all cost-of-production theories of value, they held that value essentially springs from utility, that it reflects the mind of a person who finds something useful . . . that value sanctions costs and is not caused by costs.[2]

Paraphrasing this definition in order to make it applicable to the valuation of real estate, we may say that:

1. Value arises from the uses or services which the property offers.

2. Such use value is expressed by the action of buyers and sellers in the market place.

3. Cost will not be given the sanction of value in the market

---

[1] *Summa Theologica*, circa 1250.

[2] Alexander Gray, *Development of Economic Doctrine* (New York, Longmans, Green, 1931), pp. 330 and 331.

place unless, in the production process, it has developed optimum use.

The action of buyers and sellers is the reflection of their attitudes toward what they consider to be a "just" price. The price is warranted by the interaction of the law of supply and demand and constitutes "valuation by the public." This we may accept as the objective of the market approach with one stipulation: the so-called "just" price that apparently indexes this action in the market place must be representative of transactions that conform to the definition of "market value" cited in Chapter 2. The reason for this will be discussed subsequently.

Mechanics of the Process

The "market approach," as its title implies, is a method that explores the phenomena of the market place in an attempt to relate these data to the property under appraisal and thus to determine the value that arises from the comparative result. Sales and listings of comparable properties in comparable neighborhoods are tabulated and analyzed. These are used as "bench marks" with which to measure the value of the subject property.

It is in the selection of these bench marks that we encounter our first difficulty. While recognizing that exactly similar properties may not be available, the method contents itself with using those that are reasonably similar. Using these bench marks as value templates, the method proceeds to compare the property under appraisal in accordance with the following plan:

1. *Comparison of the physical aspects* — the lot's size, shape, area, frontage, soil, topography, and location within the block; the building's architecture, interior and exterior construction, size, floor plan, equipment, livability, functional adequacy, and future life expectancy.

2. *Comparison of the social aspects* — the environing features, social and physical; comparative desirability of the neighborhood; and expected future life of the present social stratum resident therein.

3. *Comparison of market data* — present and future rental levels; present and future anticipated sales price; present offering prices and the duration of exposure to the market; and present and future anticipated listing price of the subject property.

The Reliability of Sales Prices

Seemingly, we have encountered a paradox. The objective of the appraisal process is market value; yet here we find ourselves granting academic indulgence to a technique that is based upon sales price. This poses the question: "Are price and value the same?" The generally covering answer is "No"; yet transactions in the market place between buyer and seller may be accepted as indications of value where they have congealed in them the ingredients of the market value definition — namely, where they were "normal" transactions; where free and competitive trading was present in each transaction; where buyer and seller acted freely, without duress, and were not motivated by special or ulterior purposes; and where both were fully informed of the uses to which the property could be put. Under these circumstances only may price data be accepted as evidence of value. Used in any other way, the result is apt to be disastrous, as in the following examples that tend to show the extent to which the appraiser, unmindful of the qualifications on the use of the method, may fall into error:

1. In a certain city, a mining company owned a number of houses, which it rented to its employees. The mines closed because they became too expensive to work. The company then sold these "company" houses to its tenants at a price of $250 each. Comparable housing not owned by the mining company was priced at from $2,000 to $2,500, with a well-stabilized rental level of $25 per month.

2. A new commercial development was projected for a neighborhood characterized by old residential properties. Owing to the scarcity of vacant land, it was found necessary to purchase many residential buildings in the district and to wreck them so as to make the land available for the newly projected use. The assembly was gotten under way secretly, the public having no knowledge of the reasons for which property was being purchased. The secrecy of the program gave rise to extravagant rumors. Tall tales were told that magnified many times the economic importance of the project. Speculation nourished and prices soared. Many old properties with a top utility value of $5,000 were freely traded at prices of from $10,000 to $15,000.

Each of these examples serves to show the extent to which

value levels may be distorted by transactions that do not contain the essentials of our definition of "market value." In example 1, there was the lack of freely competitive trading. The seller in this case was distressed; he had to sell, and consequently was not concerned with obtaining market value. His chief concern was to liquidate, and the price obtained was of secondary importance. In example 2, we have the case of uninformed buyers acting in ignorance and depending on fancy. Were the appraiser to use these transactions as *prima facie* evidence of value, the result would be ludicrous.

The erroneous use of price data arises largely from an inability to get at the facts that motivate buyers and sellers. The concept that market value is indicated by those transactions in which buyers and sellers act freely and voluntarily and with full knowledge of the present and future uses of the property must be accepted in valuation practice as an idealistic proposition. It would be helpful if the appraiser could know the motives underlying every transaction that he uses to index market value. But he does not know and he cannot know, for the simple reason that this is the sort of information that is not obtainable. Buyers and sellers will not divulge it. So the appraiser must accept, in his use of this approach, the sometimes doubtful character of sales prices as evidencing the definition of "market value."

Reliability of Listing Prices

Listing prices furnish a sound basis for the use of the market approach. What buyers will do may result from impulse, whim, or caprice. But the seller, in fixing the listing price, usually acts with greater deliberation. The individual owner, for example, may be assumed to have made some investigation of the existing market levels before placing a price on his property. Thus some form of market analysis, however casual, will have preceded the action of listing the property for sale.

In the case of the lending agency that has become an unwilling owner through mortgage default, this is even more true, for as a rule the listing action will have been preceded by an intelligent and thorough analysis of the market and an appraisal by one competent in this specialized field.

The listing, therefore, having followed an analysis of the market, will produce the probable value ceiling, although in most cases value levels will stabilize at some point below the asking price. How much lower? The question is difficult to answer with mathematical exactitude. Generally, it may be answered by the statement that the difference between asking prices and actual sales prices will depend entirely upon the degree of urgency with which the buyer is compelled to act or the seller is compelled to sell.

There is, generally speaking, a normal spread between the asking and the bid prices assuming that both parties to the transaction are fully informed as to the optimum use to which the property may be put. Both the asking and the bid prices are hopeful figures. In the process of higgle-and-haggle, a meeting of minds develops somewhere between the two, and the transaction is consummated. But of this the appraiser may be certain: the asking price represents the ceiling of value; the bid price represents the floor. This then is the value bracket, and if the appraiser can determine by observation where the point of agreement probably lies, a knowledge of listing prices will emerge as useful data. Thus listing prices cannot be disregarded by the appraiser as having some reliability and as a possible index to the valuation figure. In the case of the institutional owner the offering will have been preceded by appraisal; in the case of the individual owner the price asked will result from his knowledge of what comparable properties are bringing in the market. In fact, listing prices are the only form of market data available during those phases of the market cycle when buyers are completely absent.

Selection of the Bench Marks

A prime requirement in the use of the market approach is that the bench-mark properties shall be similar to the property to which they are to be compared. It is a well-worn axiom that no two pieces of real estate are exactly similar. The method must content itself then with those that, although not facsimiles, are of the same family.

There is a marked tendency here to confuse similarity with proximity. Thus the remark is often heard that the subject property "is worth .... dollars because another house *in the same block* sold for a like amount." This is to assume that because the two properties are located in the same block, they possess characteristics of similarity, which is often not the case.

The bench-mark properties need not exist in the same block or in the same neighborhood. Indeed, they may lie at the other end of the city. The test lies in their similarity to the subject property; if the social and economic levels of the neighborhoods in which they exist are similar to the neighborhood in which the appraisal problem lies, they are of legitimate usage.

Currency of the Data

The transactions used must be of reasonably current status. They must reflect the current rate of ebb or flow of the market. It is of little value to the appraiser to attempt to relate the property under appraisal to transactions concerning similar properties that occurred years ago. The sales and listing data used should reflect the current phase of the market cycle, the current ratio of supply and demand, pay roll and family income levels, and the present purchasing power of the dollar.

The True Basis of Comparison

A general misconception of the use of this method lies in an apparent willingness to compare prices as the first step in the process. This accounts for the statement, oft repeated during times of real estate prosperity, that "anyone can appraise residential property." If we think of appraisal as the mere matching of market prices, we must admit that "anyone can appraise" property and that, during a good market, almost everybody does.[3] But it is something more than that. And price is not the initial basis of comparison. Utility is, and so is the amenity content. Thus, in the selection of the bench-mark properties with which the subject property is to be compared, primary selection should first be made on the basis of comparable utility and comparable amenities. If the bench marks offer the same volume of livable services, they should be used; otherwise they should not, regardless of any other aspect of their relationship.

Necessity for the Use of Bulk Transactions

A further restriction on the use of this approach is that the bench-mark properties must be used in bulk. There must be

---

[3] And during the boom period of the 1920's everybody did. How well they did was evidenced by what came after.

several bench marks. The use of bulk data or a number of bench marks is a safeguard against being led up a blind alley by an isolated transaction containing some hidden condition of abnormality in the circumstances surrounding the sale. If the appraiser uses but one bench mark in the comparison and relies on the selling price of that particular property as accurately indexing the fair price in the market for that type of property, subsequent information may disclose that the owner was compelled to sell and that therefore the price, instead of reflecting the "fair" price for the property, reflected a distressed price and was not indicative of the fair or "going" prices for property in that class. Any value reached by the appraiser on the basis of such a comparison will obviously be out of line and may result in an entirely false conclusion of value. Therefore the data must be used in bulk; there must be many bench marks — many properties all like the subject property with which the appraiser may compare sales and listing prices — in order that the market data may be sifted and the nonstandard or nonaverage eliminated, leaving only those in which the conditions surrounding the transaction are normal.

Summary

In conclusion, the market approach has its rightful place in the valuation process. It is a useful and valuable tool in the hands of an appraiser who understands its limitations, which are principally:

1. The first limitation of the market approach is inherent in the nature of the market place. It depends for accuracy on the analysis of market phenomena, which can be nothing more than price data. Confusion will always exist on the point of whether a particular transaction is a dependable indicator of value. Thus, where the motivating impulses of buyer and seller are not known and cannot be known, there is always the off-chance that the appraiser may be inveigled into forming a conclusion of value with erroneous result.

2. The market approach is a method that is usable only when there is a market. This fact limits its value in the appraisal process, because it is well known that in a certain segment of every business cycle there is no market for real estate.[4] This does not mean

---

[4] Such was the period 1930 to 1935.

that the appraisal process must mark time pending the recurrence of active marketing conditions. On the contrary, history shows that there is more need for *expert* appraisal service during times of economic stress than during times of real estate prosperity. What happens in the absence of an active market is that the appraisal process proceeds to get along without the market approach, except in so far as current listings appear to indicate the value ceiling.

Before leaving the central theme of this discussion, there is this final word of admonition: the market approach is one that must be used with extreme care in application to the appraisal problem as explained above. Furthermore, there is no reason, because of the restrictions with which its use is surrounded, to accord it any preference over the other two tools in the process. Its principal value to the appraiser is not, as many think, to fix the level of value; rather, its advantage lies in the extent to which it acts as a check and balance on estimates of value arrived at through the approaches of cost and income.

CHAPTER 15

The Income Approach to Value

No less deep-rooted in the lore of classical economics than the approaches already discussed is the income approach to value. The principle that income or rent is an index to value was first discussed by David Ricardo.[1] Agricultural lands, Ricardo implied, were of three kinds: (1) those that produced a surplus over and above the cost of production; (2) those that produced exactly enough goods to pay the production costs; and (3) those that failed to produce enough goods to pay the cost of the labor involved in production.

The first classification he called "marginal lands," and these, because they produced a surplus over and above the costs of production — that is, the labor and sustenance of those who worked them — were "rent lands," the surplus of production being the equivalent rent. "Rent," he said, was "that portion of the produce of the earth paid to the landlord for the use of the original and indestructible powers of the soil."[2]

Ricardo, like most of the writers of his time, thought of "land" in its agricultural sense and of "rent" as farm products. Yet, we can with facility paraphrase his definition of "rent" with logical suitability to the problem of value as it applies to urban real estate. Thus, the "produce of the earth" may be considered as the power of the land to produce wealth in the form of realty — that is, improved property — and the "original and indestructible powers of the soil" may be construed as the ability of the land, when fed capital, to produce an entity of real property — that is, land and building.

---

[1] *Principles of Political Economy* (1817).
[2] *Ibid.*

It may be claimed, also, that he gave clandestine recognition to the principle of income as an index to value (although he was a disciple of the cost of production school), because of his differentiation between the rent-producing qualities of the three classes of lands that he described.

A later writer went Ricardo one better. It remained for Von Thunen, the German economist, to lay the academic groundwork for the income approach. Writing in his *Isolated State* (1840), he improved on Ricardo's theory by claiming that rent did not derive wholly from the land; that, in addition, it represented interest earned on the capital invested on or in the land; that any surplus of land production should go to pay interest on capital investment first; and that thereafter land might receive what was left, the residue being "ground rent." "Rent," therefore, according to Von Thunen, was an element of value, although he did not say so.

This is the exact theory applied in the process of finding land value by capitalization in the valuation of investment properties where the income from the property serves to pay the wages of labor (janitors, maids, elevator operators, gardeners, maintenance men, and the like), the services of co-ordination (taxes, insurance, light, power, gas, fuel, and so forth), the charges on investment capital (interest), and, finally, the land rent. This land rent, or land earnings, when capitalized at the prevailing rate for land investments, is said to equal the land value.[3]

This discussion, therefore, serves to frame, against a background of classical economics, the contention that rent is an index to value.

Income and the Subjective Theory of Value

The income approach teaches that rent tends to indicate value [4] because, in the process, it measures the intensity of the desire of the prospective user of the property.

A fixed relation always exists between the rents being paid in a certain neighborhood (or the hypothetical rents) and the prices at which properties are selling. Thus, a survey by the

---

[3] A technique of popular use in the appraisal of lands underlying income and investment properties, but not applicable to the appraisal of residential lands.

[4] "Rent is one of the best guides to public acceptance, and, hence, of market price obtainable." David Montonna, in *Review* (Society of Residential Appraisers).

appraiser may show that, in a certain residential district, the fair rental level is $100 per month and that the same properties are selling for $12,000 in the market. The per annum rental ($1200), therefore, is equivalent to 10 per cent of the sales prices. On the assumption that the transactions examined fit the definition of "market value" (as discussed in the foregoing chapter) it may be said that the percentum relationship between the rents being paid (or the rental values) are equivalent to 10 per cent of the values.

From this, we may reason as follows:

1. The rents being paid, or the hypothetical rents, index sales prices.

2. Sales prices, assumedly indicative of value, index buyer attitudes.

3. Buyer attitudes arise from the desire for and anticipation of use.

4. The degree of desire is measured by transactions in the market place. This again is the subjective theory of value, as discussed in Chapter 14.

Legal background. The income approach takes its mandate from the definition affirming that "value is the present worth of all the rights to future benefits arising from ownership." The "future benefits" are the future income; thus value is the present estimated worth of that income.

More important support, however, is lent the validity of this technique in the famed Brewer decision, quoted in Chapter 2. Here the Court defined "value" as arising from use, "from the profitableness of that use, present and potential, actual and anticipated." The Court thus states the case for the income approach. Value is the profit to be derived from use. Hence, profit is derived from income in the form of rent.

Mechanics of the approach. The mechanics of the income approach exemplify the nature of the technique to be employed. The method teaches that income bears a fixed, mathematical relationship to value. The process involves, then, the discovery of the fair rental and the translation of that result into capital value by the mathematics of capitalization. It divides itself into three steps, as follows:

1. The fair rental income of the property is estimated. If the

property is in actual rental status, the actual rent being paid is easy of ascertainment. This may not be the "fair" rental.[5] The actual rent being received by the landlord may be less than the amount for which the property should be rented; it may be more. The problem confronting the appraiser is to discover the "fair" rental, for it is upon this figure that the whole success of this method will depend. This can only be estimated by comparing the property under appraisal with similar properties offering like quantities and qualities of utility and amenities.

If the property is occupied, not by a tenant, but by an owner, the rental value is estimated in the same manner — by comparison with other bench-mark properties that are in rental status.

Here again, emphasis must be laid on the purity of the bench marks. The properties with which the comparison is to be made must be similar to that under consideration as regards the services they offer, or as reasonably similar as it is possible to discover.

In this analysis, the quality of future income must be determined. It is not enough that the present income shall have been accurately estimated. "Value," says the Court, "arises from the actual and anticipated profitableness of use." This means the actual and the *future* rent to be received. It means further that the future income must be predicted. For how long? For as long as it is possible for the appraiser to predict with reasonable certainty. The length of that prediction in relation to its accuracy will depend on: (1) the extent of his knowledge of the history of the particular district in which the property lies; and (2) his knowledge of the future trend of rental prices in the area.

An observable defect in some appraisal systems lies in the acceptance of the idea that value evolves from the capitalization of the present rentals. Any such method nullifies the principle expressed in the value definition quoted above as to the "present worth of all the rights to *future* benefits" and contradicts the ideology expressed in the Court's definition as to "actual and anticipated" profit derivable from use.

The fair income from the property is a future prediction that must be made notwithstanding the questionable accuracy of the

---

[5] Distinction should be made between the "fair" or "economic" rent and "contract" rent. This is of great importance to the appraiser in situations where rent control is in effect.

prediction. The appraiser asks this question: "What will be the fair income to be received in the form of rentals over the future remaining life of the property?" This may seem like a large order, and so it would be if accepted literally. But as has been stated, actual practice proves that it is impossible to predict the future income stream for more than a year or two with any degree of accuracy. The method, therefore, must content itself with what turns out to be a reasonable prediction, for while there is academic acceptance of the theory that the rents used should represent the fair income over the remaining economic life of the property, actual practice proves that the fair rentals used are those the appraiser believes will be constant and level over the period of the immediate future.

2. The fair rental having been estimated, the next step in the approach is to determine the ratio between that figure and the values of properties comparable to the one being appraised. This ratio evolves as the capitalization rate to be applied to the rentals in the mathematical process of determining the value.

As an example, let us assume that the property under appraisal has a fair rental value of $100 per month. The per annum rental is $1,200. Similar properties, it is found, are selling at $10,000. The ratio, therefore, of the per annum rentals to the values being placed on these properties by the purchasing public is 12 to 100. Expressed arithmetically, this equation results:

$$\$1,200 : \$10,000 :: 12 : 100$$

Stated percentum-wise, $1,200, the per annum rental is equivalent to the interest on $10,000 at an interest rate of 12 per cent. This computation indicates the rate at which the rental income may be capitalized is 12 per cent.

3. In this final step, mathematics translates income value into capital value. Having discovered that the capitalization rate to be applied to the rentals is 12 per cent, we proceed to effect that translation, which is expressed in the following equation:

$$\frac{I}{r} \times 100 = V.$$

I, equals the per annum income; r, the capitalization rate; and V, the capitalized value. Applying this equation to the above problem, we have the following:

$$\frac{\$1200}{12} \times 100 = \$10,000$$

the capitalized value of the property or the estimate of value via the income approach.

The Use of Gross Rentals

In the appraisal of properties purchased purely for money income or investment, the net income is used as the basis for capitalization. In the appraisal of single-family residential properties, however, gross income is used. Back of the principle lie custom and usage, based on the contention that expense ratios in residential properties do not vary in the same degree as do those of larger income or commercial properties. According to the Federal Housing Administration:

The use of an estimate in the gross returns in the capitalization of amenity income is justified because expense-of-ownership ratios usually are relatively constant in amenity income dwelling properties of the same kind, quality and price group in the same general locality.[6]

Obviously, this is not true in the case of investment properties, where the variable quality of management, operations expense, and fixed charges, *i.e.*, taxes, will affect pro and con, the amount of net income to the be derived from operations.[7] But management, by the owner, plays no important part in the operation of an individual residential property. Furthermore, the only expense variables are for maintenance and repairs. Taxes on properties of the same type are usually in balance. With expense ratios fairly constant, the process is not disturbed by the use of gross rentals. In fact, practice in the field indicates their use to be desirable and logical.

Selection of the Rate

Probably the most fallacious rule-of-thumb ever devised for the

---

[6] FHA, *Underwriting Manual*, paragraph 1202 (4).

[7] This is clearly exemplified in the case of hotel properties, where not only the efficiency of management but also its personality is reflected in the operating statement.

estimation of value based on income was one that had wide vogue during the 1920's and is still in use. Ease of application gave it popularity. This rule (as easily stated as it was applied) held that "100 times the monthly rent equaled the value." Thus, a property that had a rental value of $100 per month was said to be worth $10,000, or 100 times the monthly rental.

What actually transpires, in the mathematical sense, in this computation is the capitalization of the per annum rentals at a rate of 12 per cent. Since the monthly rental is $100, the per annum rental is 12 times $100, or $1,200, which is equal to 12 per cent of the assumed capital value of $10,000.

It is extremely doubtful whether the users of this rule realize that the method employed is one of translating income value into capital value. More likely it is looked upon as a short cut to the estimation of value by the use of a simple mathematical formula. But its use implies that *all* properties can be treated in this way; that 100 times the rental value will equal capital value — that is, that *all* property incomes can be capitalized at a rate of 12 per cent per annum. This is tantamount to claiming that the same quantum of elemental risk is inherent in all properties; that the buyer takes no more chance in purchasing an old property than a new one; that neighborhood age makes no difference in the degree of risk.

We know this is not true. If it were true, it would be as easy to procure a mortgage on an old property as on a new one, or on a property in an old residential district as on one in a new district.

The rate is appraised. The rate used in the income approach reflects the hazards of investment. It cannot be the same in all properties because of the variable degree of risk inherent in the properties themselves and in the neighborhoods in which they are situate. The rate, therefore, must be appraised. It must be determined by factual analysis, and its use, in this approach, must be justified in the light of accepted investment practice. How shall this be accomplished? By measuring the risk. Again, the question is: "How?" The answer lies in observing the phenomena of the market place.

The buyers of residential property bid the rate, and the appraiser, by noting the rates they bid, is able to select the rate at which the income should be capitalized. The rates bid are reflected in the percentum ratio of rental values to market values.

How these rates evolve in the market place is shown in the following schedule:

I	II	III	IV
Monthly rental	Per annum rental	Market value*	Indicated rate of capitalization
1. $100	$1,200	$20,000	6%
2. 100	1,200	15,000	8
3. 100	1,200	12,000	10
4. 100	1,200	10,000	12
5. 100	1,200	8,000	15
6. 100	1,200	6,000	20
7. 100	1,200	4,800	25

In each of the items shown above, the assumption is made that market data reveal buyers actively trading in the market place at the prices shown in column III; that the rental values in each instance are the same — namely, $100 per month, or $1,200 per annum; that the rates shown in column IV evolve from the per-centum relation between columns II and III. The capitalization rate, therefore, is the product of the action of buyers and sellers in the market place.

Many nebulous theories have been advanced for the measurement of interest rates, most of which are based upon quantitative analysis of the rate itself. Thus, it is claimed that the rate is built up of various components; that the final over-all rate consists of the "pure" rate, or the safe rate (said to be the rate for governments bonds) plus added increments for risk and management. It is true that the rate reflects these elements, but it is not true that rates can be measured by weighing them. No appraiser is as competent to measure the element of risk as are the buyers and sellers. The appraiser is competent to observe and record the actions of buyers and sellers in the market place and to estimate risk rates by analysis of the prices paid for properties in relation to the rental incomes therefrom. Rates are determined, not by any slide rule or formula in the hands of the appraiser, but by transactions in the market place.[8]

Neighborhood age as an index to risk. The age of neighborhoods connotes the degree of risk and indexes the rate to be used

---

* Arising from sales actually made that appear to fit the definition of "market value."

[8] "The public as a whole are pretty good appraisers." Montonna in the *Review,* Society of Residential Appraisers.

in the capitalization process. As neighborhoods begin to wear out and the properties therein begin to pass from the original to the second or third owners, or into rental status, the risks to ownership become greater. This condition is recognized in mortgage lending practice, where varying interest rates apply to mortgages in one neighborhood as against another. Thus, in a new neighborhood, mortgages may freely be obtained, for example, at rates of 4½-5 per cent; in older neighborhoods, the rate is higher. The rates increase in proportion to the ages of neighborhoods because of the added degree of risk attendant upon the changing social characteristics of the district and the ever-declining character of property use. In some neighborhoods, we find it impossible to obtain mortgages because capital cannot afford to run the risks that would follow investment therein.

In the schedule of indicated rates of capitalization shown above, it may well be assumed that the difference between the rate of 8 per cent shown in item 2 and the rate of 15 per cent shown in item 5 arises from the manifest difference in the ages of the respective neighborhoods in which the separate properties are located.

Reflection of risk in the loan contract. That risk influences the rate is shown by the variable pattern of mortgages. Rates vary with the ratio of the amount of money loaned to the value of the property. Where the loan amounts to only 50 per cent of the property value, the rate will be low. As this ratio increases, the rate increases. The increased rate is a hedge against possible loss because of having decreased the normal margin of security between the amount loaned and the value of the security.[9]

Risk-area maps. There has been a growing use of city maps delineating the risk characteristics of neighborhoods. In their completed form, these maps show the geographical demarcation of certain neighborhoods within the city that exhibit different qualities of investment preferment. The gradations are labeled: "excellent," "good," "fair," "poor," "definitely hazardous."

These data are valuable to the appraiser. His information plant should contain such a map of the city in which he does his work. The differences in neighborhood grades are a key to the rate of capitalization. Thus Neighborhood A, with a rating of "good," may disclose a justifiable rate of 8 per cent; Neighborhood

---

[9] This does not apply in the case of insured mortgages, where, because of the insurance of performance by the borrower, the risk to the lender is minimized.

B, with a rating of "good," 10 per cent; Neighborhood *C,* 12 per cent; Neighborhood *D,* 15 per cent; and Neighborhood *E,* 20 per cent.

A neighborhood risk-area map, once compiled and kept up to date, and supplemented by frequent surveys of the existing relation between rentals and values, furnishes a competent and reliable index to value via the income approach.

The Use of Monthly Multipliers

Reference has been made to the "rule-of-thumb" which holds that "100 times the rent is the value." It has been shown how fallacious any such rule is when applied indiscriminately, on the ground that rates vary with risk and that all property incomes cannot be capitalized at the same rate. But there is no intent to decry the use of monthly multipliers, provided the appraiser knows what they are and why they are used.

The monthly multiplier is a mathematical coefficient for the equation in capitalization shown on page 178. Its use may be approved solely on the grounds of mathematical expediency. It is simpler to multiply (by the multiplier) than it is to divide and then multiply (by solving the equation). Note the following examples:

1. Estimated fair monthly rental $100.00
   Monthly multiplier used .... × 100
   Estimated value $10,000

2. Estimated per annum rental (at 100 per month)............ $1,200
   Selected capitalization rate 12%
   Hence $1,200 × 100 equals (capitalized value) $10,000
   $\overline{12}$

In each example, the same result is obtained; hence the use of a monthly mutliplier of 100 is equivalent to capitalizing the per annum rental at a rate of 12 per cent.

If there is any objection to the use of monthly multipliers, it is grounded in the academic dictum that interest rates, established to measure the return of investment capital, are usually computed on an annual, rather than on a monthly, basis. The use of the multiplier is, in effect, a monthly interest computation. The capitalization process, by the use of the typical equation shown in example 2 above, is an annual interest computation.

There follows a schedule to show per annum interest rates and their equivalent monthly multipliers:

Per Annum Interest Rates and Equivalent Monthly Multipliers

Rate per annum	Monthly multiplier	Rate per annum	Monthly multiplier
6%	200	13%	92.3
7	171.4	14	85.7
8	150	15	80
9	133.3	17½	68.5
10	120	20	60
11	109	25	48
12	100	30	40

Advantages and Disadvantages of the Method

Advantages. The advantages of the income approach are as follows:

1. The income approach exerts a rational check and balance on the cost and market approaches. It is condemned by some writers on the grounds that it fails to measure all of the income and that the income derived by an owner is of two parts: the hypothetical money income that the property would bring if it were rented, *plus* the psychic income or the amenities to the owner. In the case of the property which is owner-occupied and has never been rented, perhaps this opprobrium is, in a measure, justified. But in the case of purely tenant property, it most certainly is not. For, with the transition that occurs from owner to tenant occupancy, a large portion of the amentities or the mental income attributable to the single-family dwelling disappears. The owner, in the selection of his place of abode, has opportunity to pick and choose his edifice and his neighborhood; the tenant, as a rule, must take what is offered and make the best of it. There may be objectionable features in the building or the neighborhood; the owner (as buyer of the existing house or builder of a new one) will have none of it. The tenant is not so discriminating; he cannot afford to be. The detached single-family dwelling is built for owner occupancy. The tenant arrives on the scene only after the once new house or the once new neighborhood has been reclassified as shopworn and damaged; he must take what he can get. We may conclude, therefore, that in the case of the property that has become renter-occupied, the rents do indeed measure the remaining small amenity content.

2. The income approach, accurately used, measures depreciation of all kinds. It is a fair assumption that the fair rental value has considered the physical disabilities of the structure, its functional inadequacies, and the objectional environmental aspects of the property.

3. The income approach is useful during phases of the business cycle when there is no market. In those times, income is one of the two remaining tools worthy of the problem. In the absence of actual sales, its use becomes more difficult because of the inability to fix the exact ratio of income to values. But listings may be available, and even though these disappear along with actual transfers of title (which is unlikely), the appraiser's experience and historical knowledge of capitalization rates will remain to furnish an opinion of value via the income approach.

4. The income approach serves as the most dependable tool in the appraisal process in old, worn-out neighborhoods, where sales have long since disappeared as a value index but where rents are well stabilized (in rooming-house areas, for example).

Disadvantages. In the case of the property built for or occupied by an owner, the charge that the hypothetical rent fails to measure the amenity income must be admitted.

The amenities are elusive of measurement and difficult of recognition. They are not the same to all owners. "One man's meat is another's poison." The near-by parochial or public school gives amenity value to the subject property according to the owner's religion. The house located in the sparsely built-up area, with buildings placed at remote distances from each other, has a special value to the sufferer from claustrophobia. But the owner who is gregarious by nature finds amenity income in the property located in a densely populated neighborhood.

Thus, any attempt to measure the quantity of owner-occupancy appeal in a single-family dwelling must be regarded as a purely assumptive proposition — a valiant but futile effort to regimentate the multifarious concepts of amenity value as construed by individual owners.

This limits the value of the income approach in properties that are the subject of owner occupancy. But this limitation is not serious; nor does it serve to invalidate the method. Amenities, could they be measured by the yardstick of dollars, would be found to be relatively small as compared to the rental value. In fact they may be as little as 10 per cent of the rental yield.[10] If this is true, no serious error can result from the use of the hypothetical rental income without consideration of the dollar value of the amenities, since the zone of error in the entire appraisal process validates a latitude of 10 per cent in the final result.

Conclusions

From this discussion of the income approach to value, we may conclude that the efficacy of the method depends on two things: (1) the ability of the appraiser to estimate accurately the fair rental value; (2) his ability to appraise accurately the rate at which the income should be capitalized. Once that is demonstrated, he is assured of having at his command another useful tool which helps to fabricate the solution to the appraisal problem.

---

[10] "The capitalized amenity income is computed by deducting from the estimated monthly rental value the amount of any monthly excessive expense of ownership and multiplying the remainder by the appropriate rent multiplier." FHA, Underwriting Manual, par. 1217.

CHAPTER 16

Valuation of Residential Land

Land, like the entire realty entity, must be appraised. The instances in which it must be appraised separately are many. It is the purpose of this chapter to treat instances affecting the mortgage lender and the owner that are most common to everyday real estate activity.

The Purposes of Land Valuation

Land value as participating collateral. This is the problem of the mortgage lender. The appraisal made to determine the collateral value of the real estate to be pledged as security for the mortgage loan must reflect the land value as separate from the improvements. The reasons for this are well known and hardly merit repetition.

Vacant building sites have little intrinsic value except in the perspective of the services they may render, if and when they have been dosed with capital in the form of income-producing improvements placed upon them in the shape of buildings.[1] Until that occurs, urban land may be classed as an agent in the production of outgo. It is frozen capital, upon which a carrying charge is levied by government in the form of taxes.

Since unimproved land produces no income of itself, is not a loanable commodity. Mortgages on vacant property are practically unknown. The well-secured residential mortgage, therefore, is the one in which land is the least participant in the collateral.

As an illustration, let us consider a choice between two mort-

---

[1] Or income-producing services, such as parking lots.

186

gages. In mortgage A, the appraisal is $12,000, of which $1,000 is in the land. In mortgage B, the value is the same, but $6,000 is in the land. Which is the more desirable security? Obviously, mortgage A, for here the greater part of the income (prospective rent and amenities) is in the building, which is where it should be in order adequately to secure the lender. In order, therefore, to surround the lending process with proper safeguards, the appraisal must discover the separate value factors — land and building.

Land value as a residue of loss. This is alike the problem of the lender and the owner, and it contemplates the situation where disaster has occurred to the property — such as fire, flood, or tornado. Intelligent treatment of this problem requires a knowledge of the land values. In the event of total loss, the question is: "What have we remaining in the form of value?" The appraisal of the land answers this question.

Land value as an index to fair purchase price. This may be the problem of the individual owner desiring to purchase additional property — the lot next door to his home, for example — or it may be the problem of the institutional owner of residential property. In the latter case, there often arises the necessity to purchase additional abutting lands to settle an encroachment or to furnish additional land capacity for the extension of existing improvements.

Land value as an index to fair sales price. In the case of the institutional owner, this is related to the situation where it is decided not to rehabilitate a property that has been the subject of a major disaster and to sell the remaining land. In the case of the individual owner or the broker, the objective is to find the market price commensurate with value. Appraisal of the land in these instances becomes necessary.

Land value as an index to fair compensation. This has reference to actions in eminent domain where the property has been condemned ostensibly for purposes of public necessity — either by the city, county, state, or Federal government — and where it is to be taken over by the unit of government and the owner compensated therefor.

In some jurisdictions, it is common practice for the condemning authority to require that valuations of land and buildings be made separately; where this is so, the land must be separately appraised.

Land value as the final step in the cost approach. The above characteristics of land value constitute the common land appraisal problem as it applies in everyday practice. But in addition to these general characteristics that have application to real estate operations, there is another factor more important to the appraisal process — namely, the relationship of land value to the cost approach.

In the use of the cost approach as one of the tools in the appraisal process, *land* is valued separately. In the market and income approaches, the *property* is valued. In the cost approach, *buildings and land* are valued. And the valuation of the land is the final step in the method.

The separate valuation of land, therefore, is an indispensable factor in the appraisal of the single-family dwelling, for, in addition to the general reasons above enumerated, the appraisal process cannot effectuate itself with any degree of precision unless all of the approaches are used, of which the cost approach, involving separate land valuation, is not the least important tool.

Methods of Land Valuation

There are three methods of land valuation: (1) the comparative method; (2) the abstractive method; and (3) the anticipated minimum use method. Each method has its individual field of application.

The comparative method. This is probably the best known of the three methods. Its nature is denoted by its title. In the process used, the lot under appraisal is compared with certain bench-mark lots, whose characteristics, in point of the usable volume of housing services, are similar in quality to that of the subject lot.

The bench marks arise from two sources: (1) from vacant and unimproved lots whose comparatively recent sales, under conditions that appear to index market value, are of record; (2) lots that are improved with buildings, which have been recently sold or appraised and where a valuation via the cost approach discloses the land value.

We must be impressed again (as in the use of the market approach to value) with the necessary legitimacy of the bench marks to be used in the process of comparison. Inherent in them must be the same quantum of utility as offered by the subject lot — no more, no less. Thus, where the subject lot is adaptable in view of its conformity and its restrictions for single-family housing, there is no point in comparing it with another lot that is adaptable for multifamily housing. The use capacities must correspond.

The bench marks need not be near-by lots. Proximity should not be confused with similarity. Provided the use-volume is comparable, the bench marks may be classed as "pure," regardless of location.

Mechanics of the method. The bench marks having been selected and their data catalogued, the method proceeds to compare the subject lot with these data in the following order:

1. *Comparison of physical characteristics.* The first point of comparison provokes the application of the principle of conformity. Does the lot conform to the other lots in the neighborhood and with the bench marks? Its size, shape, and topography must be compatible with the neighboring land development and with the lots to which it is ultimately to be compared in price.

The *width* of the lot must conform. It must be normal and compatible with other lots in the neighborhood. This is the principle of conformity in operation. The width must be sufficient to serve the class of building that ultimately will repose upon it. Where the principle is violated, value will be adversely affected. Thus, in a block platted to lots of 50 feet in width, the odd lot of only 25 feet in width (a remnant in the platting process) is of questionable value. Utility has been impaired almost to the point of complete elimination, and the valuation conclusion may reveal that the 25-foot lot is worth far less than half as much as the 50-foot lot. A general observation is that narrow lots produce cheap buildings. Thus a 50-foot lot will usually be worth more than twice as much as one only half that width, on the ground that it provides more than double the utility.

The *depth* of the lot must conform with the bulk of the homesites in the neighborhood. As has been stated, the minimum depth desirable in small-house development is 125 feet, based on a setback line of 30 feet for the building, although there is considerable current platting to 100 feet. But again, the depth should conform.

Lots shorter than the norm for the block will be of less value. Those longer will be worth more. How much more? The answer is in the measure of additional utility. A well-established principle of residential land valuation is that value increases with depth, but with ever-decreasing ratio. To illustrate the principle: "If a lot 50 feet wide by 125 feet deep is worth $750, is a lot 50 feet wide by 250 feet deep worth $1,500?" The answer is "No," because value in land is proportionate, not as to quantity, but as to usefulness. Frontage, in a residential site, is of more importance than depth. Illustrating this principle, we have the case of two lots, one of which is 30 feet in width by 250 feet in depth, and the other 75 feet in width by 100 feet in depth; both contain 7,500 square feet. Which is the more desirable? Obviously, the second. Its broad expanse of frontage will frame the building to be erected upon it with more attractiveness; the 30-foot lot will crowd the structure. Depth, in this case as in most similar cases, is of secondary importance.

The situation differs radically from that of commercial and investment land. Here, rearage is ofttimes quite as valuable as frontage, because it is usable. But the use value of a residential lot of abnormal depth is highly questionable. Ordinarily, the lot of nominal depth (125 feet) serves the nominally priced house with all that is necessary in the matter of yard space and appurtenances. Anything over that amount is responsible for maintenance costs incompatible with the value increment.[2]

The *shape* of the lot controls, to an extent, its utility. In the small-house field, the rectangular lot provides optimum utility by conveniencing the layout and placement of the building. Odd-shaped lots present problems of design that increase the cost of buildings beyond the average, and hence inhibit optimum value. This is illustrated in Figure 4.

In Figure 4, it will be noted that only routine construction problems are involved in lots numbered 1 to 5 and 19 to 22. But special problems of design and building placement arise in the odd-shaped lots, particularly those numbered 9, 11, 14, and 15. On the lots of routine plottage, the conventional house, common to the neighborhood, can be placed and oriented without great difficulty. But in the others, in almost every case the house must be tailored to fit the peculiarities of lot shape. This may well involve the services of an architect, which will increase the cost. And in the special building design found suitable to the odd-

---

[2] This does not apply in small farm developments of quarter- and half-acre tracts bought for the purpose of raising garden produce on the back end of the lot.

shaped lot, nonstandard cost items are certain to arise from the nonstandard construction problem. The adaptable building area,

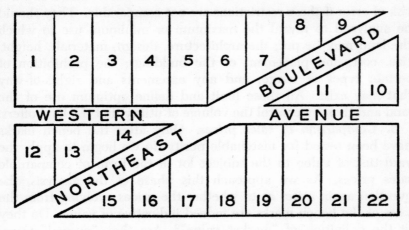

Figure 4.

compared to the lots of conventional shape, is severely restricted; the proportions are out of balance.

The question of *subsoil* conditions has been previously discussed,[3] but it is put into this continuity of comparison to remind the appraiser that this is one of the factors that must be matched against the bench marks.

The *improvements to the lot,* in the form of paving, sewer, water and gas lines, electricity, landscaping, drives, fences, walks, and sprinkler systems are all noted and catalogued. As to paving, time was when the street surfaced with reinforced concrete commanded a heavy premium over one less expensively treated. While hard-surfacing of some sort is to be desired, it is not necessary, in order to command maximum value, that the typical residential street be surfaced of the same materials used in through-highway construction. Something less than this will not only suffice but will deter high speed traffic, which is desirable. High-priced residential developments are observed where the streets are surfaced with crushed rock, gravel, or "black top," and much of the objection to loose surfaces has been removed by the application of chemicals that stay the dust.

2. *Comparison of restrictions.* The bench-mark properties to

---

[3] Chapter 9, "Analyzing the Property."

be used as comparisons must agree with the subject property in the matter of the restrictions on use, either those that run with the land or those established by local ordinance. There is grave risk of error if these restrictions are not comparable. They should be analyzed to reveal the maximum or minimum use to which the land may be put; the architecture, design, materials, height, size, cost, and placement of the buildings; the prohibition of certain types of usage; and any easements and rights-of-way that may exist. All these limit and define optimum use of the land and thereby control the volume of utility that the land offers.

3. *Comparison of sales prices.* Only after the bench marks have been tested for matchable purity do we begin to apply the yardstick of value to the subject lot in the form of comparable sales prices. As we approach this phase of the analysis, the question again arises as to whether the prices evolving from the sales of the bench marks are indeed indicative of value. Do they fit the definition of "market value"? Are they "normal" transactions? Was there complete freedom of action on the part of buyer and seller, and was each fully informed as to the present and potential benefits to be derived from the ownership of the lots in question? In the same measure that we have attempted to answer these questions heretofore in the case of the market approach to value (Chapter 14), they must be answered again as we attempt to find the value of the residential site.

These values, once established, should be reduced to a value per front foot or per square foot, as regional practice may dictate. Lot frontages vary. Usually, they vary according to the value bracket in which the property (land and building) falls. Low-cost housing is found on lots narrower than high-cost housing. To reduce the factor of error, therefore, it is advisable to reduce the values per lot to values per front foot or per square foot.

Bulk sales to builders. In the selection of the bench marks, *bulk* sales to builders should be discounted as indicating the values of the individual lot. It is common practice in the housing industry to give the builder a shorter price than that at which the individual may purchase. The reasons for this are logical. The owner of a group of lots in an undeveloped subdivision, or in a section where building is slow to start, realizes that increased building will speed lot sales. Thus, while the asking price to the individual may be, say $1,000 per lot, the price to the builder for a group of lots may be — and usually is — considerably less.

Volatility of price levels. Land, unlike buildings, is not reproducible. Its supply is definitely limited as the surface of the earth is limited.

Urban building sites are even more limited. Not that there is insufficient land; there is plenty. But it is not of the kind and in the locations demanded by potential home builders and buyers. Land of the sort adaptable to the new house must be new land — that is, new in the sense that it has not heretofore been developed as homesites. While it is true that, during periods of building activity, remaining vacant lots in the older areas are filled in by building, it is likewise true that the bulk of new building at these times occurs on new land. The supply of this new land, replete with service improvements, is limited at the start and becomes more limited as the boom develops.

The development of buying, building, or land booms has its genesis in small beginnings. Usually, it starts with the building of a few homes in a certain section by one or two builders. The houses are readily sold, provided the market is psychologically ripe. There proceeds word-of-mouth advertising by the new residents, which may be coupled with newspaper or other advertising by the operative builders. More builders, sensing that the district is "hot," are attracted to it and commence operations. More homes are built and sold; there is more word-of-mouth and newspaper advertising. The core expands and overflows its original limits.

And now speculation enters the scene. Speculators, realizing the prestige created by building and purchasing operations for the new district, buy up the land on its periphery or cover it with "shoestring" options. The builders, in their anxiety to continue operations in the "hot" district, bid the prices upward. Land prices soar. This upward movement continues until the demand for housing is satisfied or until a slump in general business occurs. This is followed by a collapse of land prices in those areas surrounding the core of the "hot spot." The "shoestring" options are forfeited; the market is flooded with sacrifice offerings with no takers; and whatever sales are made are at prices far less than value reckoned from the basis of utility.

These recurring surges make for a highly volatile land market and for sharp peaks and valleys in the historical curve of land prices. The trend of such a price movement is reflected in the actual history of lot values as shown by Figure 5, which traces

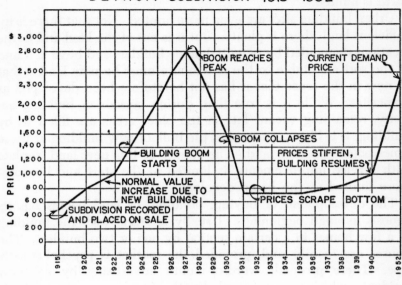

HISTORICAL PRICE CURVE OF LOTS IN A
DETROIT SUBDIVISION 1915—1952

Figure 5.

the history of land prices in a Detroit suburban subdivision over
a period of 35 years.

Value versus price. Recognizing that land prices are highly
volatile, the question will naturally follow: "Does the value curve
follow the price curve?" The answer is "Yes, but not in exact
mathematical sympathy." In the price curve, shown in Figure 5,
a substantial share of the high land price was due to the high
cost of junior financing. The bonuses paid for second mortgage
money, plus the item of second mortgage discount, accounts in
this example for a price curve far higher than the norm of value.
The second mortgage discount squeezes out of the land price a
portion of the "water" that exists in the sale of the whole property. And where a premium is paid for second mortgage money,
that cost must be added to the sales price of the property, thus
adding to the value of the land an increment of price attachable to the whole property.

Furthermore, when land speculation becomes rife and the land
speculator steps in, as between the owner of the land and the
consumer (that is, the operative builder), additional profit is

taken that further inflates the price levels and further distorts the relation between price and value.

In attempting to determine the relationship that exists at a given time, the appraiser should invoke the theory of substitution, which teaches that value cannot exist in any amount greater than the price that must be paid in the market place to obtain a lot similar to the one that is offered in the "hot spot" or contiguous area, and one that will offer the same quantum of utility and amenities. The application of this theory will always tend to limit the value ceiling, and it will tend to discount the fictitious "values" manufactured by land speculation.

The ratio of land value to building cost. There always exists, particularly in the new-building area, a well-stabilized ratio between the demand price of the land and the cost of the new building. This ratio should be observed and recorded, because it is an index to land values. To a degree, it controls the value of land by indexing its utility. For example, if, in a given situation, it is found that the majority of lots valued at $1,200 are improved with buildings costing $9,600 (or in the ratio of 8 to 1), it is a reasonable assumption that other lots in other locations that provide a comparable volume of housing services will be worth a like figure.[4]

Depth tables as measuring devices. From the time the appraisal of real estate first began to exhibit some slight affinity for scientific heritage, there have been the depth tables. These tables, of which there are several, were evolved some years ago (in most cases, by those influenced by tax assessment method) for the purpose of attempting to measure value by developing a mathematical coefficient for variable depth.[5] In other words, this is another attempt to measure value by the process of mathematics. These tables are based on mathematical formulas, and, with slight variation, the formula is the same in each. The formula used is expressed as follows:

$$V = F \times U \times \left(\frac{\sqrt{d}}{\sqrt{s}}\right)$$

In the equation shown, *V* equals value; *F*, the number of front

---

[4] Assuming, of course, that there is no scarcity of land available for and adaptable to similar types of buildings.

[5] Facsimilies of these tables may be found in Stanley McMichael, *Appraiser's Manual* (New York, Prentice-Hall, 1951), Ch. 35.

feet in the lot; U, the unit price per foot; d, the actual depth of the lot under appraisal; and s, the standard depth of the majority of the lots in the particular area under survey.

As an example of the use of this formula, assume that there is to be appraised a lot 50 feet wide and 225 feet deep, in a neighborhood where the majority of the lots are 50 feet wide and 100 feet deep, and where the unit value per front foot has been established at $15 per foot. Applying the formula, the problem is expressed as:

$$50' \times \$15 \times \left(\frac{\sqrt{225}}{\sqrt{100}} \right) = \$1,125$$

And the solution is reached in this way:

1. 50 feet multiplied by $15 equals $750.
2. The square root of 225 equals 15.
3. The square root of 100 equals 10.
4. 15 divided by 10 equals 1.5.
5. $750 (item 1) multiplied by 1.5 (item 4) equals $1,125.

The solution of the problem shows, therefore, that if the standard lots 100 feet deep in the subject neighborhood are worth $750 (item 1 above), the nonstandard lot 225 feet in depth will be worth $1,125 (item 5 above). It shows further that, while value increases with depth, the increase is in ever-decreasing ratio. In the example it is noted that, while the subject lot is two and a quarter times as deep as the surrounding lots, it is only one half times more valuable.

Depth tables as value-measuring devices have been given an entirely unwarranted popularity by appraisers because of their acceptance by assessors, on the ground that they assist in fixing an equity of assessment between parcels of land. They enjoy a mistaken importance also because of insistence on their use by the counsel of Federal, state, and municipal bodies in eminent domain practice, on the ground that this is a simple method of explaining variable value arising from variable depth which juries in condemnation cases can easily understand.[6]

But the whole thing is a snare and a delusion, for the depth table attempts, with resulting futility, to prove that value is in the material quantity of the thing (the objective theory again!)

---

[6] A contention that is an admission either that the intelligence quotient of juries sitting in condemnation cases is minus par or that the "expert" witnesses used are sadly limited in the degree of their "expertness."

instead of in the services the land offers in the form of housing. It is another vain attempt to confine within the strait jacket of mathematics the subjective theory of value as registered by the buyers in the market place. The variable of quantity is expressed as value; the variable of utility is ignored. Where utility is ignored, value is absent.

Corner influence. Four decades ago when residential home-sites in the large city were still being platted to thirty-five foot widths, it was the custom to accord some premium of value to the corner lot in the block. This was justified in light of the crowding of residential buildings on lots far too narrow to allow a sufficiency of light and air. But modern town planning and subdividing have long since recognized that the single-family dwelling must have sufficient land around the building to generate maximum owner-occupancy appeal. The influence of government agencies [7] in the field of housing has stimulated this idea, with a resultant trend toward wider lots.

With the disappearance of the crowded conditions that resulted from the use of narrow lots, there has disappeared also the value premium that heretofore attached to corners. In fact, in most cases the attitude of buyers has swung to the other extreme; the corner lot is less desirable to a majority of the market. It is claimed that the corner location decreases the element of privacy; the property is exposed to traffic hazards on two sides; the lot must bear the expense of paving on both streets.

The corner lot (in the opinion of the author) is not entitled to any increment over the inside lots, where the latter are of sufficient width to afford the building attractive placement and to enable development of an acceptable floor plan.

Advantages and limitations of the method. The comparative method of land valuation is useful and practical only in an active lot market. Unlike the market approach (detailed in Chapter 14), only sales are a reliable index to value. List prices, especially during a real estate slump, are of little help to the appraiser because, in a receding market, list prices of vacant property seldom follow the market down. The owners (because their capital investment and carrying charges are far less than those of the owner of an improved property) continue to hold at high prices; in most cases, they are unwilling to yield to the attack on values made by a diminished demand for lots. They continue to hold

[7] FHA particularly.

their vacant property, paying the small carrying charges against it in the form of taxes, in the meantime hoping for the return of a prosperous real estate market. Thus, of themselves, listings fail to furnish much assistance to the appraiser seeking to find the value of vacant residential land during a dull market. But in an active market, the method works within such limitations as have been discussed above.

The abstractive method. If the comparative method is one that works only in an active market, how, the reader may well ask, may we find land value in an inactive market?

One answer is found in the abstractive method. This is a process of abstracting land value out of property value, of squeezing out of the value of the entire property the value of the lot. In this process, the usual mechanics employed in the approaches to value are put into reverse. There, we started with certain data and worked toward a result. Here, we start with a result and work toward the definition of certain data — in this case, the land value.

The field of use. In order to define clearly the circumstances under which this method may be used with safety, let us assume that the area or the neighborhood in which we wish to apply it is characterized by a thoroughly inactive market. There is a complete absence of sales records, possibly over a period of years; there are few listings. There are sufficient properties rented, however, to establish with reasonable accuracy the stabilized rental index.

Specifically, this might be a residential area, densely built, with the buildings classified as being in early or midlife, where the question of land values is on the isolated lot or lots that have not been improved with buildings, or where it is necessary to establish land values for use with the cost approach. The question confronting the appraiser in this situation is: How shall he determine the underlying land values?

Mechanics of the method. The mechanics of the method divide into three steps. In step 1, the value of the surrounding properties is found by capitalization. On the assumption that there is a stabilized level of rental values, this should not be difficult. The capitalization rate is assumed to be known to the appraiser because of his experience with similar situations, or because there are sufficient listings available that indicate the ratio between rental income and possible sales prices. The values of these properties established by capitalization are used as bench marks with which to measure ultimately the land value of the lot under appraisal.

In step 2, the net depreciated worth of the bench-mark buildings is computed by the process described in Chapter 12. The cost, new, is calculated; then physical deterioration and functional and economic obsolescence (that part of it attributable to the building) are deducted, thereby producing the net depreciated value of the buildings.

In step 3, the result of step 2 is deducted from the result of step 1. The final result is said to be the value of the lots underlying the bench-mark buildings, which is said to indicate the land value of the lot under appraisal.[8]

Example. In this example, the neighborhood in which the lot to be appraised by the abstractive method is located is about 20 years old. In the immediately prior years, no sales have been made, either of lots or of properties. There are a few listings of record, ranging from $13,000 to $15,000. About 60 per cent of the occupants are renters; the remainder are owners. The rents are well stabilized at $150 per month. It cannot yet be termed a rooming-house district, although many of the owners and renters are known to keep "paying guests." After applying the mechanics outlined above, the following computation develops:

1. Rental income of the bench-mark properties,
   per annum ($150 per month × 12) .... $ 1,800
   Indicated capitalization rate 15%
   Value of the bench-mark properties by capitalization of income ($1,800 ÷ 15 × 100) $12,000
2. Estimated reproduction cost of the bench-
   mark buildings, new 20,000
   Less depreciation
   Physical deterioration, curable and incur-
   able $2,600
   Functional obsolescence, curable and in-
   curable 3,600
   Economic obsolescence (attributable to the
   buildings) 4,800
   Total depreciation 11,000
   Net depreciated value of the buildings 9,000   9,000

3. Residue of value imputed to the land............ $ 3,000

[8] In this method, as in the method of land value by comparison, it must be assumed that the quantum of utility in the bench-mark lots is similar to that existing in the lot being appraised.

Thus the land value by abstraction in this example is said to be $3,000.

Limitations of the method. There are many limitations to the use of this method, all of which are fraught with many risks to accuracy of the ultimate findings.

1. It is necessary to re-emphasize the necessity for the selection of bench-mark properties, the lands which are similar in their output of utility to the lot under appraisal. The use capacities must be equal. If, for example, the buildings on the bench-mark lots represent the highest and best use of the land, and if the lot under appraisal possesses a high and good use that does not correspond to the others, the result will be error (it is difficult to conceive of the situation where this might be true, but it could happen).

2. The land value that is abstracted in this process depends for its accuracy on two estimating processes, neither of which is simple: (a) the estimate of reproduction cost, new; and (b) the estimate of depreciation. The estimates of cost, new, involve the ability to calculate the cost as of today, based on the use of the same or closely related materials. In the case of a residential building in midlife, the changes in architectural style, construction method, and materials may cause difficulty in arriving at a proper cost, new.

Depreciation estimates in the sample problem are even more tricky. The method of measuring functional obsolescence, incurable, is described in Chapter 12 as one of estimating the dollar loss of rental value. In the above example, it is reported that there have been no sales in the immediately prior years. How shall the item be estimated in this instance? Only by the appraiser's opinion, based on his experience and judgment of the dollar amount of rental loss that the property would suffer if and when it were offered for rent.

In the measurement of economic obsolescence, the same tactics must be used as described in Chapter 12. Comparison must be had with the ideal neighborhood in order to measure the dollar amount of rental loss present and so capitalize that sum and estimate the dollar penalty of that type of depreciation. It may be difficult to visualize the "ideal" neighborhood to which, in fancy, the bench-mark buildings may be transported to effect the recapture of the rent loss now existent.

All these are serious limitations on hoped-for accuracy. But they cannot completely invalidate the use of the method, because it is the only one known for the valuation of residential lands under conditions described in the example above. And these are not unusual conditions. The appraisal operation is frequently faced with circumstances of the kind herein described Old properties as well as new must be appraised. Lot valuation must be had during times of market activity and inactivity. If the method exhibits aspects of academic desperation, it is because the end justifies the means, for, despite all the limitations with which its use is encompassed, it is at least one method that can be used where no market data are currently available. And any sort of method in these cases, however faltering some part of its gait may be, is more to be desired than some totally unsupported idea of land value that, in the final analysis, may prove to be little more than a figment of the appraiser's imagination.[9]

The anticipated minimum use method. There yet remains one situation that is bothersome in the appraisal of homesites in the absence of market data. This is the case of the vacant lot in a dormant subdivision where all of the surrounding lots are unimproved and where no sales have occurred for probably several years prior to the appraisal date. To meet this situation, there has been developed the anticipated minimum use method, so called because it is based on the comparison of unimproved residential lots with the proven utility value of improved residential lots, having the minimum value controlled by the minimum restrictions on use.

Three factors condition the use of this method.

1. The lot to be appraised must bear minimum restrictions running with the land that, based on use-volume in terms of square feet or cubic feet, set the minimum dollar cost of the building which it is permitted to serve.

2. There must be reasonable grounds for the belief that these restrictions will be sustained.

3. The lot must be adaptable for building (as of the appraisal date).

4. It must be assumed that there is a fixed ratio between the

---

[9] The author has long been intrigued by those systems of appraisal that demand that the appraiser file reams of detailed information concerning the neighborhood and the building, yet accept his estimates of land value in the same report without a shred of supporting evidence!

value of the completed property and family income of the prospective users.

If these conditions are present in the problem confronting the appraiser, the method may proceed.

Mechanics of the method. In step 1 of this method, the appraiser analyzes the restrictions imposed on the subject lot by virtue of the restrictive covenants in the deed that define minimum uses based on minimum dollar cost or building volume of the buildings that may be erected on the site. In step 2, certain bench marks are established. These take the form of improved properties in other localities where the cost of the buildings is now, or recently was, approximately the same as the minimum cost of the building that may be erected on the subject lot. In the selection of these bench marks, care is taken to see that the lots underlying the buildings are of the same size, shape, and utilitarian capacity as the lot under appraisal. As far as can be determined, the environing factors should be similar.

In step 3 a determination is made of the relation between the values of the bench-mark properties and the family income of the owners. In step 4 a determination is made of the relation between the value of the land and buildings of the bench-mark properties. In step 5 that ratio is applied to the present problem and the land value deduced from that finding.

Example. An appraisal is necessary of a lot located in a subdivision in which no building has as yet occurred and in which no sales are of current record. The restrictions running with the land which define the design and building volume prohibit the erection of any building at a cost of less than $10,000. Bench marks are sought, preferably in the near-by general district in which the minimum restrictions are approximately the same as in the subject lot. These, we assume, have been catalogued as follows:

Subdivision "A." Minimum restrictions $10,000; all lots same size and shape as subject lot; property sales occurring at prices that average $10,000 to $12,000. Analysis by the cost approach shows building values at $10,000 and land values at $1,200, or in the approximate relation of 90 per cent to 10 per cent.

Subdivision "B." Minimum restrictions, $12,000; property sales occurring at prices that average $13,500 to $14,000; analysis by the cost approach shows building values at $11,200 and land values at $1,400, or in the relation of 87.5 per cent and 12.5 per cent.

Subdivision "C." Minimum restrictions, $11,000; property sales occurring at prices that average $12,000 to $12,500; analysis by the cost approach shows building values at $11,000 and land values at $1,300 or in the relation of 88 per cent to 12 per cent.

From an analysis of these data, it seems logical to conclude that, if and when building is commenced in the subdivision in which the subject lot is located, the relation of the lot values will approximate 12 per cent of the total property value. Assuming, then, that the cost of the buildings to be erected will approximate the minimum restrictive amount, or $10,000, the solution to the problem may be expressed by this equation:

$$\text{"X"} = \frac{10,000}{88} \times 100 \times .12 = \$1,363$$

Thus, the conclusion drawn is that the value of the subject lot, based on *minimum utility* is approximately $1,350.

Limitations of the method. The method has its limitations as well as its advantages, as follows:

1. The restrictions of record in the bench-mark properties must be similar in design and use-volume, or reasonably so, as has already been mentioned.

2. There must be reason to believe that as they appertain to the subject lot they will continue in force.

3. The restrictions on estimated building cost must not be so high as to discourage or prohibit development of the land.

4. The value ascribed reflects minimum utility only. It is possible, of course, that once building gets under way, the minimum restrictions may be exceeded. Examples are many in actual practice where a minimum restriction has been exceeded by every building in the subdivision.

5. It must be reasonably certain that the people who will eventually purchase and use the land under appraisal will represent about the same social and economic level as those who now inhabit the near-by active areas. As a matter of fact, this entire method of land valuation leans heavily on the comparison of family incomes and the comparative ratio of family income to

housing cost, for the assumption must be made that the future users of these lots can afford housing in the $12,500-$15,000 price bracket.

With these limitations clearly in mind, the method may be used to arrive at an estimate of value based upon minimum land utility as defined by the restrictions of record. This result, it should be emphasized, is the lower limit of value which should be maintained pending the establishment of neighborhood character as indexed by the development yet to come.

Value versus price. It may be that the first sales in this area may occur at prices below that found by this method, a fact that is understandable in light of the evident surplus of land available, as indicated by the present lack of building. The first prices of record, also, may be the result of bulk sales to builders, which reflect the desire of owners to sacrifice value to price in order to stimulate the early development of the district. But the value of these parcels of vacant property in the final analysis results from utility. The minimum quantum of utility that the lots offer is reflected in the restrictions, both physical as to the building and economic as to family income. These indicate the value found by the use of this method.

Conclusions

Thus, we have three methods of land valuation: (1) the comparative method, for use in an active market where sales are brisk and there is a sufficient volume of active trading under conditions between buyer and seller which index market value; (2) the abstractive method, for use during a sluggish market or where, because of the age of the neighborhood, sales are no longer frequent; and (3) the anticipated minimum use method, for use in the valuation of vacant sites in areas that are totally composed of unimproved residential lots or during times when the market is oversupplied with vacant property.

All of these methods have their advantages and disadvantages, most of which have been explored and detailed. None of them is a precision tool. All three, like the tools of the appraisal process, are dependent to a large extent on the manner of their use, the proper selection of the method that will fit the appraisal circumstances, and, finally, on the experience of the appraiser and the quality of his judgment.

CHAPTER 17

Appraising the New Home

Up to this point, we have been engaged in a discussion of the theory of the appraisal process. Methods of analysis have been detailed, techniques explored, and principles expounded. We are now ready to put these to the test. It is the intent of this chapter to apply these methods to the valuation of actual, new properties. For this purpose, four case studies have been selected from actual field practice.

In each of these four cases the buildings are new. The appraisal, it is assumed, is being made immediately following the completion of construction.[1] The range of values is from $15,800 to $30,000, with emphasis on those falling within the $15,000 to $20,000 range.

In only one of these cases does simple treatment result. In the remaining three, depreciation is present in some form, thus exemplifying a point made in our discussion of depreciation in Chapter 11 — namely, that depreciation, because it is not alone a matter of building age, may be found in the newly completed dwelling.

Definition of the problem. The valuations are made for the purpose of finding market value, as defined in Chapter 2. The market value may be desired for ascertaining the worth of the property when pledged as security for a long-term first mortgage loan, for determining a fair sales or purchase price, or for determining fair compensation for the taking of the entire property by the state in cases of eminent domain. In the author's

---

[1] At this point it seems advisable to restate a sentence from the preface of this book; the figures used in these studies *do not* represent actual construction costs or value. They are purely hypothetical.

opinion, the differences in these purposes do not affect the value to be found. In each case, market value, as heretofore defined, is the objective.

Method of presentation. It is assumed that all of these properties are located in the same city, where they are equally affected by the general social, political, and economic factors that affect the city as a whole.

The neighborhood data in each case portray the social and economic background of each of the districts in which the particular case property is located. The comparative data furnish information as to comparative costs, sales, and rentals. The physical structure is described, as well as the important aspects of the site. These data are then interpreted in light of the particular appraisal problem, and, by the use of the three approaches — market, cost, and income — we arrive at a final market value estimate.

Case Property I

Description of the property. *Neighborhood data.* The area in which this property is located was subdivided about 12 years ago, but it was 10 years later before the first buildings were erected. As of the appraisal date, it may be classified as a new residential district barely three years old. The investment quality is considered good; the neighborhood is approved for insured mortgages, and there is keen competition among lenders to place loans on the properties being developed within it.

The area of the neighborhood is about one square mile. The nature of the terrain is level with good natural drainage.

About 60 per cent of the land is improved with single-family residential dwellings. The area is zoned for Class A residential usage, and the deed restrictions provide for 1- and 1½-story single dwellings of brick or brick-veneer construction, with a minimum of 1,000 square feet of dwelling space.

Although the streets are not hard-surfaced, they have been gravel-treated and are frequently dustproofed by the application of chemicals. The street system is comprehensive, giving convenient access to the surrounding main thoroughfares. There are no alleys; a 4-foot easement at the rear of each lot provides the necessary space for telephone and power lines.

Transportation for the neighborhood is furnished by high-speed

CASE PROPERTY No. 1

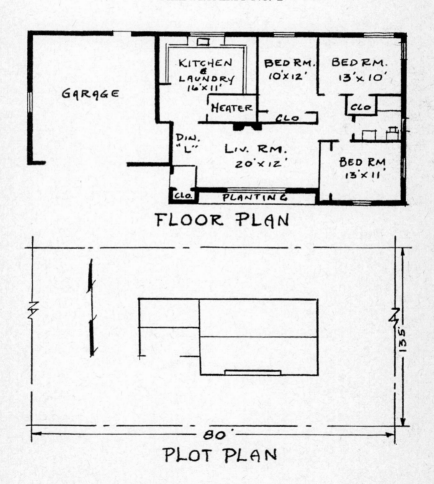

FLOOR PLAN

PLOT PLAN

CASE PROPERTY No. 2

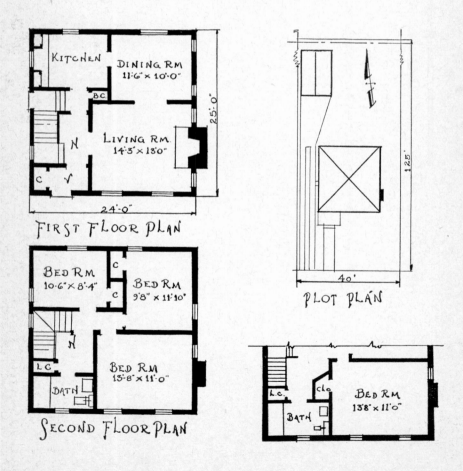

KITCHEN
DINING RM
11'-6" × 10'-0"
B.C.
LIVING RM.
14'-3" × 13'0"
25'-0"
N
C
24'-0"

FIRST FLOOR PLAN

PLOT PLAN

125'
40'

BED RM
10-6" × 8'-4"
C
C
BED RM
9'8" × 11'10"
N
L.C.
BED RM
13'-8" × 11'-0"
BATH

SECOND FLOOR PLAN

L.C.
clo
BATH
BED RM
13'8" × 11'0"

CASE PROPERTY NO. 3
(Courtesy of Corning and Moore, Architects.)

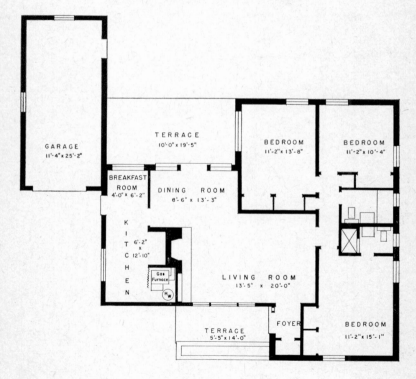

CASE PROPERTY NO. 4

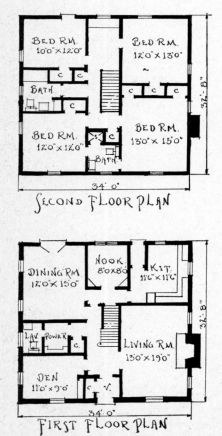

SECOND FLOOR PLAN

FIRST FLOOR PLAN

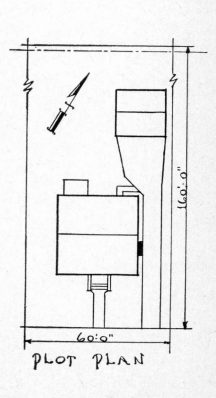

PLOT PLAN

busses along the main streets that bound the district at the north and south, and a 10-cent fare carries the residents to the downtown area 50 minutes distant.

Within a mile, there is a well-diversified retail area composed of many of the national chain stores and a first-run motion picture theater.

With the exception of the near-by school playground, there are no recreational facilities aside from a large city park, which is four miles away.

All public utilities — including gas, electricity, city water, sewer, and telephones at reasonable cost — are available.

The inhabitants are mostly well-paid factory and clerical workers. Many of them were former renters in the older section of the city who have become homeowners for the first time. The average age of the family heads is under 35, but there is a sprinkling of older couples who formerly owned larger homes in the older sections which, upon the marriage of their children, were found to be too large for their needs. On the whole, they are patriotic American citizens who believe in homeownership.

At the date of appraisal, only three rented homes could be found in the entire area.

The average family size is three.

Public and parochial grade schools are within convenient distance. The nearest high school is four miles away. Churches of all the prominent denominations are within a mile of the center of the neighborhood.

The average family income is $4,500 to $6,000 per year. The range of value of residential properties in the district is $12,000 to $16,000. The stability of the family incomes is fair as it applies to the factory workers and good as it pertains to the clerical workers.

Real estate is active. Considerable building is being carried on, and the completed properties are finding ready absorption in the market. No record of foreclosure could be found. The tax load is equitable and conforms with the average of city taxes found in other neighborhoods of like economic and social caliber. Retail operations serving the neighborhood are well stabilized, as indicated by the presence of the local and national chains already noted.

Site data. All lots in the neighborhood are platted to dimensions of 80 feet in width and 135 feet in depth. They are level, and the mean grade is about three feet above the street. Each has a 4-foot easement at the rear.

Specifications

Architecture — Rambler type, as shown by the floor plans
Attic — None
Basement — None
Footings — Poured concrete 20" x 8"
Foundation — Poured concrete 12" thick over a bed of sand covered with waterproof membrane
Exterior walls — Face brick veneer
Framing — Studs, No. 2 yellow pine or fir
Sheathing — ¾" celotex
Heating — Radiant floor — copper coils set in concrete floor 12" O.C. with booster pump and control valves on each circuit — oil-fired hot-water system
Insulation — 2" insulating blanket on sidewalls and 4" blanket on ceilings throughout
Interior Trim — White pine — 15' of base and 15' of wall cabinets — Wardrobe-type sliding doors on bedroom closets with built-in drawers
Floors — Asphalt tile in bedrooms, hall, and kitchen, balance to be carpeted at owner's expense
Plastering — Two coats on rock lath
Plumbing — Double-shell tub with overhead shower — 1-wall lavatory, 2-piece water closet — 30-gallon automatic oil-fired hot-water heater
Tile — Bath floor and wainscot 4' — 7' over tub
Roof — 210# asphalt shingles — galvanized iron flashings, gutters, and downspouts
Windows — Double-hung, mutton sash, weatherstripped
Garage — 24' x 22' solid face brick
Driveway — 15' wide, solid concrete

Solution of the problem. *Interpretation of market data.* As stated, the real estate market is active. Until a short time ago, many new buildings were being constructed and were finding quick sale in the market place. Sales were ranging between $14,000 and $16,500, with the average selling price at around $15,500-$16,000.

Interpretation of cost data. The indicated cost of the subject building is $14,400 covering the building itself, the extras, garage, and landscaping as detailed in the schedule of the cost approach which follows. The land value is indicated to be about $2,000.

Interpretation of income data. Little income data was found as indicated. Only three properties were in rental status. The estimated rental income from the property under appraisal, if it were rented, probably would be $125-$130. Based on the scant information available in regard to income data, the relation of per annum rents to sales prices would probably be in the neighborhood of 11 per cent.

Depreciation analysis. Inasmuch as the building represents the highest and best use of the land and there are no undesirable factors in the floor plan or in the functional utilities within the building, it is concluded that no depreciation exists.

Case Property I — Valuation A
Valuation date: completion date of construction

1. **COST APPROACH TO VALUE:**

1151 sq. ft. @ $9.50	$10,900

Extras:
Radiant heat
Natural fireplace
Automatic hot-water heater

Storms and screens	1,800
Garage	1,000
Landscaping, drive and walks	400
Terrace	300

	$14,400	($12.50 sq. ft.)
Plus land value (by comparison)	2,000	

Estimate of value by the cost approach........	$16,400

2. **MARKET APPROACH TO VALUE:**
Value as indicated by recent sales
of comparable properties ....$15,000-$17,000

3. **INCOME APPROACH TO VALUE**
(See "Rental data" above)
Rental of three similiar properties in the neighborhood (125 plus 125 plus 115 ÷ 3) 122.00, or $1,464 per annum
Indicated capitalization rate
(Based on ratio of rents to sales prices) 11%

Thus $1,464 per annum ÷ 11 × 100 =	$13,300

4. **FINAL MARKET VALUE ESTIMATE** $16,500

Conclusions. This is a simple appraisal problem. However, it is the problem faced most often by the mortgage lender and by the appraiser. The building is new; it is located in a good neighborhood that is economically suitable in every way. The prices paid by informed buyers, who do a pretty thorough job of shopping, approach the replacement cost.

As has been indicated, the income approach here offers very little help. There are only three properties rented in the area and because the rental data are so scarce, the income approach as shown above at $13,000 is hardly indicative of the value. If there were more renters in the neighborhood it might be possible to establish an index sufficiently reliable to justify an estimate of value by the income approach. However, the appraiser should not scorn this approach because, it must be remembered, at those times in the market cycle when there is no market and when there are no sales to be used as bench marks in the comparison process, we will usually find plenty of rental data from which an estimate of value can be made. The conclusion, therefore, is that the market approach and the cost approach tell us the entire story in this instance, and they tell it so conclusively as to justify our fixing the final market value at $16,500.

Case Property II

Description of the property. *Neighborhood data.* The neighborhood in which this property is located is a comparatively new one. Although it was platted some years ago, no building had been started until recently. An active promotional program by builders soon convinced many prospective purchasers that it was a desirable place in which to live. This, coupled with the favorable attitude of mortgage lenders, soon started a mild boom in the district.

Physically, it is readily adaptable to the development of attractive homesites. The lots are level, with a slight elevation above the street. The entire area is about a half square mile in extent.

About 60 per cent of the lots now bear homes all built within the past three years. The district is zoned A residential. The restrictions running with the land permit 2-story brick or brick-veneer dwellings of colonial design to be erected with a minimum floor area of 800 square feet. The street pattern is rectangular, and all streets are hard-surfaced with cement curbs. Good bus service is a quarter mile distant. A well-balanced retail section containing many local and national chain stores is the same distance. Two and a half miles away is one of the largest city parks, with tennis courts, golf course, small lakes, wading pools, and picnic grounds. The district is served with all public utilities at reasonable cost.

Most of the present owners are former renters coming from the older sections of the city. Many of them formerly occupied apartments. Predominantly, they are American whites whose forebears were born here. They are self-respecting and law-abiding, "solid" citizens. Their standard of citizenship is high, as denoted by the manner in which they keep up their homes and yards. Ninety-eight per cent of the homes are owner-occupied. The average family size is four. Both public and parochial grade schools are within a half mile; high school is within two miles; and all churches (of the prominent denominations) are within one mile.

Family incomes range from $5,000 to $7,000; the range of housing values is from $15,500 to $18,000. There is a fair stability of incomes, although many of the residents are employed in the automobile industry. Others come from clerical occupations and minor executive posts.

The real estate market is active. As of the appraisal date, more than 30 homes were under construction, all of which were finding ready absorption in the market. No record of recent foreclosure could be found. The taxes are in line with the accepted city assessment practice and rate. Retail operations are well stabilized.

Site data. All lots are platted to dimensions of 40 by 125. They are level, and show a mean elevation of three feet above the street level. There is a 4-foot easement at the rear of each lot.

Cost data. The average cost of buildings similar to Case Property II is found to be $14,500. Frame single garage and side drive are usually added, at a cost of $750. The present demand price of the lots is $1,500.

Rental data. As of the appraisal date three properties were found to be rented. Two of these were bringing $130 and the third $125.

Specifications

Attic — unusable; hatch opening

Basement — 7 feet in the clear; concrete block walls; concrete floor; coalbin; fruit closet; 2-inch stair treads with no risers

Electrical — Romex cable; fixture allowance $100

Exterior walls — common brick veneer

Fireplace — wood mantel and tile hearth

Floors — living rooms, select oak; kitchen, pine with linoleum covering; bath, unglazed tile; vestibule, glazed tile

Framing — studs, No. 2 yellow pine or hemlock; first-floor joists, 2 by 10, 16 inches on centers; second-floor ceiling joists, 2 by 6, 16 inches on centers; second-floor joists, 2 by 8, 16 inches on centers; roof rafters, 2 by 6, 16 inches on centers

Heating — forced warm air, mineral- or glass-wool-filtered

House walks — street to front and grade entrances

Insulation — 4-inch mineral wool over second-floor ceiling; celotex sheathing

Interor trim — gum; 20 square feet of linen closet, 60 square feet of kitchen cupboard, ironing board, and broom closet

Landscaping — rough grade only
Linoleum — kitchen floor
Built-in equipment — milk receiver; metal-lined clothes chute; steel medicine cabinet; steel kitchen cabinets; formica drainboards and splash
Plastering — 2 coats on rock lath
Plumbing — double-shell tub with overhead shower; wall lavatory; closet combination; flat-rim 2-compartment sink; automatic gas heater with 30-gallon storage tank
Roof — wood shingles; galvanized iron flashings, gutters, and conductors
Terrace — 48 square feet at front entrance
Tile — bath, 4-foot tile wainscot and unglazed tile floor
Windows — double-hung, weatherstripped
Garage — 12 by 20 frame; wood-shingle roof; ordinary doors and hardware
Side driveway — 2 24-inch concrete ribbons 4 inches thick

Solution of the problem. *Interpretation of market data.* The market is active with 30 new homes under construction. These are being sold as quickly as completed, and there is no overhang of unsold new properties. Sales prices range from $15,500 to $18,000. Properties similar to the subject property are selling at about $15,000.

Interpretation of cost data. The estimated cost of the subject building is $14,300, of the garage and side drive, $750, and of the lot $1,500 — a total of $16,550.

Interpretation of income data. There are but few properties in actual rental status. The estimated rental value of the subject property is $120 per month. The ratio of per annum rentals to sales prices is about 9.5 per cent.

Depreciation analysis. Examination of the second-floor plan shows that the hallway is superadequate and that the master bedroom has no clothes closet. This is a serious functional deficiency. To an extent, it is curable by taking sufficient space from the hallway to develop a clothes closet. (See amended second-floor plan, Case Property II.)

When this is done, some functional inadequacy will still exist, because the master bedroom closet will be irregular in design and will contain fewer cubic feet than the closets in the auxiliary bedrooms.

Depreciation estimate. The estimated cost to cure this deficiency as per the foregoing is $200. Some resistance to the sale of the property will still remain, however, on the grounds that the master bedroom, normally accommodating two persons, is equipped with the smallest clothes closet. The appraiser believes that, by comparison with other similar buildings that do not possess this deficiency, the property will be harder to rent, except at a lower figure than could be obtained for a similar property in which this deficiency is absent. This amount he estimates at $5 per month. The depreciation, therefore, is of two sorts and is itemized as follows:

Functional obsolescence, curable $200
Functional obsolescence, incurable and resulting from
  rental loss of $5 per month or $60 per year capitalized
  at 9.5% viz; $\dfrac{60}{9.5} \times 100 =$ 630

Total functional obsolescence $830

The valuation of the property then proceeds as follows:

Case Property II — Valuation B
Valuation date: completion date of construction

Estimate of value by the market approach
A sufficient number of investigated comparable properties
have been recently sold to justify a value by comparison
of $17,000
    Market approach estimate $17,000
Estimate of value by the cost approach
Replacement cost of the building $14,300
Less functional obsolescence (as above) 830

                                              $13,470
Plus garage and drive, $750 750
Plus land value 1,500

    Cost approach estimate $15,720
Estimate of value by the income approach:
Estimated monthly rental .... $ 120
Estimated yearly rental 1,440
Indicated capitalization rate 9.5%
Computation: 1,440 ÷ 9.5 × 100 .... $15,150
    Income approach estimate $15,150
Final market value estimated (called) $15,800

Conclusions. The original replacement cost of the land and the building in this case does not correspond to value because of the factor of decreased desirability noted in the floor plan of the dwelling. Since it is possible to measure the loss in value that occurs from this source, the cost approach, rather than the market or income approach, is accorded preferential recognition in the approach to value. Here again, there is insufficient rental data to justify dependence on the selected capitalization rate; hence the income approach must be considered weak.

Case Property III

Description of the property. *Neighborhood data.* The district to the north of this property is about 20 years of age. It is known as a "class" neighborhood. It is well liked by mortgage lenders who are actively bidding for 80-90 per cent insured loans at rates down to 4¼ per cent interest. The exact "neighborhood" consists of a single street culminating in a cul-de-sac. On it have been built in the last year 20 new homes, all of the same kind as the property under appraisal. The floor plans are identical; elevational design has been varied.

This particular piece of land was a "hold-out." Its use was frozen by litigation while the abutting areas were being built up. Now it is entirely built up along both sides of the street. There are no remaining sites for sale.

The street is zoned "A" residential with restrictions running with the land that prohibit the construction of any building of less than 1,000 square feet of livable area.

This single street leads into a main drive through the district which, in turn, feeds into the main traffic arteries serving this section. Bus service is available and adequate one block distant. The central shopping section containing national food chain stores is less than two miles distant. A golf and country club with swimming pool, with fees within the reach of most of the residents, is one mile distant. Public parks and playgrounds are two miles away. All public utilities are available.

The inhabitants are junior and senior executives or men engaged in business for themselves. The average family size is three. School enrollments are heavy; there is a comfortable density of population in the area. All churches and schools — public and parochial — are conveniently near.

Family incomes range from $8,500 to $12,000. Property values in the general area range up to $50,000 with a very few properties going much beyond that figure. In the exact neighborhood — the street on which this property is located — all of the houses were sold within the last year at $22,500 to $24,000. One block south of this street is an area about six blocks square built up within the last three years with cheaply constructed homes that sold for $11,500 to $13,000.

There is an active real estate market throughout the area and more houses in this price bracket could be sold on this street if there was any more land available.

Because of location outside of the municipality and within the county, taxes are low — about $180 per year.

Directly to the rear of this property there is a run-down 12-acre farm owned and operated by a family whose social and economic background is much lower than that of the new community. Although the farm is directly in the path of development, the owner thus far has refused to sell. When and if he does, the farm will undoubtedly be subdivided into lots for house building. Since there are no municipal zoning restrictions (the farm is in the county where there is no zoning law) the natural use will evolve as a supplement to the cheaper $11,500-$13,000 homes directly south and east of our property and now right up to the farm line.[2]

Site data. All lots on the street are built up with single-family homes, the same as the property under appraisal. The dimensions are 80 feet along the front and 125 feet deep. The mean grade is about four feet above the street with a 4-foot easement at the rear. All street improvements are in. The street is paved with black top with concrete curbs and gutters.

Cost data. The cost of this building has been estimated at $18,500; the garage and driveway at $1,500 and the lot (including sodding and planting) at $3,500 (10,000 square feet).

Income data. One house on the street, well removed from the appraised property, was found to be rented at $150 per month. Several other houses in the general area of comparable size and utility were rented at that figure. There are indications that the rental value of the subject property is $150 per month.

Market data. There are plenty of these. As was stated, all of the houses on this street were built and sold during the past year at prices of $22,500 to $24,000. They are all reasonably comparable.

Specifications

Attic — subfloor in place; 4½ feet to ridge; pull-down stairway

Basement — none.

Electrical — BX cable; fixture allowance, $100

Exterior walls — common brick, cinder-block backing; frame sections, No. 1 yellow pine backed with 2" insulator bats

Floor — 5" mesh-reinforced concrete slab; W/P membrane; 6" gravel fill

Finished floor — parquet blocks in mastic; kitchen, linoleum over plywood; baths, tile

Footings — 8" poured concrete to below frost line; inside of exterior foundation wall, fiber-glass insulated

Framing — studs, No. 1 yellow pine; first floor, 2 x 6 over bedrooms; 2 x 8 over living area; rafters, 2 x 6; all 16" o.c.

[2] This situation does not in fact exist. It is a fiction invented by the author to point up one of the environing conditions that generate economic obsolescence and to demonstrate the technique to be applied in the appraisal process. The fact is that the neighborhood is the subject of good planning, excellent building placement, and architectural treatment in the best tradition.

Heating — forced warm air, gas fired; earth-imbedded concrete pipe ducts
House walks — front door to driveway; 190 feet of concrete terrace at dining entrance
Insulation — 4″ rock wool bats in ceiling
Interior trim — Ponderosa pine, No. 1
Landscaping — rough grading; front yard, sodded; planting allowance $85
Kitchen work counters and splash — formica
Built-in and furnished equipment — steel medicine cabinets; sliding closet doors; garbage disposal; dishwasher; clothes washer; 8 c.f. refrigerator
Fireplace — common brick breast and hearth; wood storage niche
Plastering — 1 double rough and 1 finished coat on rock lath
Plumbing — 1 tub-shower; 1 stall shower; 2 wall lavatories; 2 closet combinations; flush-type sink; 30 gal. automatic hot-water heater
Roof — 220# asphalt shingles; galvanized gutters and conductors
Tile — ceramic 3′ 6″ wainscot; 7′ over tub and in stall shower
Windows — "Ceco" steel residential casement
Garage — common brick; cinder block backing; asphalt shingle roof
Driveway — 6″ concrete, street to carport

Solution of the problem. *Interpretation of market data.* This appears to be no problem. The recent sales (during the past year) of all 20 homes appear to bracket the market price firmly.

Interpretation of cost data. These speak for themselves also. Since the house was built so recently the costs are easy to check. Applying the square foot method we get (for the house) 1,120 square feet of livable area at $16.50 per square foot or 24,640 cubic feet (1120 s.f. x 22 ft.) at $0.75 per cubic foot, both of which computations come out to $18,500. Adding the garage and driveway at $1,500 and the lot at $3,500, gives us a total of $23,500.

Interpretation of income data. We found one house rented at $150. This was located at the other extreme of the street from the subject property. Our estimate of the rental value of the appraised property is $150.

Depreciation analysis. There are two factors in this problem which tend to deteriorate the value of this property. First, there is the presence of a socially undesirable family directly to the rear of the property and 150 feet distant from the rear wall of our house. Second, there is the potential encroachment of the cheaper housing immediately to the south and stopped, temporarily, by the farmer who still holds the fort against the onrush of housing progress. These facts point up the presence of economic obsolescence in this particular dwelling, evidenced by a lack of demand because of the socially inharmonious situation across the backyard.

Depreciation estimate. The amount of economic obsolescence attachable to the subject building is estimated by the process and the technique described in Chapter 12; the rental loss is determined, and that amount capitalized to find the dollar value of the economic loss that has been sustained. Application of the procedural steps outlined in Chapter 12 to this particular case produces the following computation:

1. Estimated rental value of the subject property .... $ 150
2. Estimated rental value if located in a neighborhood void of the present social and economic risks 175
3. Resulting monthly rental loss 25
4. Resulting yearly rental loss 300
5. Indicated capitalization rate for the "ideal" neighbor-hood 8%
6. Capitalized value of the rental loss ($300 ÷ 8 × 100) 3750
7. Percentum relation of land to buildings in the ideal neighborhood; land, 20%, buildings, 80%
8. Estimated economic obsolescence imputable to the building; ($3750 × 80%) 3000

Case Property III — Valuation C

Valuation date: 6 months following completion of construction

Estimate of value by the market approach
All of the houses on the street sold for $22,500 to $24,000. Because of the remarks noted under "Depreciation analysis" this property must be worth less than the one sold at the lowest price,

Market approach estimate	$21,000
Estimate of value by the cost approach	
Replacement cost of the dwelling, new $18,500	
Less depreciation:	
Physical deterioration, none	
Functional Obsolescence, none	
Economic Obsolescence (as above) 3,000	
	$15,500
Plus garage and driveway 1,500	
Plus land value 3,500	
Cost approach estimate	$20,500
Estimate of value by the income approach	
Estimated rental value .... $ 150	
Estimated yearly rental value 1,800	
Indicated capitalization rate 10%	
Computation: 1800 ÷ 10 × 100 .... $18,000	
Income approach estimate	$18,000
Final market value estimate	$20,500

Conclusions. The market approach is of some help here because of the sales made of almost duplicate properties within the past year on this same street although none of them is affected by the depreciatory influence in the same degree as the property under appraisal. A safe assumption, therefore, is that the property we are appraising is worth less, because of the conditions mentioned, than the house that sold at the lowest figure, that is, some figure less than $22,500.

The cost approach (provided the rental estimates and the capitalization rates can be justified) appears to nail down what seems to be the fair value. The income approach also is within hitting distance of the optimum figure. All approaches seem to justify the appraiser's final figure of $20,500.

Case Property IV

Description of the property. *Neighborhood data.* The neighborhood in which this property is located is a small suburb 14 miles distant from the center of a large industrial city. It was subdivided about 25 years ago and about 30 per cent built up at the commencement of the depression of the thirties. For some years there was no building, but lately an active building program has gotten under way. As of the appraisal date, the investment quality is rated as "good" by mortgage lenders; 80 per cent insured mortgages are being secured at the going rates of interest.

The physical aspects are attractive. The gently rolling terrain lends itself to a platting scheme that takes full advantage of the contours. The street system winds through the district following the low areas; the homesites are on the knolls and higher ground.

The district is zoned A residential. The deed restrictions provide that all buildings shall be single-family residential (there is no retail district in the immediate subdivision). The construction shall be of frame or brick veneer; it shall set back at least 40 feet from the front lot line, with a minimum of 10 feet from the side lines of the abutting lots; each structure shall contain not less than 1,000 square feet of ground floor area.

Transportation of various kinds is conveniently available. One-half mile from the center of the neighborhood there are streetcar and bus lines. One and one-half miles distant, there is railroad commuter service.

At one edge of the area, there is a small retail section consisting of grocer, butcher, and drugstore. There is a 100 per cent shopping area one mile distant.

Within a five-mile radius, there are three private golf clubs and a municipal course, one of the largest city parks, and a zoological park.

All public utilities are available; and the rates, although not as cheap as in the near-by large city, are not prohibitive.

The inhabitants of this neighborhood are distinctly "white-collar"; they are department heads and junior executives, with a salary range of from $8,000 to $12,000 yearly. Their standards of citizenship are high; they believe in the American way of life and are respectors of law and order. Ninety-five per cent of the homes in this area are owner-occupied. The average family size is three. The cultural institutions are convenient and adequate; they consist of schools, churches, and a public library.

New and used property values range from $22,000 to $30,000. In the subject block and across the street, the ceiling of value, new, is $27,500. Since most of the inhabitants are salaried workers, the stability of their incomes is high. The real estate market is active. There is a healthy demand for new and used homes in the area. Foreclosures are few. The tax situation is favorable. The municipality has no bonded debt, and the rate is 35 mills on assessments, which approximate 60 per cent of market values.

Site data. All lots in this block are platted to dimensions of 60 by 160. Elevations above the street levels vary according to the roll of the terrain, but in nearly all cases the building locations are on the highest points. There are no alleys; easements take their place.

Cost data. The cost of the subject property has been estimated at $32,000, of the garage (which is detached) $1,500, and of the land (based on demand prices) $3,500—a total of $37,000.

Rental data. There are but few houses rented, and these vary from $175 to $225 per month. The estimated rental value of the subject property is $200 per month. There are no vacancies. In the same block are two properties renting at $175 per month.

Market data. Comparable sales of new and used housing indicate a value range of from $22,000 to $30,000 for the district and an average of $27,500 for the block.

Specifications

Attic — 10 feet to the ridge; stairway; rough floor
Basement — 7 feet, 6 inches in the clear; brick walls; concrete floor; fruit closet;

2-inch stair treads with pine risers; hand rail; plastered recreation room with floor covering of asphalt tile

Calking — all openings

Electrical — Romex cable; fixture allowance $350; door chimes and kitchen vent fan

Exterior walls — common brick veneer

Fireplace — wood mantel with marble hearth and trim

Floors — Living rooms, select oak; kitchen and nook, linoleum over pine; baths, unglazed tile; lavatory, glazed tile

Framing — Studs, No. 2 yellow pine or hemlock; first-floor joists, 2 by 10, 16 inches on centers; second-floor joists, 2 by 10, 16 inches on centers; second-floor ceiling, 2 by 6, 16 inches on centers; rafters, 2 by 6, 16 inches on centers; 2 steel "I" beams

Heating — winter air conditioning with humidity control, oil fired

House walks — street to front and grade entrances

Insulation — 4-inch mineral wool and air-o-cell foil-surfaced board behind exterior walls and over second-floor ceiling

Interior trim — gum; 30 square feet of linen closet, 80 square feet of kitchen cupboards, ironing board, and broom closet

Landscaping — full lot, graded, seeded, and shrubbed; allowance $300

Linoleum — kitchen and nook floor

Formica — kitchen counters and splash

Built-in equipment — milk receiver; metal-lined clothes chute; steel medicine cabinets

Plastering — 2 coats on rock lath

Plumbing — double-shell tub with overhead shower; 1 pedestal and 2 wall lavatories; closet combinations; stall shower with glass door; 50-gallon oil-fired water heater with thermostat control

Roof — good grade wood shingles laid double butt, each 5 courses; galvanized iron flashings, gutters, and conductors

Terrace — 48 square feet of concrete floor at front entrance; 80 square feet of concrete floor at dining room exit

Tile — master bath, 4-foot wainscot and 7 feet in shower stall; general bath, 4-foot wainscot and 7 feet over tub; lavatory, Yankee fiber tile, 4-foot wainscot trimmed with chromium strips

Water pipe — copper

Windows — double-hung mutton sash, weatherstripped

Garage — 18 by 20 solid brick; wood shingle roof and overhead doors

Driveway — 7 feet solid concrete

Solution of the problem. *Interpretation of market data.* The market for real estate is active. New and used housing is in demand, with values ranging from $22,000 to $30,000. The ceiling of value is $27,500 for properties along both sides of the street in the block in which the subject property is located.

Interpretation of cost data. The cost of the subject building is $32,000, of the garage, $1,500, and of the land $3,500—a total of $37,000.

Interpretation of income data. Five per cent of all the properties in the area are rented. The rental range is $175 to $225. In the subject block, two properties are being rented at $175 per month. The indicated capitalization rate is 8 per cent for the area as well as for the block. The estimated rental value of the subject property is $200.

Depreciation analysis. The building is an overimprovement of the land. The total cost, new, is $37,000. The value ceiling for the area is $30,000, and for the block $27,500. The improvement, therefore, is in violation of the principle of conformity, resulting in decreased appeal to the typical purchaser of homes in this particular neighborhood.

Depreciation estimate. By application of the procedural steps outlined in Chapter 12:

1. Estimated rental value as at present located	$ 200
2. Estimated rental value if located in a neighborhood economically suitable	250
3. Resulting rental loss per month	50
4. Resulting rental loss per year	600
5. Indicated rate of capitalization in the conformable neighborhood	8%
6. Capitalized value of the rental loss	$7,500
7. Indicated ratio of building to land value in the ideal neighborhood 6 to 1, or (expressed in percentages) building 86%, land 14%.	
8. Estimated economic obsolescence imputable to the building ($7,500 × 86%)	6,450

Case Property IV — Valuation D
Valuation date: completion date of construction

Estimate of value by the market approach:
Neighborhood ceiling, $30,000; ceiling for the block $27,500; cost, new, subject property, $37,000. Hence no comparable properties with which to make accurate comparison based on actual sales.

Market approach estimate	$32,000

Estimate of value by the cost approach:

Replacement cost of the dwelling	$32,000	
Less economic obsolescence (as computed above)....	6,450	
Depreciated value of the dwelling	$25,550	
Plus garage value	1,500	
Plus land value (based on present demand price)....	3,500	
	$30,550	
Cost approach estimate (called)		$30,000

Estimate of value by the income approach:

Estimated monthly rental	$ 200	
Estimated yearly rental	2,400	
Indicated capitalization rate	8%	
Capitalized rental value (2,400 ÷ 8 × 100)............	$30,000	
Income approach estimate		$30,000
Final market value estimate		$30,000

Conclusions. The market approach in this case is weak. Because the building is an overimprovement, there are no comparable sales of new housing with which it may be compared. The norm for the area is $22,000 to $30,000; the norm for the block is $27,500, with that figure indicating the value ceiling. Since the new cost of the subject property is estimated at $37,000, any attempt to fix value by the medium of comparative sales will only tend to prove the distortion that exists between cost and value, without lending any assistance toward fixing value as emanating from sales prices. The appraiser, in this instance, concludes that while cost and value are not identical, any sale of the property would not necessarily be limited to the value ceiling observable in the subject block, on the ground that some purchaser will be found who will pay a price somewhat higher than the prices paid for the conformable dwellings in the block. This he estimates to be $32,000. To an extent, this figure is picked out of thin air, except in so far as his experience with similar overimprovements tends to prove the observable ratio between the margin of overimprovement and the amount the *occasional* (not the typical) purchaser is willing to pay in excess of the value ceiling in the subject location.

The cost approach is more dependable. The exact costs are known. The only item subject to question is the depreciation estimate, which again is computed by capitalizing the rental loss occasioned by having failed to environ the building among its own kind. The question, of course, is on the estimate of the present rent the property would command if offered for rent.

The income approach speaks with considerable authority. The ratio between rents and sales prices is known — 8 per cent. The normal value for properties in the block is said to be $27,500; the going rents are $175 per month or $2,100 per year. Thus the indicated capitalization rate is proved to be 8 per cent. If, as estimated by the appraiser, the subject property will rent for $200 per month, or $2,400 per year, then the value by the process of capitalization is $30,000 ($2,400 ÷ 8 × 100$).

Leaning heavily, therefore, on the cost and income approaches to value the appraiser concludes that the fair market value is $30,000.

CHAPTER 18

Appraising the Used Home

This chapter presents four case properties in the field of used housing. The values range from $8,250 to $28,000. The ages of the buildings vary from 10 to 20 years. The neighborhoods in some cases have begun to exhibit unmistakable forms of social blight.

These characteristics amplify the appraiser's problem. It has been demonstrated in Case Property I that where the building on the lot develops the land to its highest and best use, cost will usually correspond to value. But where building and neighborhood age has accrued, functional and economic absolescence has been generated, and as a result the problem becomes more complex.

Because the four studies that follow are used properties, depreciation treatment becomes a major phase of the valuation process.

The method of presentation is the same as in Chapter 17; the description of the neighborhood and the property is followed by the solution to the appraisal problem. In each case market value, as defined in Chapter 2, is the objective.

Case Property V

Description of the property. *Neighborhood data.* As a neighborhood, this district is about 30 years of age. Its investment quality is rated by mortgage lenders as only "fair." Very few new mortgages are being placed; the bulk of lending activity is in refinancing. Mortgage interest rates are at 5½ to 6 per cent, which is higher than in the newer districts, and loans are limited to 60 per cent of appraisal.

Physically, the district is flat and well drained. Its area is about a half mile square.

Ninety-eight per cent of the usable residential land is improved with buildings, most of which are more than 20 years old. No new construction is noted. It is zoned B residential, permitting the building of singles, two-flats, or apartments. The block in which the subject property is located is limited to single-family usage, the deed restrictions calling for frame or brick buildings of a minimum ground-floor area of 800 square feet.

The street system is rectangular; the main residential streets are paved; the side streets are unpaved.

The district is well served with good transportation facilities. One-quarter mile distant there are bus and streetcar lines. Within easy walking distance there is a large retail center, containing many prominent national chain stores and two first-class motion picture theaters. Within two miles there is a large public park. All public utilities are available at nominal cost.

The inhabitants are shop and factory workers. Many of them —particularly the remaining owners—have lived here many years. The standard of citizenship is high, as indicated by the well-kept homes and yards. Tenant occupancy is on the increase. As of the appraisal date, 70 per cent of the occupants were found to be renters. There is an excellent rental demand because of the convenient transportation system giving access to the near-by industrial areas in which many of these people are employed.

The average family size is four to five. School enrollments indicate a density of population in the neighborhood. Public and parochial grade schools are within walking distance, and the nearest high school is two miles away.

Family incomes range from $3,600 to $5,000 per annum. Housing values range from $7,500 to $10,500. Stability of family income is fair. Many of the resident workers are employed in a near-by industry whose products are in seasonal demand.

There is a good demand for used single-family homes. The two-flats in the area are slow to sell, except at bargain prices. There were few foreclosures noted. The tax load is equitable.

Site data. All lots in the subject block are platted to dimensions of 30 by 125 feet. They are level and well drained, with a mean elevation about three feet above the street. There are paved alleys at the rear.

CASE PROPERTY No. 5

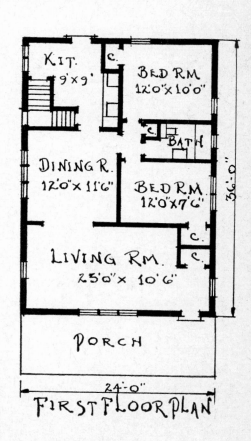

KIT.
9'x9'

C.

BED RM
12'0"x10'0"

C. BATH

DINING R.
12'0"x11'6"

BED RM
12'0"x7'6"

C.

LIVING RM.
25'0"x 10'6"

C.

36'-0"

PORCH

24'-0"

FIRST FLOOR PLAN

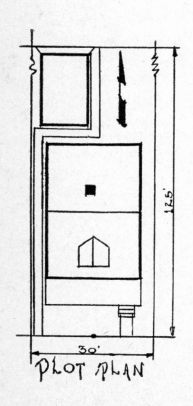

125'

30'

PLOT PLAN

CASE PROPERTY No. 6

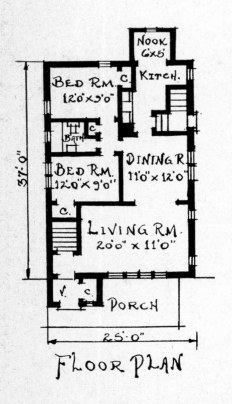

BED RM.
12'0" x 9'0"
C.
NOOK
6'x5'
KITCH.

BATH C.

37'0"

BED RM.
12'0" x 9'0"
C.
DINING R
11'0" x 12'0"

C.

LIVING RM.
20'0" x 11'0"

V. C.
PORCH

25'0"

FLOOR PLAN

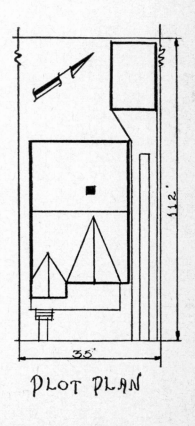

112'

35'

PLOT PLAN

CASE PROPERTY No. 7

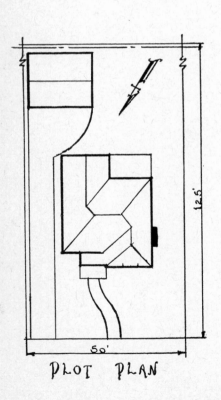

PLOT PLAN

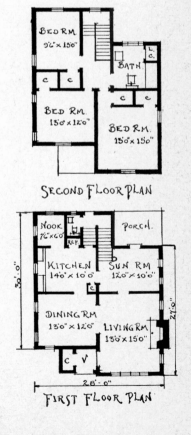

SECOND FLOOR PLAN

FIRST FLOOR PLAN

CASE PROPERTY No. 8

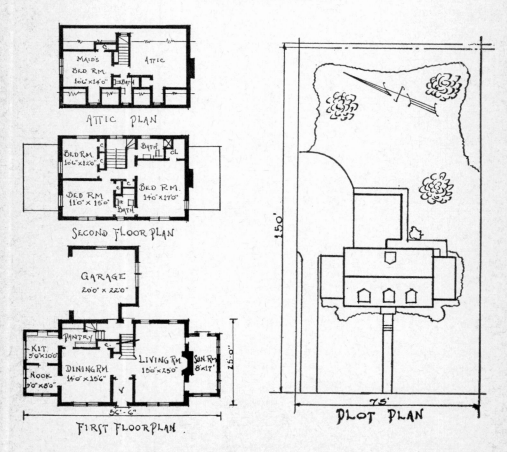

ATTIC PLAN

MAID'S BED RM. 10'6" x 14'0"
ATTIC
BATH

SECOND FLOOR PLAN

BED RM. 10'6" x 12'0"
BATH
CL.
BED RM. 11'0" x 15'0"
BED RM. 14'0" x 17'0"
BATH

FIRST FLOOR PLAN

GARAGE 20'0" x 22'0"
PANTRY
KIT. 5'0" x 10'0"
NOOK 5'0" x 8'0"
DINING RM. 14'0" x 15'6"
LIVING RM. 15'0" x 25'0"
SUN RM. 8' x 17'
25'-0"
50'-6"

PLOT PLAN

150'
75'

Cost data. The subject building, it is estimated, could be constructed new today for $12,350; the garage, for $400. The land cost is $1,800.

Rental data. Single-family homes in the neighborhood are rented at $80 to $100; multifamily dwellings, at $60 to $80 per unit. There are practically no single-family vacancies.

Specifications

Attic — 9 feet to the ridge; rough flooring; stairway from kitchen
Basement — 7 feet in the clear; cement block walls; coalbin; fruit closet; 2-inch stair treads with no risers; 2 laundry trays
Electrical — BX cable; old-style fixtures, center-hung
Exterior walls — cypress lap siding over building paper and yellow pine sheathing
Fireplace — none
Floors — all living rooms except kitchen, oak; kitchen, pine, linoleum-covered; oak floor in bath
Framing — studs No. 2 yellow pine; first-floor joists, 2 by 8, 16 inches on centers; ceiling joists, 2 by 8, 16 inches on centers; rafters, 2 by 4, 16 inches on centers
Heating — gravity hot air, coal fired
House walks — street to front and to rear porch
Insulation — none
Interior trim — oak; linen closet and kitchen cupboards
Landscaping — front and rear lawn
Linoleum — kitchen floor only
Built-in equipment — clothes chute; framed medicine cabinet
Plastering — 2 coats on wood lath
Plumbing — roll-rim enameled cast-iron tub; wall lavatory; closet combination; old-style kitchen sink; side-arm gas heater with 30-gallon storage; old-style plumbing fittings
Roof — 160-pound asphalt shingles; galvanized iron flashings, gutters, and conductors
Porches — 24 by 7, covered at front; 6 by 5 covered at rear
Garage — frame, 13 by 16; asphalt shingle roof; cinder floor

Solution of the problem. *Interpretation of market data.* There is an active market for used housing. Apparently, the neighborhood is well seasoned, as indicated by the density of building; 98 per cent of the usable land is improved with buildings. The data further indicate that offerings are quickly sold at prices ranging from $7,500 to $10,500.

Interpretation of cost data. The estimated cost of the subject dwelling is $12,350, of the garage, $400. The demand price of the land is $1,800. The total cost, new, of the entire property is $14,550.

Interpretation of income data. There are few vacancies, despite of the fact that 70 per cent of the inhabitants are renters. The percentage of rental occupancy is high as compared to the age of the district. This is due, in all probability, to the congested character of the area. With 98 per cent of the usable land improved with buildings, both single and multiple, overcrowding has resulted, with consequent decreased desirability from the owner viewpoint. Rental properties, however, are in demand. The excellent system of transportation that serves the district taps the large near-by industrial area, offering convenient service to those who live here and work in the plants. The rental range is $80 to $100. The subject property rental is estimated at $80 per month. The indicated capitalization rate for the neighborhood is 12 per cent.

Depreciation analysis. All three main classes of depreciation are present: physical, functional, and economic. The physical condition of the house, as of the appraisal date (it is assumed), is poor. Maintenance items have been neglected. Exterior and interior painting, in addition to minor heating, carpentry, and plumbing repairs, are necessary. The linoleum floor covering in the kitchen needs replacement. There is considerable loose plaster that must be renewed. The roof still gives good service, but new gutters and conductors are needed.

Functional obsolescence is manifested in the outmoded electrical, heating, and plumbing equipment, and in the layout of the rooms. The kitchen plan is obsolete, as is also the entire floor plan. (One bedroom has no cross ventilation, and there is no direct access from the front to the rear of the house, except via the dining room. The reader should compare this plan with the one shown in Case Property I.) The floor plan fails to function in comparison with the modern building.

Economic obsolescence is present because of diminution of owner-occupancy appeal. The tenants are in the majority and are on the increase. This is clearly evidenced by the fact that there is practically no new construction activity, and by the reluctance of mortgage companies to lend in this district at the same rates and in the same relative amounts they are now lending in newer districts.

Depreciation estimate. Depreciation is estimated by the process described in Chapter 12. A survey is made of the reconditioning necessary to cure deferred maintenance. This amount is $1,170 and is classified as "physical deterioration, curable." A further $650, the appraiser estimates, is the resultant physical damage to the structure of the building based on its age; this is classified as "physical deterioration, incurable." The cost of modernizing the outmoded items of plumbing, heating, and electrical equipment, to include a revamping of the kitchen layout, is estimated at $1,520. Capitalized rental loss emanating from the general floor plan is estimated at $750.

Economic obsolescence is estimated in the same manner as detailed in the depreciation estimate for Case Property IV. The factors involved in the present case are an estimated rental loss of $15 per month, or $180 a year, arising out of the decreased owner-occupancy appeal, manifested in the real estate economy of the subject neighborhood; an indicated capitalization rate of 10 per cent for the ideal neighborhood; an observable ratio of building to land in the ideal neighborhood of 5 to 1, or buildings 83.4 per cent and land 16.6 per cent. This gives expression to the following equation:

$$\$180 \div 10 \times 100 \times 83.4\%$$

the solution of which is $1,500, the estimated amount of economic obsolescence attributable to the building.

The total depreciation is itemized as follows:

Physical deterioration	
Curable	$1,170
Incurable	650
Functional obsolescence	
Curable	1,520
Incurable	750
Economic obsolescence	1,500
Total depreciation	$5,590

Case Property V — Valuation E
Valuation date: twentieth year of the life of the building

Estimate of value by the market approach
Comparative sales indicate a price range of $7,500 to $10,500, dependent on age and condition.

Market approach estimate		$8,500
Estimate of value by the cost approach		
Replacement cost of the dwelling, new	$12,350	
Less depreciation (as detailed above)	5,590	
Depreciated value of dwelling	$ 6,760	
Plus depreciated value of garage	200	
Plus land value (by comparison)	1,800	
	$8,760	
Cost approach estimate (called)		$8,750
Estimate of value by the income approach		
Estimated monthly rental value	$ 80	

Estimated yearly rental value 960
Indicated capitalization rate 12%
Computation: 960 ÷ 12 × 100 8,000
      Income approach estimate $8,000
Final market value estimate $8,250

Conclusions. The property is being appraised in an "as is" condition. In order to find accurate bench-mark properties that have recently been sold for use as templates with which to measure the value of the subject property, there is the further requirement that such bench marks shall exhibit the same factors of decreased desirability as are present in the appraised property. Because these properties were originally built on a production basis, it is a simple task to find many of them similar to the one being appraised where the title has recently changed hands and where, so far as can be learned, the transactions reflect the informed buyer and seller and all other stipulations made by the definition of "market value" discussed in Chapter 2. But it is not so simple to find in these bench-mark properties the exact quantum of physical deterioration and functional and economic obsolescence correspondent to the subject property. In fact, it is well nigh impossible to do so. This clouds the market approach with some doubt as to its accuracy, although, as will be noted, it is reasonably within the "zone of error."

All of the approaches are in line, but because there is an abundancy of income data, the appraiser is inclined to lean upon it with considerable dependency. The importance of the income approach as a guide to market value cannot be overlooked in any situation where 70 per cent of the neighborhood inhabitants are renters.

Case Property VI

Description of the property. *Neighborhood data.* This neighborhood is about 25 years old. Its investment quality is rated by mortgage lenders as being only fair. There is practically no new building being carried on, and such mortgages as are being placed arise from the necessity for refinancing. Interest rates are comparatively high, and loans are limited to 50 to 60 per cent of appraisal.

The nature of the topography is level. There are no physical hazards, and the entire area is well drained. The size of the area is one square mile.

Eighty-five per cent of the usable residential land is improved with single-family and multifamily dwellings. The district is zoned *B* residential, a classification that permits of 1-, 2-, 3-, and 4-family buildings. The deed restrictions on those streets that are restricted to single-family dwellings provide for a minimum content of 20,000 cubic feet. The street system is rectangular, with the principal streets paved and the side streets hard-surfaced. Good transportation, in the form of streetcar and bus lines, is within a half-mile radius. Within the same distance there is a well-balanced retail area of local and national chains, and a second-run motion picture theater. The nearest public park is four miles away. All public utilities are available in the district.

The inhabitants are skilled mechanics, foremen, and office workers. They are good citizens, exhibiting pride in their homes. The neighborhood is 50 per cent tenant-occupied. The average family size is four. Directly opposite the subject property are a grade school and playgrounds. A high school and all churches are within half a mile.

The average family income is $3,600 to $5,000. Values of single-family homes range from $12,500 to $15,000. The stability of the incomes of the clerical and office workers is fair, while that of the skilled mechanics is less so, because of seasonal unemployment. There is a good demand for homes in the district and few foreclosures. The tax load is equitable.

Site data. All single-family residential lots are platted to dimensions of 35 by 112 feet. The lots are level and well drained. Each block is bisected by a 16-foot gravel-surfaced alley.

Cost data. The replacement cost, new, of the subject building is estimated at $15,000; that of the garage, at $500; that of the lot improvements, at $200; and that of the lot, at $1,500.

Rental data. The range of rental values is from $80 to $115 for single-family homes. There are practically no vacancies.

Specifications

Attic — 12 feet to the ridge; rough flooring; stairway from living room entry

Basement — 7 feet, 6 inches in the clear; cement block walls; concrete floor; coalbin and fruit closet; 2 laundry trays

Electrical — BX cable; modern fixtures

Exterior walls — face brick veneer to the belt and shingles above; front gable ends, all brick

Fireplace — dummy with floor plug; no flue

Floors — kitchen and nook, linoleum over pine; bathroom, unglazed tile; all others, oak

Framing — studs No. 2 yellow pine; first-floor joists, 2 by 8, 16 inches on centers; second-floor joists, 2 by 8, 16 inches on centers; rafters, 2 by 6, 16 inches on centers
Heating — gravity hot air, coal fired
House walks — street to front and grade entrances
Insulation — none
Interior trim — enameled gum; linen closet and kitchen cupboards
Landscaping — front and rear lawns, and shrubbery
Linoleum — kitchen and nook floors
Built-in equipment — metal-lined clothes chute and steel medicine cabinet
Plastering — 2 coats on wood lath
Plumbing — flat-rim kitchen sink, single-shell tub, tile faced; overhead shower; wall lavatory; closet combination; side-arm gas heater with 30-gallon storage; porcelain bath fittings
Roof — wood shingles
Tile — 4-foot tile wainscot in bathroom; tile drains and splash in kitchen
Terrace — 160 square feet of concrete floor at front entrance
Garage — 12 by 18 frame with concrete floor
Driveway — 2 24-inch concrete ribbons

Solution of the problem. *Interpretation of market data.* The market for used housing is active. There is very little new building, probably because of the age of the neighborhood, the fact that it is 85 per cent built up, and the consequent difficulty of securing favorable mortgages. But there is quick absorption on easy terms of such used housing as is being offered. The market reflects a price range of $12,500 to $15,000.

Interpretation of cost data. The estimated replacement cost, new, of the subject dwelling is $15,000; of the garage, $500. The land cost is $1,500, based on the average demand price of the few remaining lots still for sale in the area.

Interpretation of income data. The rental range is $80 to $115. Thirty per cent of the properties in the neighborhood are in rental status. Survey shows less than 2 per cent vacancy. The indicated rate of capitalization for the district is 11 per cent. The subject property has an estimated rental value of $100, which is lower than the average, the reason for which is explained in the depreciation analysis that follows.

Depreciation analysis. The property is being held vacant awaiting sale. One week prior to the appraisal, a major reconditioning program was completed that had the effect of curing all items of deferred maintenance and improving the functional adequacy of the dwelling. This consisted of roof repairs, exterior and interior painting and papering, floor refinishing, new door and cupboard hardware, new linoleum floor, new formica sink drains and splash, new chromium plumbing fittings, new kitchen sink, rehabilitation of the heating plant, new electrical fixtures, and additional wall plugs. Physical deterioration and functional obsolescence, curable, have, in the opinion of the appraiser, been eliminated. There still remains, according to his estimate, $1,100 worth of physical deterioration, incurable, because of wear and tear on the "bone structure" of the building, and $1,200 worth of functional obsolescence, incurable, caused by the deficiencies in the floor plans as compared to a modern building. (This is discernible in the room arrangement, the lack of cross ventilation in one bedroom, and the insurmountable difficulty encountered in attempting to streamline the kitchen.)

Economic obsolescence arises chiefly from the specialized location of the property within the neighborhood; it is directly across the street from a grade school and playground. For nine months of the year, therefore, the conditions of agreeable living in this property are affected negatively by the incidental noise of the children who attend this school and use the playground. The estimated rental loss is $20 per month—meaning that, if the building were located where this nuisance did not exist, it would command a rental $20 in excess of that which it will now command. In arriving at the amount of economic obsolescence, this rental loss is treated in the same manner as detailed in the depreciation estimate for Case Property IV, with the use of the following factors that are applicable to this case:

Estimated monthly rental loss	$ 20
Estimated yearly rental loss	240
Indicated ideal rate	10%
Relation of building value to total value in the ideal location	83%
Computation: 240 ÷ 10 × 100 × 83%	1,992
Estimated economic obsolescence	1,992

The depreciation estimate, therefore, evolves as follows:

Physical deterioration	
Curable	$ ——
Incurable	1,110
Functional obsolescence	
Curable	——
Incurable	1,200
Economic obsolescence	1,992
Total depreciation	$4,292

Case Property VI — Valuation F
Valuation date: fifteenth year of the life of the building

Estimate of value by the market approach
  Properties reasonably comparable to the subject have been
  recently sold at prices ranging from $12,500 to $15,000.
          Market approach estimate $11,000
Estimate of value by the cost approach

```
Replacement cost of the dwelling, new ..................... $15,000
Less depreciation (as computed above) .................    4,292

Depreciated value of the dwelling ........................... $10,708
Plus depreciated value of the garage ........................     200
Plus land value (based on demand price) ..............   1,500
                                                          _____
                                                          $12,408
        Cost approach estimate ............................................. $12,408
Estimate of value by the income approach
    Estimated monthly rental value ...............................  $   100
    Estimated yearly rental value ...................................   1,200
    Indicated capitalization rate for the neighborhood....     11%
    Computation: 1200 ÷ 11 × 100 ...............................  $10,900
            Income approach estimate .......................................... $10,900
Final market value estimate ......................................................................... $11,000
```

Conclusions. In the use of the market approach, the appraiser is confronted with difficulty in finding comparable sales that will act as a guide to the value of the property. The market for used housing is active, and apparently there is plenty of market data available. But in this case, the appraiser is faced with a situation that departs from the normal. The property is located across the street from an influence that detracts from its optimum desirability. Properties for sale that are similar in size, style, and equipment to the subject house do not show the same abnormality as regards its peculiar location. The appraiser knows that the value range for comparable housing, based on current sales, is $12,500 to $15,000. He knows further that the value of the subject property will be lower than the minimum of the range because of the disagreeable influence by which it is affected. This reasoning accounts for his estimate by the market approach of $11,000.

Here again, the cost approach attempts to measure the dollar value of the factor of decreased desirability arising from location; and, on the assumption that the loss in rental can be accurately measured, it indicates by the same token that market value will result from the cost treatment.

In the treatment by the income approach, it is assumed also that the going rental value of the property in the present location is indeed $100 per month, and that the rate of 11 per cent applicable to the district is justified by the income data.

Case Property VII

Description of the property. *Neighborhood data.* This neighborhood is about 25 years old. Although platted that long ago, until 15 years ago there was comparatively little building within it. It is located at the edge of a large industrial city perhaps 16 miles from the loop area. Its topography is varied; part of it is level, while other parts are gently rolling.

Investment quality is considered fair. Although insured mortgages are not available, there appears to be little difficulty in obtaining loans at 5-5½ per cent interest for new construction.

The area contains about three square miles, in which there are 300 homes, about two thirds of which are about 15 to 20 years old. Since it is not within the city limits, it is not zoned, but there are well-established restrictions running with the land defining the character of the buildings that may be erected. These provide for 2-story single-family homes of brick veneer, or brick and frame, containing not less than 25,000 cubic feet.

The street system is well planned to give access to the surrounding main highways, as well as to lend attractiveness to the general layout. The streets wind through the area, are graveled, and have concrete curbs. There are no alleys. A suburban bus line passes one edge of the district, making it two miles distant from the farthest part of the neighborhood. The land company operates its own private bus line, which makes four trips daily to the only available shopping area, which is four miles from the center of the neighborhood. Recreational facilities are distant; the nearest city park is seven miles away. Public utilities are available in the form of electrical power and telephones; there is no gas service. All sewage is handled by individual septic tanks installed in each property.

The district is inhabited by those whose occupations are foremen, chief clerks, junior executives, and proprietors of small enterprises. Their attitude toward government and their respect for the principle of homeownership leaves nothing to be desired. About 10 per cent of the homes are occupied by tenants. The average family size is four. The land company built the grade school that lies at one end of the district; high school and churches are four miles away.

Family incomes range from $5,000 to $7,200; residential property values, from $15,000 to $22,500. Family incomes are fairly stable. There is an active market for new homes currently being constructed; used homes are slower to move. Investigation shows that practically all of the used homes vacated by owners have been forced into rental status because of slow marketability.

Practically no record of sales of used houses could be found. Taxes are comparatively reasonable, and not so burdensome as to discourage buyers.

Site data. The lots are platted to dimensions of 50 by 125. The majority are level to gently rolling. There is a 4-foot easement at the rear of each lot.

Cost data. The replacement cost, new, of the subject building is estimated to be $19,500; that of the garage, $750; that of the lot improvements (to include the graveled driveway), $300; and that of the lot, $1,800.

Rental data. The rental range of the tenant-occupied properties is $125 to $150. As of the appraisal date, there were no vacancies.

Specifications

Attic — unusable; hatch opening; partial rough flooring

Basement — 7 feet in the clear; concrete floor; brick walls; 2-inch stair treads with pine risers; coalbin; fruit storage; 2 laundry trays

Electrical — modern fixtures; BX cable; vent fan in kitchen

Exterior walls — common brick veneer; celotex sheathing

Fireplace — tile mantel; brick breast and hearth

Floors — kitchen and nook, linoleum over pine; lavatory, bathroom and vestibule, unglazed tile; all others, select oak

Framing — studs No. 2 yellow pine; first-floor joists, 2 by 10, 16 inches on centers; second-floor joists, 2 by 10, 16 inches on centers; second-floor ceiling joists, 2 by 8, 16 inches on centers; rafters, 2 by 6, 16 inches on centers

Heating — steam, coal fired

Insulation — 4-inch rock wool, second-floor ceiling

Interior trim — gum; linen closet, kitchen cupboards, and cedar closet

Landscaping — front and rear lawn; shrubbery in the rear yard

Linoleum — kitchen and nook floors, sink drains, and splash

Built-in equipment — broom closet; ironing board; mirror door in vestibule; 1 steel medicine cabinet

Plastering — 2 coats on wood lath

Plumbing — closet combinations; wall lavatories; double-shell tub with overhead shower; chromium fittings; flat-rim sink; 50-gallon automatic electric water heater

Windows — steel casements

Roof — good grade wood shingles

Terraces — 20 square feet of concrete floor at front entrance; 80 square feet at rear

Garage — 20 by 18 frame with concrete floor

Driveway — gravel with concrete curbs

Condition — completely reconditioned immediately prior to appraisal to include exterior painting, interior decorating, kitchen and bathroom modernization, and second-floor ceiling insulation

Solution of the problem. *Interpretation of market data.* Apparently, there is a fair market for new housing. The market for used homes is slow; it is found that many of the once new homes originally occupied by owners have been forced into rental status, assumedly because they are difficult to sell. We are further informed that insured mortgages are not available. The value range is indicated by comparison to be $15,000 to $22,500.

Interpretation of cost data. The replacement cost, new, of the subject building is $19,500, of the garage $750, of the lot improvements $300, and of the land, $1,800—a total of $22,350.

Interpretation of income data. A survey shows about 30 rented properties, most of which vary in age from 15 to 20 years. No vacancies are noted. The rental value of the subject property is $125 per month. The indicated capitalization rate is 12 per cent.

Depreciation analysis. The appraisal is made following the completion of a reconditioning program that has had the effect of developing optimum marketability and rentability. A thorough decorating job was done inside and out; bathroom and kitchen were modernized as far as was practicable; all heating and electrical repairs were made; and the second-floor ceiling was insulated. Physical deterioration, incurable, is of course present in this 18-year-old structure. All functional deficiencies, curable, have been cured. Functional obsolescence, incurable, results from the heating system, which is a one-pipe steam job. The installation of a modern system is economically unsound because of the difficulty of installing the necessary ducts in the walls of the building. It results also from the floor plan, as indicated by the stair arrangement, which is at the rear of the building and which affects the optimum utility of the room from which it leads.

Economic obsolescence results from lack of demand for used housing in this area. This lack of demand has its source in the remoteness of location, the inadequacy of near-by shopping facilities, and the uncertainty of transportation. To an extent, this is a pioneering project that entails considerable risk to the investments in homeownership. All this is clearly indicated in the lack of a market for used properties.

Depreciation estimates. There is no physical deterioration, curable, present in the structure. Physical deterioration, incurable, is estimated, based on structural age, at $2,100.

No functional obsolescence, curable, is noted. The incurable items (heating plant and floor plan) that affect optimum rental value are estimated at $2,400.

Economic obsolescence is measured by the process used in

Case Property IV, with the following factors that are applicable to the present case: rental loss, $300 per year; indicated rate, 10 per cent; relative building value to property value, ideal location, 85 per cent. The equation is as follows:

$$\$300 \div 10 \times 100 \times 85\% = \$2,550, \text{ economic obsolescence}$$

Total depreciation is itemized as follows:

Physical deterioration	
Curable	$ ——
Incurable	2,100
Functional obsolescence	
Curable	——
Incurable	2,400
Economic obsolescence	2,550
Total depreciation	$7,050

Case Property VII — Valuation G
Valuation date: tenth year of the life of the building

Estimate of value by the market approach		
No record of recent sales of comparable used properties; listings range from $15,000 to $22,500		
Market approach estimate		$17,500
Estimate of value by the cost approach		
Replacement cost of the dwelling	$19,500	
Less depreciation (as above)	7,050	
Depreciated value of the dwelling	$12,450	
Plus depreciated value of the garage, driveway, landscaping	700	
Plus land value (demand price)	1,800	
	$14,950	
Cost approach estimate (called)		$14,950
Estimate of value by the income approach		
Estimated monthly rental value	$ 125	
Estimated yearly rental value	1,500	
Indicated capitalization rate for the neighborhood....	12%	
Computation: 1500 ÷ 12 × 100	$12,500	
Income approach estimate		$12,500
Final market value estimate		$15,000

Conclusions. It is difficult in this situation to find any evidence of "valuation by the public," as expressed by actual market transactions, upon which to base an estimate of value by the market approach. The used housing is being rented; the listings show a wide range of price, representing, perhaps, the variable desperation of the prospective sellers. The appraiser's estimate of $17,500 by this approach, therefore, is to some extent a shot in the dark, although he has been able to bracket the comparable listings between $15,000 and $22,500. The value of $12,500 as found by the income approach the appraiser feels is on the low side. There is not a good rental market. The district lacks appeal. The appraiser concludes that this approach reflects the lower limit of value.

The cost approach appears to indicate the upper limit of value. True, some homes in the area have sold for higher figures and this home, when offered for sale, may bear a higher asking price. However, as reflecting the long-term swing of the market, or as security for a long term mortgage loan, the appraiser concludes that $15,000 represents the market value.

In the above valuation and in the depreciation analysis it will be noted that two capitalization rates are used, one of 12 per cent for the neighborhood in which the appraised property is located and one of 10 per cent for the "ideal" neighborhood in which the factors of undesirability do not exist. This makes sense. Obviously the risks to investment in the "ideal" neighborhood are *less* than they are here where, because of the remoteness of location, uncertainty of adequate public transportation and the consequent lack of demand for used housing, the risks to investment capital (either as owner or mortgagee) are greater — probably greater than the risk represented by the spread between 10 and 12 per cent.

Case Property VIII

Description of the property. *Neighborhood data.* The subject neighborhood is approximately 30 years old. It is known as a "class" suburb of the large city that it adjoins and whose downtown retail area is eight miles distant. Its investment quality is rated "good." Mortgages are being made at 66⅔ per cent of appraised value at rates of 5 to 5½ per cent.

The topography is level, and the entire district, consisting of one square mile, slopes gently toward the shores of a small lake that forms part of the Great Lakes chain.

It is known as a good social address, which, added to the scenic beauty that it possesses, makes it an attractive place in which to live. It is zoned as A residential. The restrictions running with the land prohibit the building of any house of a cost of less than $25,000, and many of the streets running through this area carry higher restrictions. All buildings are required to be built of brick veneer or stone, with restrictions as to setbacks and orientation, making for pleasing placement on the lots.

The streets are irregular and wind through the area; many are boulevarded, and all are concrete-paved. Bus lines within a half-mile radius furnish good transportation. Within the same distance there is a complete shopping area, with many branches of the main downtown stores and all prominent chains. A 1,600-seat, first-run motion picture theater is also convenient. A municipal park is half a mile away, where, in addition to the usual recreational facilities, boating and bathing may be enjoyed.

The street on which the subject property is located is three blocks from the limits of this suburban community. Just over the corporate line and within four blocks of the subject property is a recently opened amusement park, consisting of riding devices and a midget auto track, where, during the summer, racing is held nightly from 8 to 11 P.M.

The incidental noise and traffic constitute a nuisance — so much so, in fact, that many former owners have either sold or rented their dwellings and moved to other, more desirable locations.

The inhabitants are of the upper social strata, with the bulk of occupations in the executive and professional fields. All homes and yards in the area are well kept. As of the appraisal date, 25 per cent of the single-family residences were found to be occupied by renters. The average family size is from four to five. Grade and high schools and all prominent churches are half a mile distant.

The range of family incomes is $10,000 and up. The range of housing values is $25,000 to $35,000. The real estate market may be considered fair as it pertains to this class of property, which is slow to change hands and where vacancies awaiting sale may extend over many months. Several pending foreclosures were noted. The tax load is comparatively heavy; assessments are high compared to values in the market.

Site data. Lots in the immediate area of the subject property are platted to dimensions of 75 by 150. They are well drained, with elevation about three feet above the street level. There are no alleys.

Cost data. The estimated replacement cost of the subject building is $32,500; that of the garage, $1,500; that of the lot improvements, $1,000; and that of the lot, $5,000.

Rental data. Rental prices range from $250 to $300; the estimated rental value of the subject property is $275 per month. There are few vacancies.

Specifications

Attic — contains 1 maid's room and bath; also ample storage room

Basement — 7 feet in the clear; separate furnace and hobby room; fruit storage; 3 laundry trays; 2-inch stair treads with pine risers and hand rail; concrete block walls

Electrical — BX cable; fixtures semimodern; vent fan in kitchen

Exterior walls — face brick veneer to the eaves

Fireplace — wood mantel and face; tile hearth and trim

Floors — pantry and kitchen, linoleum over pine; vestibule, nook, sunroom, and second-floor baths, unglazed tile; third floor, all pine; all others select oak

Heating — vacuum steam, oil fired

House walks — street to front and rear entrances

Insulation — none

Exterior trim — enameled pine; closets and cupboards as per floor plans

Landscaping — front and rear lawns, and shrubbery

Built-in equipment — clothes chute; milk receiver; steel medicine cabinets; disposal; dishwasher

Plastering — 2 coats on metal lath

Plumbing — flat-rim two-compartment kitchen sink; 1 double- and 1 single-shell tub; 3 wall lavatories; 4 closet combinations; stall shower; 1 40-gallon automatic gas water heater

Roof — 220-pound asphalt shingles; galvanized iron flashings, gutters, and conductors

Porches — small brick platform at main entrance

Tile — front bath, 4-foot tile wainscot; rear bath, 4-foot tile wainscot and 7 feet in shower stall

Windows — double-hung weatherstripped

Garage — 20 by 22 attached; face brick to match main building; concrete floor; tilt doors

Driveway — 8 feet solid concrete and apron

Condition — completely reconditioned 18 months prior to appraisal to include interior and exterior decorating; modernization of bathrooms and kitchen; new oil burner, hardware, and plumbing fittings. Part of this has been dissipated, owing to rental occupancy. Needs interior decorating and minor repairs.

Solution of the problem. *Interpretation of market data.* There is a fair market for properties in this area, although it is less active than is found in the lower price brackets. This is the expected situation as we ascend to a higher price level; there are fewer buyers for $30,000 houses than there are for $15,000 houses.

The sales of comparable housing that have occurred in the past year, as well as the current listings, indicate a price range of from $25,000 to $32,500.

Interpretation of cost data. The cost of the subject dwelling is $32,500, of the garage $1,500, of the improvements to the lot (to include the driveway, walks and landscaping) $1,000, and of the land $5,000 — a total of $40,000.

Interpretation of income data. The rental value of the subject property is $275. The indicated rate of capitalization for the neighborhood is 12 per cent. There are very few vacancies. Twenty-five per cent of the properties are in rental status.

Depreciation analysis. The building is being appraised at the twentieth year of its life. Eighteen months ago, it was thoroughly reconditioned and modernized. After this, it was offered for sale for several months; and, no buyers appearing, it was rented during the winter season. As of the date of appraisal, it is vacant. Tenant occupancy has dissipated a part of the reconditioning that was previously performed, making necessary a nominal expenditure for decorations and minor repairs, the cost of which is classed as "physical deterioration, curable." Physical deterioration, incurable, is present, owing to age.

Functional obsolescence, curable, is noted in the absence of insulation. Functional obsolescence, incurable, is detected in the lack of a downstairs lavatory and in the obsolete heating equipment.

Economic obsolescence arises from the decreased desirability of the district because of the proximity of the near-by nuisance, previously detailed.

Depreciation estimates. Physical deterioration, curable, consists of the cost of complete interior decorations plus minor plumbing and carpentry repairs, cleaning furnace, tuning oil burner, and so forth. This is estimated at $750.

Physical deterioration, incurable, is estimated at $2,200.

The cost of applying insulation to the inside of the roof (made difficult because of the third-floor partitions) is estimated at $400, which is the estimate of the functional obsolescence, curable.

Functional obsolescence, incurable, is estimated at $2,500, representing the capitalized rental loss due to lack of a downstairs lavatory and a modern heating plant.

Economic obsolescence is estimated (as in Case Property IV) by calculating the capitalized value of the rental loss that exists because of the near-by nuisance. The factors in this case are: estimated rental loss of $50 per month, or $600 per year; an indicated ideal capitalization rate of 10 per cent; relative building value to property value, ideal location, 80 per cent. The equation is:

$$\$600 \div 10 \times 100 \times 80\% = \$4,800, \text{ the estimated amount of}$$
economic obsolescence

Total depreciation, therefore, is itemized as follows:

Physical deterioration
Curable .... $ 750
Incurable 2,200

Functional obsolescence
    Curable 400
    Incurable 2,500
Economic obsolescence 4,800

    Total depreciation $10,650

Case Property VIII — Valuation H
Valuation date: twentieth year of the life of the building

Estimate of value by the market approach
    Reasonably comparable properties are observed selling at
    prices of $25,000 to $32,500.
            Market approach estimate $30,000
Estimate of value by the cost approach
New replacement cost, dwelling $32,500
Less depreciation (as above) 10,650

Depreciated value, dwelling $21,850
Depreciated value, garage 1,000
Depreciated value, lot improvements 500
Land value (demand price) 5,000

                                                                            $28,350
            Cost approach estimate $28,350
Estimate of value by the income approach
Estimated monthly rental value .... $ 275
Estimated yearly rental value 3,300
Indicated capitalization rate 12%
Computation: 3300 ÷ 12 × 100 .... $27,500
            Income approach estimate $27,500
Final market value estimate $28,000

Conclusions. The final estimate of market value is well supported by all three of the approaches. None is all-conclusive. No other property is affected to the *exact* degree as the subject property, in its relative location, by the near-by undesirable influence. This fact imperils the accuracy of the market approach.

The factor of economic obsolence in the cost approach is affected by the presumed accuracy of the current estimated rental value. Rentals, in this situation, are highly volatile. The incidental noise and heavy traffic induced by the amusement park in the neighborhood may affect different tenants in different degrees of rental desirability, all measured finally in the rent they are willing to pay.

Fortunately, the property has some actual rental history, and it is assumed that the capitalization rate has been carefully appraised. That being the case, the income approach is entitled to some preferment as indicating the lower limit of value.

CHAPTER 19

The Appraisal Report

We come now to the final step in the appraisal process: the writing of the report. This last step is as important as any that have gone before. Perhaps it is more so when judged by the rule that the proof of the pudding is in the eating. The skillful doctor must demonstrate his ability to render his diagnostical findings into a written report. The able lawyer must be capable of briefing his petitions in intelligible and readily understood language. In like fashion, the appraiser must be able, as the final step in his diagnosis of the appraisal problem, to narrate his analyses in readable form. There must be demonstrable ability to tell the story.

The "Certificate Appraisal"

Through the years there has developed the practice of issuing a simple certificate in the form of a brief letter, setting forth in a few sentences the valuation found in a particular problem. This has become known as the "certificate appraisal." Until the early 1930's, is was used quite generally. However, following the real estate collapse of that period and the volume of inquiring research in the field of real estate economics that followed, the certificate appraisal began to disappear; in its place appeared the printed forms of many of the governmental agencies active in the field of housing, as well as those of the large insurance companies. This was a clear-cut indication of the unwillingness on the part of owners of real estate and mortgage lenders to accept, unchallenged, the unsupported words of the appraiser as to value. For the first time, he was being asked to detail his findings and to

242

expose the technical processes (or lack of them!) that lead to his conclusions.

The printed form had another advantage: it served to plot the course of the appraisal narrative. It acted as a check sheet, a memory jogger, which prevented the careless omission of important data.

Today, the printed appraisal form is in general use, and its scope varies between the single page with printing on two sides, as used by many of the savings and loan associations, and the more elaborate four-page form used by many large insurance companies lending on investment real estate. The certificate appraisal is still in circulation, but its use is evidenced principally in those instances where the appraiser, lacking sufficient professional attainment, is unable to tell the appraisal story, or is prohibited from doing so because the amount of his fee will not justify the value of the time involved.[1]

In the discussion that follows, the assumption is that the appraiser is not working with a printed form but is required to prepare a specific brief of his findings, to consist of whatever number of pages is necessary to detail the appraisal story in proper and pleasing arrangement. This statement should not be misconstrued to mean that we have in mind the compilation of a manuscript, encyclopedic in volume. Only enough text is necessary to support the valuation conclusion with something more than vague or sketchy opinion.

General Character of the Report

As has been indicated, the report is more than a simple unsupported statement of the value found. It contains all the necessary supporting data — the information that forms the structure on which the valuation conclusion is erected. It recites, and frankly so, the facts on which the appraiser relies in arriving at the value to which he has certified. It details the reasoning that he used in forming his conclusions. The report, as duBois says,

---

[1] Notwithstanding that the governmental agencies have taken the lead in the matter of paying adequate fees (as witness the Veterans Administration base fee of $15.00 for a residential appraisal), there are many residential appraisals made today at lower fees. In some localities, the "going" fee is $5.00 — which should remind us of the story of the client who asked his lawyer for some "free" advice and later found that the counsel he received was worth no more than he had paid for it. And so it is with the $5.00 appraisal; it may be worth $5.00 to the appraiser's employer, but chances are that it will be worth less.

should "lead the reader along the identical paths [of thought] which the appraiser has traversed." [2]

This teaching departs radically from the underlying philosophy of the still used certificate appraisal, which told all and yet told nothing — probably purposely so, for it must be admitted that among those who practice the valuation of real estate as a profession a relative few remain whose methods lie well within the realm of necromancy and are inexplicable.

The appraiser who has done good work on his assignment and is sure of his ground will not consider it treasonable to his profession to inform his principal *in detail* of the methods used in arriving at his opinion.

The textual scheme. This will vary according to the purpose for which the appraisal is made. For example, if the appraisal is made to determine the fair sales or purchase price, emphasis will probably be on the detail of the three approaches to value. If it is made to determine equity of assessment, it will contain considerable comparative assessment data on similar properties. If it is made to determine fair compensation to the owner in an action in condemnation, the report will be constructed as a primer for the expert testimony to be given in the litigation that may follow.

The Format

The report should be well organized and attractive, both internally and externally. A book is not to be judged by its cover; yet good binding commands respect.

The paper used should be of good quality, preferably eight and a half by eleven. This size is recommended because it is the size of the average letter file. Schedules, exhibits, and maps used in the report should be folded to meet these dimensions.

It should be bound, book style, in the left-hand margin; reports so bound are easier to hold and to read than those bound at the top or tumble fashion. Each page should be numbered for easy reference.

The text should be typewritten, and the typing should be neat. Erasures, if at all necessary, should be carefully made; and strikeovers, because they have far-reaching implications as to the appraiser's professional ability, should not be permitted.

---

[2] Ayers duBois, in the *Appraisal Journal* (April, 1936).

Page margins, right and left, should be evenly spaced, and the necessary headings, subheadings, and paragraph captions used to facilitate ease of reading.

The report should be literate.[3] Poor grammar, misspelled words, and improper punctuation reflect indirectly on the appraiser's ability.

The cover should be of durable material and in good taste. The firm or individual specializing in appraisal work will have specially printed covers. For the individual who does an occasional appraisal job, suitable paper covers, with an embossed panel in which to type the title of the report, can be obtained at any stationer at nominal price.

Synopsis of the Report

The text of the report should be grouped into three subdivisions labeled Parts I, II, and III. This makes for easy reading and effects a proper grouping of the material in the order of its importance to the reader. These three parts and the title of their contents are as follows:

PART I

1. Title page
2. Table of contents
3. Letter of transmittal
4. Photographs
5. Qualifications of the appraiser
6. Statement of limiting conditions

PART II
Analysis and Conclusions

7. Purpose of the appraisal
8. Legal description of the property
9. City data
10. Neighborhood data
11. Property data
    a. The building
    b. The site
12. Analysis of highest and best use
13. Detail of the cost approach estimate
14. Detail of the income approach estimate
15. Detail of the market approach estimate
16. Interpretation of the estimates
17. Certification and final market value estimate

---

[3] This means simple, clear (not professorial!) language.

PART III
Addenda

18. Location map
19. Occupancy and use map of neighborhood
20. Plot plan
21. Floor plans
22. Exhibits, extra photos, etc.

In Part I above, each item, from 1 to 6 inclusive, should be allotted a separate page. In Part II, items 7 to 17 should follow one another on the same page as separate paragraphical captions. In Part III, items 18 to 22, as their titles indicate, call for separate pages.

Specifications for Part I. Part I is the essence of the report. Its object is to place before the reader a flashlight picture of the completed appraisal. It contains no detail and no supporting data. The appraisal of a parcel of real estate, as we have said previously, is a problem. The valuation found is the answer. Part I recites the answer quickly and tersely, satisfying the first question of the appraiser's employer upon receiving the report: "What is the value?"

The route pursued in arriving at that value is told in Parts II and III, which may be read at leisure. But the decisions to be made, the action to be taken, and the policies to be formed, which have been waiting upon the receipt of the answer to the problem, may now proceed for the desired information has been received.

Item 1: title page. The text of the title page should include:

1. The name (or street address) of the property
2. The name of the individual or firm for whom the appraisal is made
3. The name of the individual making the report
4. The date

First impressions are lasting. The first impression the reader receives is from the cover. The second is from the title page; consequently, this page should be well arranged, with the proper use of capital letters and spacing.

Item 2: table of contents. The titles of items 1 to 22 are listed; opposite each item the page number is shown on which the titles may be found.

Item 3: letter of transmittal. The purpose of item 3 is to transmit formally the report and to inform the appraiser's employer of the value found. A sample of such a letter reads as follows:

Mr. Frank D. Hall, Vice President,
Universal Trust Corporation
248 Griswold Street
New York, N. Y.

Dear Mr. Hall:

In accordance with the request made in your letter of the 21st, I have appraised the property known as No. 2648 Atkinson Boulevard and legally described as Lot No. 986 of Schmutz' Subdivision of the City of McRossie, Westchester County, New York. I made a careful personal inspection of the property and analyzed all of the discoverable factors that index its value. The results of this investigation are contained in my accompanying report of 12 pages.

In my opinion, the market value of this property for purposes of securing a long-term first-mortgage loan, at January 1, 19___, is —

TWELVE THOUSAND FIVE HUNDRED ($12,500) DOLLARS.

Sincerely yours,

(Signed)   JOHN DOE [4]

The above letter contains all the minimum essentials of the report — namely:

1. The legal description and street address of the property appraised

2. Certification as to personal inspection and thorough investigation

3. The purpose for which the report was made

4. The value estimate

5. The date on which it applies

6. The appraiser's signature

Item 4: photographs. It is advisable to follow the letter of transmittal with a page containing one or more photos of the property. This enables the reader to tie in the information contained in the letter of transmittal with a visualization of the physical aspects of the property. The number of photos used should depend on their size. Where the usual commercial photograph is used, of the approximate dimensions four and a half by six, one is sufficient. Any additional photographs should show side and rear views and facing properties.

The character of the photography should neither flatter nor disparage; it should give equal advantage to the favorable as well as the unfavorable aspects of the property. If snapshots are

---

[4] If the appraiser is a member of either the Society of Residential Appraisers, the American Institute of Real Estate Appraisers, or other professional body, his signature should be followed by the proper initials designating such membership.

used, they should have good definition and correct orientation.

Item 5: qualifications of the appraiser. Where the report is being made for a new client for the first time, these should be detailed. The employer, if the appraiser is hitherto unknown to him, has a right to know something of the background and experience of the appraiser.[5] Obviously, this will not be necessary where the appraiser has been employed in repeated instances by the same principal. But where it appears to be necessary and advisable, such a statement should be included and should cover the following points:

1. Length of residence
2. Character and duration of business experience
3. Education, general and technical
4. Membership in trade and professional organizations and offices held therein
5. Important appraisal assignments handled
6. Articles or books written and published
7. Record as an expert witness
8. Participation in educational work; professional contributions

Item 6: statement of limiting conditions. The reader will recall a typical statement appearing in the advertisements and prospectuses of stockbrokers, reading: "While the information contained herein is not guaranteed, it is gathered from sources which we believe to be correct."

The statement of limiting conditions is related to something of this kind. In it, the appraiser attempts to protect himself from the accusation that he has accepted hearsay as fact. As has been stated previously, the appraiser deals with data of two kinds: factual and inferential. The deductions made, therefore, from purely inferential data must be qualified in this statement.

As an example, let us assume that the appraiser is called upon to make an appraisal to determine the value of the property as security for a mortgage loan and that the building is yet to be built. He is given the identity of the lot and the architect's plans and specifications. In the process of appraisal, therefore, he must proceed under certain assumptive conditions leading to the conclusion that the property will be worth a certain sum as of the

---

[5] The author's favorite technique for reviewing an appraisal report is first to appraise the appraiser who made it.

completion date of construction. Hence, his completed report must contain a statement of the assumptions made in the process of appraisal. Such a statement should embrace the following points:

1. That the plans and specifications furnished him are correct, and that the building will be built in accordance therewith

2. That the construction project will be completed by a certain date (as a protection against any fluctuation in building costs in the interim)

3. That the title will be marketable as of the date construction is completed

It is good practice to set up in all reports a general statement of limiting conditions covering the following points:

1. That the title is marketable (there can be no market value of something that is not marketable)

2. That no responsibility is assumed by the appraiser for legal matters, especially those affecting title to the property

3. That the legal description furnished him is correct

4. That certain opinions and/or estimates furnished him by others (properly identified here) are correct.

There are countless situations where an escape clause of this kind is vitally necessary. Thus, in the appraisal of a certain residential property, the appraiser found evidence, we shall say, of a mutual driveway serving the subject as well as the abutting property. If this mutual easement is not of record and was not disclosed to him as a title defect at the time he received his assignment, he should recite it as a limiting condition on which his value is based, since definitely to establish its legal existence is clearly a matter for the lawyer.

Specifications for Part II. The flashlight picture of the valuation having been presented to the reader, Part II follows in substantiation. This is the narrative story of the appraisal, backing up in detail the conclusions of Part I. In this section, the reader is invited to analyze the appraiser's thinking and to check his judgment.

Item 7: purpose of the appraisal. Although this has been stated in the letter of transmittal, it should be included here again in Part II as a part of the continuity of the narrative. The purpose

of the appraisal defines the objective of the problem. It serves to
make clear to the reader just what the appraiser was about. With
the purpose clearly stated, the reader understands why certain
steps were taken, why certain data were gathered. It reveals
the appraiser as understanding the nature of the problem and as
carrying out the instructions of his principal. This protects him
from possible criticism. Furthermore, if the objective of the
report is to find market value, it is advisable to incorporate in
this paragraph the appraiser's definition thereof, thus clarifying
for the reader just what kind of "value" is, in the present instance,
being sought.

Item 8: legal description. Recitation of the legal description
eliminates all doubt as to what was appraised. This, too, may have
been stated in the letter of transmittal, and usually is in those
cases where the legal description is brief. But where there is a
lengthy description by metes and bounds, it is customary to give
a rough description of the property in the transmittal letter and
to detail it in Part II under this item. Thus the appraiser dealing with a property that is described by metes and bounds may,
in the letter of transmittal, refer to it as the "Warren Morris residence, located on Ostendorf Road in Kniskern Township, the
legal description of which is detailed on page 7 of Part II of this
report."

Item 9: city data. The amount of information relative to the
social, economic, and political background of the city that should
be included in this section of the report is variable in proportion
to and dependent on the location and place of business of the
appraiser's employer. Where there is employment in repeated
instances by the same employer of the same appraiser, and where
both are resident in the same city, it may be argued logically
that any large amount of these data is superfluous, on the ground
that the employer is fully conversant with local conditions. This
should be true. If it is, there is no reason for the appraiser to fill
up his report with information already known to his employer.
It may be advisable, however, to recite some comparisons between the various important facets of the city's real estate economy now as against the prior year or two. Thus some comment
on the comparative rental and sales prices, vacancies, employment, and pay rolls tends to round out the appraisal story as well
as to keep the employer informed on current trends.

This should be augmented in cases where the headquarters of the appraiser's employer is located at some point remote from the scene of appraisal.

Item 10: neighborhood data. The important facts relating to the neighborhood, as gleaned from the program of neighborhood analysis outlined in Chapter 8, should be written into this paragraph. Those of most importance to the reader are in the following outline:

1. Physical characteristics of the neighborhood
   a. Buildings — use types, sizes, replacement costs, ages, and condition
   b. Number of vacant parcels of land
   c. Potential uses of vacant land
   d. Potential encroachment of nonconforming uses
   e. Availability of public utility services
   f. Fire, police, and health services
   g. Availability and cost of transportation
   h. Distance to schools, stores, parks, and playgrounds
   i. Topography and drainage
2. Social characteristics of the neighborhood
3. Financial characteristics of the neighborhood
   a. Family incomes
   b. Ratio of owners to renters
4. Prospects of infiltration by socially undesirable groups, or prospective changes in use-character

Item 11: property data. This paragraph should be divided under two captions denominated: (1) the building; and (2) the site. Under the paragraph devoted to the building, a word picture of the structure should be detailed. This description should include all of the principal physical characteristics — such as the over-all width and depth, height, shape, school of architecture to which it belongs, materials, number of rooms and sizes, floor area, and cubical contents in feet — and a description of the mechanical equipment. The age and condition of the building should be stated, and comment made on the functional efficiency and adequacy of design and equipment. If reconditioning is necessary, either as a matter of preservation of the structure or modernization, or both, this should be explained, and an estimate of the cost of this work given.

The data appertaining to the site should describe its physical characteristics, such as the position of the lot in the block; its frontage, depth, shape, area, topography, and surface; and subsoil conditions. Limitations on optimum use, such as restrictions — both public and private — reservations, easements, and rights-of-way, as well as zoning regulations and fire and building ordinances, should be noted.

Item 12: analysis of the highest and best use. This information is important to the client, and good practice requires that the appraiser shall analyze this element of the problem and make report of his opinion. If the present structure improves the land to its highest and best use, the report shall so state. If it does not, it should define that use to which the land should be dedicated and clearly state the reasons why such use is economically logical.

Item 13: detail of the cost approach estimate. This paragraph should contain an itemized schedule of the cost approach estimate, to include an analysis of the depreciation estimates and the land value.

Item 14: detail of the income approach estimate. This should include the comparative rental data and a discussion of the rate used. A sufficient number of comparative instances should be cited to justify the conclusions formed, especially as to the observable ratio between sales prices in the market place and the going rents.

Item 15: detail of the market approach estimate. It is not sufficient, at this point, to dismiss the market approach estimate with the mere statement: "Many similar properties were noted selling at approximately the same figure as the value quoted in this report." The "similar properties" should be identified, exact listing or sales data stated, and plus or minus characteristics explained and justified.

Item 16: interpretation of the estimates. This paragraph recapitulates the findings of the three approaches, recites the weakness and strength of each, and tells why the appraiser chooses to lean toward the conclusions of one, two, or all three of them, as the case may be. In it, he tells the reader why he chose to discriminate between results shaped by the three tools of the process and why he has decided that certain of the approaches point with greater certainty at that which appears to be so. The cards are laid face up on the table, and the reader is invited to examine the appraiser's holding.

Item 17: certification and final market value estimate. This paragraph formally concludes the report. It should certify as to the following:

1. That the appraiser has no undisclosed interest in the property, present or contemplated
2. That the appraiser's employment and his compensation are *not* contingent upon the valuation found
3. That he personally and thoroughly inspected the property
4. That, according to the best of his knowledge, everything contained in the report is true, and that no important facts have been withheld or overlooked
5. That the appraisal has been made in accordance with the standards of practice or code of ethics of that professional group or association in which he may hold membership
6. That the market value of the described property is a certain number of dollars as of a certain date
7. His signature

Specifications for Part III. The "Addenda" is a supplement to the report. It should contain supporting data that is of lesser importance than those contained in Part II. It is designed more to identify the property than to present evidence of the value.

Item 18: location map. The location map gives geographical identification to the property in relation to the larger corporate area in which it lies. Usually, the reader is interested in knowing where the property lies in relation to the geographical pattern of the city. This he can see at a glance if the report includes a map of the city (and preferably one that shows distances in mile circles from the loop area) on which the location of the property has been spotted.

Item 19: occupancy and use map of the neighborhood. The object of this record is to show the uses of the surrounding properties, and it is particularly informative in those problems where a mixture of uses exists. This exhibit consists of a simple line sketch to show the subject and the immediately surrounding blocks, with each block lined off to indicate the lots encompassed within it (the scale and style of Baist's, Sanborn, or fire insurance maps are best) and each parcel identified by the present-style title of the building, such as: "frame, single-family dwelling"; "brick-veneer, two-flat"; "brick, four-family apartment"; "gas station"; "double store and flat building"; or whatever local terminology may dictate. The subject lot should be prominently identified.

Where the uses are predominantly of one character, a blanket description for an entire block may be used, to read "similar dwellings."

Item 20: plot plan. The plot plan is a single-line scale drawing showing the dimensions of the lot and the location of the buildings that are on it. The over-all dimensions of all buildings should be shown, as well as the location of driveways, fences, retaining walls, and all other improvements above the surface.

Item 21: floor plans. Again, only single-line sketches are called for. These should show the door and window openings, the room sizes and their arrangement, and the location of plumbing and heating fixtures.

Item 22: exhibits, extra photos, etc. Include here extra photographs that influenced the valuation conclusion, particularly those of other properties used in the market (comparative) approach to value. Include also such exhibits as may be necessary to amplify any nonstandard condition found in the appraisal analysis. Thus, in the valuation of a residential property that, through a change in the character of the neighborhood, had become susceptible to use as a parking lot, the appraiser wisely included in the Addenda a parking lot plan of the lot to show the number of parking stalls into which it could be divided.

Conclusions

When we get to this point, we may expect to hear the apprentice appraiser say: "This is indeed a large order." And from a few of the bearded patriarchs of long service in this particular field, we may confidently expect to hear swift and summary condemnation, on the ground that such a report as we have described above is entirely "too technical."

This discussion is premised, as stated earlier in the chapter, on the assumption that the appraiser is obliged to prepare an individualized report. In actual practice, particularly where the employment is by some agency of the Government or some real estate or lending institution in which appraisal is an everyday function, the printed form will be found in use. Examination of most of the printed appraisal forms used by institutions where appraisal is an almost daily function will show that these forms contain most of the items discussed in this chapter.

The Society of Residential Appraisers once had for its motto: "We have no moral right to decide on the basis of opinion that which may be determined as a matter of fact." The author's interpretation of this statement is that, while value cannot of course be "determined as a matter of fact," most of the data from which the opinion of value is constructed can be determined factually. And therein lies the argument for a report that covers *all* the avenues of investigation and gathers in all the loose threads of the fabric, knotting them together into one completed whole.

There can be no conclusion without a premise; a premise is a "proposition stated or assumed as leading to a conclusion." The type of report outlined above is one in which the premises are stated. The "certificate" form of appraisal report is one in which we attempt a conclusion without a stated premise.

But aside from this, there is the important conclusion that the report documents the appraiser's intelligence, skill, analytical ability, reliability, judgment, and craftsmanship. These things proclaim his professional ability. It is the only medium through which he may ethically advertise his wares.[6] Thus, if he is to be known by his works, the skill of which he is capable must be reflected by his expert handling of this final step in the appraisal process — the appraisal report.

---

[6] The code of ethics of the American Institute of Real Estate Appraisers prohibits all but the most conservative type of professional advertisement.

APPENDIX

RULES OF PROFESSIONAL ETHICS

of the

AMERICAN INSTITUTE OF REAL ESTATE APPRAISERS

(As amended November 19, 1949)

ARTICLE I
Fees

SECTION 1. It is unethical for an appraiser to accept an engagement to appraise a property if his employment or fee is contingent upon his reporting a predetermined or specified amount of value, or is otherwise contingent upon any finding to be reported.

SECTION 2. It is unethical for an appraiser retained in cases where monetary damages are involved to make his compensation contingent upon the amount of, or to fix his compensation as a percentage of, the damages which may be agreed upon or finally decreed.

ARTICLE II
Commissions and Favors

SECTION 1. It is unethical for an appraiser to accept any commission, favor, or emolument in connection with the appraising of a property other than a fair professional fee for the responsibility entailed and the work and expense involved.

ARTICLE III
Disinterested Appraisals

SECTION 1. It is unethical for an appraiser to issue an appraisal report if he is acting or intending to act in the capacity of broker, loan broker, or manager, or if he has an ownership, contemplated future ownership, or any other interest in connection with the property appraised unless such interest or interests be fully disclosed in the appraisal certificate

ARTICLE IV
Hypothetical Appraisals

SECTION 1. It is unethical for an appraiser to issue an appraisal report in which the reported valuation is based upon predicated rentals and expenses unless he describes in detail in his report the basis for his prediction.

In particular, it is unethical for an appraiser to certify a valuation predicated upon assumed rentals and expenses which he does not feel certain are highly probable of achievement under ordinary competent management.

SECTION 2. It is unethical for an appraiser to issue an unqualified appraisal report on an investment property which does not reflect the effects of existing leases upon the value of the property.

SECTION 3. It is unethical for an appraiser to issue an appraisal report in which the reported value is based upon the completion of public or private improvements which are not assured unless he clearly states that the appraisal is made on that hypothesis. In any event, he must state in his report the conditions with regard to such improvements which he assumes in determining the value reported.

SECTION 4. It is unethical for an appraiser to issue an appraisal report in which the reported value is based upon the assumed absence of any legal restriction unless such assumption is reasonable or in accord with legal opinion accepted by the appraiser, and unless the legal authority and his opinion are quoted in the appraisal certificate, and it is expressly stated that the appraisal is contingent on such lawful restriction being changed or absent in accordance with the assumption.

ARTICLE V*
Fractional Appraisals

SECTION 1. It is unethical for an appraiser to issue an appraisal report on only a part of a whole property unless he specifically states that it is a fractional appraisal and as such can be used only in a manner consistent with such limitations.

SECTION 2. In appraising the security for a loan it is unethical for an appraiser to issue a certificate covering anything less than all of the property designated as security for the loan unless conditions and limitations of the use of the report are clearly stated.

(*It is not intended that anything in these Articles V and VI shall be construed to prevent an appraiser from preparing and presenting fractional appraisals or summation appraisals where such appraisals are required for rate making, cost accounting, and other special purposes where the concept of cost independent from value may be appropriately involved.)

RULES OF PROFESSIONAL ETHICS

SECTION 3. In appraising the security for a leasehold loan, it is unethical for an appraiser to issue a certificate of value of the improvement only, omitting the value of the leasehold, which latter may be positive, zero or negative.

ARTICLE VI*

Summation Appraisals

SECTION 1. It is unethical for an appraiser to issue an appraisal report on a property in which the total reported value is derived by adding together the values of fractional parts of the property unless the limitations are clearly stated or other and conclusive evidence is given that this result equals the total value of the property considered as a whole.

ARTICLE VII

Economic Probabilities and Value of Property

SECTION 1. It is unethical for an appraiser to issue an appraisal report on a construction project which does not give the appraiser's opinion on the economic soundness of the project.

SECTION 2. It is unethical for an appraiser to issue an appraisal report on a construction project without also reporting his estimate of the reasonably expected earnings of the project and an opinion as to the reasonable time required to attain normal occupancy.

ARTICLE VIII

Duty to Hold Findings Confidential

SECTION 1. It is the duty of an appraiser to hold as confidential the results and other findings of his appraisal until released from his obligation by the client or by due process of law

ARTICLE IX

Expert Testimony

SECTION 1. In giving testimony as to the value of real property in any court or before any other legally constituted tribunal, an appraiser may follow rules of procedure as to appraisal method legally binding in that jurisdiction even though such rules may be at variance with the provisions of these Rules of Professional Ethics.

SECTION 2. When a member accepts employment to make a real estate appraisal or employment to testify as to the value of real estate before a court of law, the appraiser will complete an adequate written appraisal of the property, signed by him, and retain a copy thereof in his files which shall be delivered to the Governing Council or the Professional Ethics Committee on request for the purposes of any investigation of the professional conduct of the member.

ARTICLE X

Contents of Appraisal Reports

SECTION 1. It is unethical for an appraiser to omit any of the following from his appraisal report:

a. An unequivocal and reasonably complete description of the property appraised.

b. A statement of any contingent conditions upon which this appraisal has been based. For example: (1) the validity of legal, engineering, or auditing opinions used; (2) the completion of projected public or private improvements; (3) that management is assumed to be competent and the ownership to be in responsible hands.

c. The date or time at which the value obtains.

d. The amount of the value.

e. A statement that the appraiser has no present or contemplated future interest in the property appraised; or a statement disclosing all such interests which the appraiser may have in the property appraised.

f. In case the property appraised is a fractional part of the property of a type covered by these Rules of Professional Ethics, a statement that the value reported is invalidated if used in making a summation appraisal of the property as a whole unless conditions and limitations of the use of the report are clearly stated.

AMERICAN INSTITUTE OF REAL ESTATE APPRAISERS

SECTION 2. It is recommended that each appraisal report should contain a statement or certificate, substantially in the following form:

'1 (We), the undersigned do hereby certify that to the best of my (our) knowledge and belief the statements and opinions contained in this appraisal are correct, subject to the limiting conditions herein set forth; also, that this appraisal has been made in conformity with the Rules of Professional Ethics of the American Institute of Real Estate Appraisers of the National Association of Real Estate Boards."

ARTICLE XI
Advertising

SECTION 1. It is unethical for a member of the Institute to advertise his professional attainments or services except in a dignified manner in keeping with high professional standards.

Public notices preferably should be limited to an advertisement of the name, professional titles including M.A.I. (Member of the American Institute of Real Estate Appraisers of the National Association of Real Estate Boards), class of service, and address of the advertiser without any other qualifying word or letters, or in the case of announcement of change of address, the plain statement of the fact for the publication of which the announcement purports to be made.

Cards permitted by this rule when appearing in newspapers shall not exceed two columns in width and three inches in depth; when appearing in magazines, directories, and similar publications, cards shall not exceed one fourth of a page in size. This rule shall not be construed to inhibit the proper and professional dissemination of impersonal information among a member's own clients or personal associates or the properly restricted circulation of bulletins containing professional information.

SECTION 2. It is ethical, however, for an appraiser of the Institute to carry an announcement in a classified directory, as follows: "JOHN DOE, M.A.I., Address, Telephone Number" under the subdivision REAL ESTATE APPRAISALS.

ARTICLE XII
Relations with the Institute and
Fellow Members

SECTION 1 No member shall conduct himself in such manner as to prejudice his professional status or the reputation of the Institute.

SECTION 2. Any oral or written statement by any member with reference to his affiliation with the Institute that is not specific and exact shall be construed to be professional misconduct and subject to immediate disciplinary action.

SECTION 3. It is unethical for any member to injure falsely or maliciously, directly or indirectly, the professional reputation, prospects, or business of another member.

SECTION 4. It is unethical for any member to accept an appraisal assignment without having had previous experience and/or general knowledge of such character as to qualify him to accept such an assignment unless either:

a. He has associated with him in the making of the appraisal an appraiser who has had experience in the valuation of the type of property under appraisement, or

b. Unless the facts are fully disclosed to the client.

Code of Ethics
Society of Residential Appraisers

Preamble

The relationship between the individuals of any group engaged in the same line of endeavor, and between the group as a whole and the public, can best be established by strict adherence to certain basic principles by the members of the group. Such principles, commonly known as ethics, are the self-imposed rules of conduct which express the ideals of the group.

The establishment of such principles is desirable regardless of the nature of the endeavor. It is necessary in those lines of endeavor which are classified as professional in character. Appraising, because of the nature of the work, is professional in character, so the establishment of certain principles to which those engaged in appraising should adhere is not only desirable, but necessary.

1. Definitions

a. Property—All rights to the future benefits arising from ownership.

b. Value—The present worth of all future benefits.

c. Residential Property—A building whose principal use is the provision of dwelling units for no more than four families.

d. Appraisal—An estimate of value based upon an individual's best judgment and reasoning as a result of his experience and his study of a particular property upon which the estimate of value is made.

2. Fees

It is unethical for an appraiser—

a. To accept an order to appraise a property if his employment or fee is contingent upon his supporting a pre-determined conclusion.

b. To make his compensation contingent upon the amount of damages which may be decreed by the court deciding the issues from the exercise of the rights of eminent domain, or other similar issues.

3. Appraisal Reports

It is unethical for an appraiser to omit any of the following from his appraisal report—

a. A complete description of the property appraised.

b. A statement of any special assumptions upon which his appraisal has been based, for example: (1) the completion of projected public or private improvements; or (2) the validity of legal, engineering or auditing opinion used if he has reason to doubt them.

c. The date at which the value obtains.

d. The amount of the value.

e. A statement of any present or contemplated future interest in the property appraised if the appraiser has such interest.

4. Professional Practice

It is unethical for an appraiser—

a. To conduct himself in any manner which will prejudice his professional status or the reputation of any appraisal organization with which he is connected.

b. To use the advantages of a salaried position to compete unfairly with other appraisers.

c. To injure falsely or maliciously, directly or indirectly, the professional reputation, prospects, or business of any other appraiser.

d. To attempt to supplant another appraiser after definite steps have been taken toward the employment of the appraiser

e. To compete with another appraiser on the basis of professional charges by reducing his usual charge, and in this manner attempting to underbid after having been informed of the charges named by another appraiser.

f. To reveal in any way, before he has been permitted to do so by his client or by due process of law, that he has been employed to make an appraisal or after making the appraisal to disclose any of the conclusions at which he has arrived.

g. To issue a separate appraisal report when another appraiser assigned to appraise the same property has had a part in the formation of the opinion on value.

Adopted by the Board of Governors July 23, 1945   Chicago

VETERANS ADMINISTRATION APPRAISAL REPORT

1	EXISTING CONSTRUCTION ☐	PROPOSED CONSTRUCTION ☐	ALTERATIONS AND IMPROVEMENTS ☐
2	LENDER		ADDRESS
3	VETERAN		PRESENT ADDRESS
4	ADDRESS OF SECURITY		

5 PLOT PLAN AND PHOTOGRAPHS OF PROPERTY

Show street names, location of subject property on plot, one front-view photograph and one other view of buildings. Show dimensions of lot on plot plan. Give lot and block or other brief legal description if available.

PASTE UPPER EDGE OF PHOTOGRAPHS HERE

Sketch outline of shape of building, including porches, attached garage, etc., give dimensions and height of building from basement floor to roof.

ESTATE APPRAISED ☐ Fee simple ☐ Leasehold ☐ Other

6 BRIEF DESCRIPTION (Building lot, district, zone, violations, lot size)

7	ANY EVIDENCE OF TERMITES	DRY ROT	DAMPNESS	SETTLEMENT	NO EVIDENCE

8 CHARACTER OF NEIGHBORHOOD IS—

NEIGHBORHOOD ACTIVITY

MAJOR STRUCTURES	CONSTRUCTION	TYPICAL CONDITION	AGE TYPICAL BLDG.	BUILT UP	OWNER OCC.	VACANCY	ZONING	TRANSITION TO—
Neigh.				%	%	%		
Block				%	%	%		

UTILITIES	AVAIL.	CONNECTED	STREET IMPS.	CONVENIENCES	BLK.	MI.	TYPICAL INFLUENCES	
Water			Walks	G. School			Racial	
Sewer			Curb	H. School			Occupn.	
Gas			Paving	Stores			Income	
Elec.			Alleys	Church			Rentals	

IS SUBJECT TYPICAL OF NEIGHBORHOOD? (Describe)

Superior ☐ Typical ☐ Inferior ☐

DESIRABILITY OF FLOOR PLAN—

PROPERTY ADDRESS	UNITS	ROOMS	CONSTRUCTION	CONDITION	SALE PRICE	DATE SOLD

10 BUILDING SPECIFICATIONS—CONDITIONS AND CALCULATIONS:

	MAIN BUILDING		OTHER BUILDING	
	Description	General Condition	Description	General Condition
Number rooms, baths				
Bedrooms				
Age				
Use				
Type				
Stories				
Units				
Construction				
Roof				
Foundation				
Basement				
Floors				
Interior walls				
Bath finish				
Heating plant and fuel				
Fireplace				
Closet space				
Gutters and drain spout				
Stove				
Refrigerator				

11

MAIN BUILDING:

Square feet / or Cubic feet	
Rate per foot	
Replmt. cost new	$
Depreciation @ _____ % per yr.	
for _____ yrs.	$
Depreciated value	$

OTHER BUILDING:

Square feet / or Cubic feet	
Rate per foot	
Replmt. cost new	$
Depreciation @ _____ % per yr. for _____ yrs.	$
Depreciated value	$

OTHER IMPROVEMENTS at depreciated value of improvements	$
Total depreciated value	$
Land valuation	$
Total depreciated value of property	$

12 FUTURE ECONOMIC LIFE

MAIN BLDG. _____ YEARS   OTHER BLDG. _____ YEARS

Assessed Valuations		Annual Taxes	
Land	$	General	$
Main building	$	Special	$
Other building	$	Other	$
TOTAL	$	Total taxes	$

Comment on any special assessments:

13 MULTI-UNIT PROPERTIES ONLY

MONTHLY RENTAL UNFURNISHED

Unit	"As Is"		AFTER NECESSARY REPAIRS	
	Actual (1)	Fair (2)	Allowable (3)	Fair (4)
A				
B				
C				
D				

Is actual rent set under rent control?	
Estimated gross income (Annual)	$
Estimated expense and vacancy (Annual)	$
Estimated net income (Annual)	$

VA FORM 4-1803
MAR 1946

16—44888-2

14. If leasehold case: (a) Unexpired term _____ yrs.; (b) Renewable for _____ yrs.; (c) Annual leasehold rental, $ _____ ; (d) Does lease limit lessee in the sale or assignment of leasehold _____ ; (e) Is leasehold redeemable _____ ; give date and terms. _____

15. COMMENTS: (a) Describe detrimental influences; (b) Justify capitalization rate if multi-unit property involved; (c) Describe real estate market in community; (d) Suitability of intended use; (e) Explain depreciation.

_____

_____

_____

_____

_____

_____

_____

_____

_____

_____

_____

_____

_____

16. Show below ONLY repairs necessary to protect property and make it suitable for occupancy. Comment in section 17 on additions or improvements that might be desirable and increase the value of property but that are not necessary.

EXTERIOR REPAIRS	ESTIMATED COST	INTERIOR REPAIRS	ESTIMATED COST

TOTAL INTERIOR REPAIRS	$
TOTAL EXTERIOR AND INTERIOR REPAIRS	$

TOTAL EXTERIOR REPAIRS $

17 COMMENTS:

APPRAISER'S CERTIFICATION

18

I HEREBY CERTIFY that (a) I have carefully viewed the property described in this report, INSIDE AND OUTSIDE, so far as it has been completed; that (b) it is the same property that is identified by description in my appraisal assignment; that (c) I have no interest, present or prospective, in the applicant, property, or mortgage except:

and that (d) I estimate the "Reasonable Value" "as is" $

When the repairs outlined above are made the reasonable value will be increased by at least the amount of the cost of such repairs.

COMMENTS:

DATE

APPRAISER'S SIGNATURE

APPRAISER'S ADDRESS

APPRAISER'S NAME TYPED

U. S. GOVERNMENT PRINTING OFFICE   16—44833–2

UNDERWRITING REPORT

AMENITY-INCOME PROPERTY

ARCHITECTURAL REPORT

6. CALCULATED AREA ▲   SQ. FT.

7. DESCRIPTION OF MAIN BUILDING

8. VARIATIONS   −   +

Fdns.
Frpl.
Ext. w.
Shg.
Subfl.
Fin. fl.
Rfg.
L. & pl.
Plbg.
Htg.
Insul.
Other

9. TOTAL VARIATIONS

10. NET VARIATION (Carry forward) $

---

11. MAIN BUILDING ▲ *a* YEAR BUILT

b BUILDING TYPE
- ☐ DETACHED
- ☐ SEMIDET.
- ☐ ROW
- ☐ END ROW

c NO. STORIES ◄
d NO. LIV. UNITS ◄
e RMS PER UNIT ◄
f BASEMENT ___ %
g NON RES. USE ___ %

h LIV. RMS.
i DIM. RMS.
j KITCHENS ◄
k BEDRMS. ▲
l BATHS

m GARAGE
- ☐ BUILT-IN
- ☐ ATTACHED
- ☐ DETACHED
- NO. CARS. ▲
- OTH. USE.

n STREET IMPR.
| | PAVING | CURB | GUTTER | SIDEWALK | STORM SEWER |

o UTILITIES

	PUB.	COM.	INDV.
WATER SUP	☐	☐	☐
GAS	☐	☐	☐
ELECTRIC	☐	☐	☐
SEWER	☐	☐	☐ C.P. S.T. ☐

12. NET VARIATION (from line 10) $
13. COST FROM ___
14. SUBTOTAL
15. ATTACHED GARAGE
16. PORCHES
17. ATTACHED TERRACES
18. DETACHED GARAGE
19. WALKS AND DRIVEWAYS
20. OTHER ON-SITE IMPROVEMENTS
21. ALL BLDG. IMPROVEMENTS
22. GEN. OVERHEAD AND PROFIT ___ %
23. BLDG. IMPROV. UNADJUSTED
24. ADJ.: LOC. ___ % QUAL. ___ % COMB. ___ %
25. BLDG. IMPROV. ADJUSTED
26. ARCHITECTURAL SERVICES
27. REPL. COST BLDG. IMPROV., NEW COND. $

---

28. EASILY REMOVABLE REAL ESTATE ITEMS ___

29. UNUSUAL CHARACTERISTICS ___

30. PRESENT CONDITION OF BLDG.:
☐ EXCELLENT   ☐ GOOD   ☐ FAIR   ☐ POOR

31. EST. COST REPAIRS PROP'D. $ ___   REQU. $ ___

PHYSICAL SECURITY FEATURES	REJ.	1	2	3	4	5	RATING
VISUAL APPEAL OF PROPERTY	4	8	12	16	20		
LIVABILITY OF PROPERTY	4	8	12	16	20		
NATURAL LIGHT AND VENTILATION	2	4	6	8	10		
STRUCTURAL QUALITY	4	8	12	16	20		
RESISTANCE TO ELEMENTS AND USE	2	4	6	8	10		
SUITABILITY OF MECH. EQUIPMENT	4	8	12	16	20		

RATING OF PHYSICAL SECURITY

ADJUSTMENT FOR NONCONFORMITY	16	12	8	4	0

RATING OF PROPERTY — *Rating of Physical Security minus Adjustment for Nonconformity*

SITE

44. DIMENSIONS ___ FT. X ___ FT. OR ___ SQ. FT.

45. ☐ EXCESS LAND, IF ANY, EXCL. FROM VAL. (SEE REMARKS.)

46. UNUSUAL ☐ FILLS ☐ CUTS ☐ FOUND. ☐ RET. WALLS WITH COST OF $ ___ NOT INCLUDED IN

VALUATION REPORT

NEIGHBORHOOD

32. GENERAL LOCATION ___

33. LAND USES ___

34. ☐ ADVERSE CHANGE IN ☐ USE ☐ OCCUPANCY ☐ IS TAKING PLACE ☐ IS ANTICIPATED. (SEE REMARKS)

---

38. AVAIL. MKT. PR. TYP. PROPS. $ ___ TO $ ___
39. AVAIL. MO. RENTAL TYP. PROPS. $ ___ TO $ ___
40. DEMAND FOR AMENITY INCOME PROPS.
41. DEMAND FOR RENTAL INCOME PROPS.
42. EXCEPTIONALLY FAVORABLE OR UNFAVORABLE

50. AVAIL. MKT. PRICE EQUIV. SITE ▲
51. LANDSCG., PLNTG. AND FIN. GRDG.
52. MISC. ALLOWABLE COSTS
53. EST. REPL. COST OF PROP. ▲ $

35. BUILT-UP _____%. PROSPECT FOR FUTURE DEVEL...
OPMENT UNDER ☐ PRESENT ☐ ANTICIPATED USES
IS ☐ LITTLE ☐ GOOD ☐ EXCELLENT. ☐ SEE RE-
MARKS.
36. AGES OF TYPICAL BLDGS. _____YRS. TO _____YRS.
37. OWNER-OCC. ___%. TENANT-OCC. ___%. VAC. ___%

43. DEMAND FOR PURCHASE OF COMPETITIVE PROPER-
TIES IN ECONOMIC B. AREA: ☐ NONE ☐ LITTLE
☐ MODERATE ☐ STRONG

54. LOWEST PRICE ASKED RECENTLY FOR EQUIVALENT PROPERTIES $
NEARLY EQUIVALENT $_____ TO $_____
55. LOWEST PRICE PAID RECENTLY FOR EQUIVALENT PROPERTIES $
NEARLY EQUIVALENT $_____ TO $_____
56. ESTIMATED AVAILABLE MARKET PRICE OF PROPERTY ▲ $
57. MONTHLY RENTAL VALUE ▲ $ **58.** EXCESS MONTHLY EXP. $
59. REM. ECON. LIFE ▲ _____ YEARS.   **60.** OWNER-OCCUPANCY APPEAL
61. MAINT. AND REPAIR $ **62.** HEATING AND UTIL. $ **63.** HAZ. INS. $
64. TAXES $ **65.** PAYMENTS FOR NONPREPAYABLE SPEC. ASSESS. $
66. TOTAL ANNUAL OPERATING EXPENSE $
67. MO. RENTAL VAL. MINUS EXCESS MO. EXPENSE X RENT MULTIPLE =
ESTIMATE OF CAPITALIZED INCOME IN FEE SIMPLE $
68. ASSUMING COMPLETION OF PROPOSED CONSTRUCTION, ALTERATIONS, REPAIRS AND REQUIREMENTS
AND THAT PROPERTY IS ☐ UNENCUMBERED BY SPECIAL ASSESSMENTS.
☐ ENCUMBERED BY NONPREPAYABLE SPECIAL ASSESSMENTS.
ESTIMATE OF VALUE IN FEE SIMPLE ▲ $

69. LEASEHOLD ESTATE $ _____ YEARS. **71.** UNUSUAL LEASE PROVISIONS
70. REMAINING TERM OF LEASE _____ YEARS. **73.** CAPITALIZATION OF LEASED FEE AT _____% = $
72. ANN. GROUND RENT $
REMARKS:

CERTIFICATION: *I have analyzed the property and I have no personal interest, present or prospective, in the property, applicant, or proceeds of the mortgage.*

Date	☐ Constr. Exam.	☐ Per diem	Date	☐ Valuator	☐ Per diem
APPROVED			APPROVED		
Date	☐ Chief Architect	☐ Deputy	Date	☐ Chief Valuator	☐ Deputy

---

47. SPEC. ASSESS. ☐ PREPAYABLE ☐ NONPREPAYABLE.
TOTAL AMT. $_____ ANNUAL PAY. $_____
@ _____% INT. REMAINING TERM _____ YEARS.
48. ☐ EASEMENTS, ENCROACHMENTS, VIOLATIONS OF
RESTRICTIONS, MINERAL RESERVATIONS

SITE DESIRABILITY FEATURES	REJ.	1	2	3	4	5	RATING
PROTECTION AGAINST INHARM. LAND USES	4	8	12	16	20		
PHYSICAL AND SOCIAL ATTRACTIVENESS	4	8	12	16	20		
AD. OF CIVIC. SOC. AND COMMER. CENTERS	4	8	12	16	20		
ADEQUACY OF TRANSPORTATION	2	4	6	8	10		
SUFFICIENCY OF UTILITIES AND SERV.	2	4	6	8	10		
LEVEL OF TAXES AND SPECIAL ASSESS.	2	4	6	8	10		

RATING OF SITE DESIRABILITY

RELATIVE MARKETABILITY	16	12	8	4	0

RATING OF LOCATION — Rate of Site Desirability minus Adjustment for Relative Marketability

49. DIFFERENCES: ITEM 5 AND RTG. OF LOC. (SEE RE-MARKS)

CASE NUMBER
F.I.-D.T. NO. _____
ADDRESS

     Number   *Street*

*City*_____
*County*_____ *State*_____

1. PREVIOUSLY PROCESSED AS CASE NO. _____
2. CONTRACTOR_____
3. BASIC CASE_____
4 SUBDIVISION FILE NO. _____
5. ESTABLISHED RATING OF LOCATION_____

Method of Calculating Building Volume

In order that the cubical contents of buildings may be computed correctly and uniformly, the following general instructions are given and illustrated.

The cubical content is the actual space enclosed within the outer surfaces of the outside wall and contained between the roof surfaces and six inches below the finished floor of the basement. Bay windows, dormers, and porches with walls and sash also shall be allowed the full volume contained therein. D stands for depth; W for width; L for length; and H for height. All measurements are in linear feet.

TYPICAL EXAMPLE

A. Basement: full volume $= L \times W \times H$.
Height measured from finished surface of basement floor to bottom of first-floor joists, plus 6″.
$L = 28'$ $W = 26'$ $H = 7'$
$28 \times 26 \times 7 = 5{,}096$ cu. ft.

B. Main Structure: full volume $= L \times W \times H$.
Bottom first-floor joists to top of ceiling joists.
$L = 28'$ $W = 26'$ $H = 19'$
$28 \times 26 \times 19 = 13{,}832$ cu. ft.

C. Attic: full volume $= L \times W \times H$.
Top of ceiling joists to average height of roof.
$L = 28'$ $W = 26'$ $H = 4\frac{1}{2}'$ (½ of height to roof peak)
$28 \times 26 \times 4\frac{1}{2} = 3{,}276$ cu. ft.

D. Exterior porch: open; part volume $= L \times W \times H \times \frac{1}{3}$.
$L = 26'$ $W = 8'$ $H = 12'$
$26 \times 8 \times 12 \times \frac{1}{3} = 832$ cu. ft.
Note: The proportion of full volume taken depends upon the type of construction and its cost.

E. Bay window: full volume $= L \times W \times H$.
$L = 7'$ $W = 2\frac{1}{2}'$ $H = 8'$
$7 \times 2\frac{1}{2} \times 8 = 140$ cu. ft.

F. Open outside areaway: full volume $= L \times W \times H$.
$L = 6'$ $W = 4'$ $H = 4'$
$6 \times 4 \times 4 = 96$ cu. ft.

G. Dormer: full volume $= \dfrac{L \times D \times H}{2}$
(Measurements to be made as shown on diagram.)
$L = 8'$ $D = 4'$ $H = 5'$
$\dfrac{8 \times 4 \times 5}{2} = 80$ cu. ft.

H. Summary:
$5{,}096 + 13{,}832 + 3{,}276 + 832 + 140 + 96 + 80 = 23{,}352$ cu. ft.

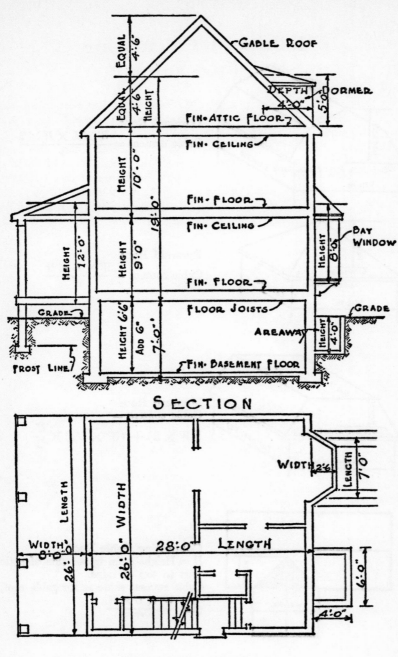

SECTION

FLOOR PLAN

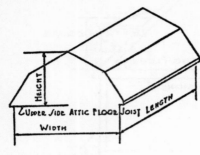

Gambrel Roof

Cubic content $= \dfrac{W \times L \times H \times 2}{3}$

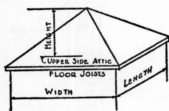

Pyramid Roof

Cubic content $= \dfrac{W \times L \times H}{3}$

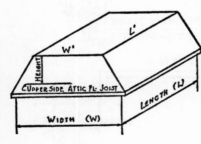

Mansard Roof

Cubic content =

$$[(W \times L) + (W' \times L')] \times \frac{H}{2}$$

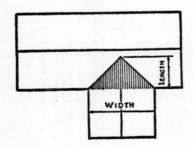

Connecting Gable Roof

$H =$ Height from upper side of attic joist to top of ridge.

Cubic content same as for gable roof,

plus $\dfrac{W \times L \times H}{6}$

Income Tax Depreciation
for Buildings *

The useful life of a building for business purposes depends to a large extent on the suitability of the structure for its use and location, its architectural quality, the rate of change in population, the shifting of land values, and the extent of maintenance and rehabilitation.

The extent to which the equipment of a building, such as heating, plumbing, electrical wiring and fixtures, elevators, and other improvements, must be replaced is an important factor in determining the over-all rate of depreciation to be applied to the building and its equipment. Such a rate contemplates that the cost of new equipment will be capitalized, and that the cost of the equipment replaced will be charged to the depreciation reserve. In instances, however, where it is not feasible to determine the cost of the old equipment, the cost of the new equipment may be charged to the depreciation reserve. Where this method of accounting is followed and in the absence of special circumstances, the composite rates of depreciation set forth in the table below are considered reasonable:

	Composite rate (per cent)		
	Type of construction		
	Good	*Average*	*Cheap*
Apartments	2½	2½	3
Banks	2	2	2½
Dwellings	2	2½	3
Factories	2¼	2½	3
Farm buildings	2	2	2½
Garages	2	2½	3
Grain elevators	1½	2	2½
Hotels	2½	2½	3
Loft buildings	2	2	3
Machine shops	2	2½	3
Office buildings	2	2½	3
Stores	2	2	2½
Theaters	2½	3	3½
Warehouses	1½	2	2½

* Reprinted from the *Prentice-Hall Federal Tax Service;* ¶ 14,160-K. Copyright 1942 by Prentice-Hall, Inc.

Appraiser's Field Kit

Nos. 1 and 2. One six-inch engineer's scale and one six-inch architect's scale

No. 3. One four-colored ball point pen to assist definition of a field sketch. The varied colors are used to show different types of property or different types of property uses.

No. 4. One two-and-one-half power reading glass, for reading reproduced material such as ozalids, blue-prints, Sanborn Maps, and Baist's Atlases

No. 5. One fifty-foot plastic tape

No. 6. One flashlight

No. 7. Army musette bag (purchasable at any army surplus store for about $1.50); it holds ALL of the equipment shown. It contains three large and three small pockets. The shoulder sling permits free use of the hands at all times.

No. 8. One six-foot folding rule; handy for measuring ceiling heights

No. 9. A supply of co-ordinate paper, 10 squares to the inch, for making rough sketches to scale

No. 10. One letter-size clipboard. Useful when working outside, especially on a windy day

Nos. 11 and 15. Flashholder and extra bulbs; used on interiors, especially on industrial properties for shooting equipment such as open-hearth furnaces, heat-treating batteries, traveling cranes, machine shops, loading docks, railroad spurs, etc.

No. 12. Extra film; Eastman Super XX, emulsion speed daylight 100; 20 exposures

No. 13. Camera; brand, Argus C3; small and compact; shoots 35 mm film, 20 exposures to the roll

No. 14. One Weston exposure meter

No. 16. One notebook — with numbered pages and spiral binding. When the job is finished the pages are torn out, stapled together, and placed in the completed work file.

An Appraiser's Field Kit. (*Courtesy Lambert and Freeman*)

Bibliography

Magazines, Periodicals, and Statistical Services

Architectural Forum ("The Magazine of Building"); monthly, Time, Inc., N. Y.

Boeckh's Cost Index, Rough Notes Co., Indianapolis, Indiana.

Engineering News-Record, monthly, McGraw-Hill, N. Y. (for Comparative Construction Costs)

Headlines, weekly, National Association of Real Estate Boards, Chicago, Illinois, and Washington, D. C.

Land Economics, quarterly, University of Wisconsin.

National Real Estate Journal, monthly, Stamats Publishing Co., Cedar Rapids, Iowa.

Real Estate Analyst, Roy Wenzlick & Co., St. Louis, Missouri.

Review of the Society of Residential Appraisers, monthly, Society of Residential Appraisers, Chicago, Ill.

The Appraisal Journal, quarterly, American Institute of Real Estate Appraisers, Chicago, Illinois.

Urban Land, monthly, Urban Land Institute, Washington, D. C.

Books

American Institute of Real Estate Appraisers, *The Appraisal of Real Estate,* Chicago, 1951.

American Institute of Real Estate Appraisers, *Appraisal Reporting Techniques,* Vols. I, II, and III, Chicago, Author, 1947-51.

American Institute of Real Estate Appraisers, *Appraisal Terminology and Handbook,* Chicago, Author, 1950.

American Institute of Real Estate Appraisers, *Farm Course Text,* Chicago, Author, 1944.

Babcock, F. M., *The Valuation of Real Estate,* New York, McGraw-Hill Book Co., 1932.

Barnes, F. E., *Estimating Building Costs and Appraising Buildings,* New York, McGraw-Hill Book Co., 1931.

Benson, Philip A., and North, Nelson L., *Real Estate Principles and Practices,* New York, Prentice-Hall, Inc., 1947.

Boeckh, E. H., *Manual of Appraisals,* Indianapolis, Rough Notes Co., 1937.

Bonbright, J. C., *Valuation of Property*, 2 Vols., New York, McGraw-Hill Book Co., 1937.

Chapman, H. H., *Forest Valuation*, New York, McGraw-Hill Book Co., 1947.

Dingman, C. F., *Estimating Building Costs*, New York, McGraw-Hill Book Co., 1944.

Ely, Richard T., and Wehrwein, George S., *Land Economics*, New York, The Macmillan Company, 1940.

Equitable Life Assurance Society of the United States, *Appraising For Farm Loans*, New York, Author, 1951.

Federal Housing Administration, *Underwriting Manual*, Washington, Author, 1947.

Finance Publishing Co., *Financial Compound Interest and Annuity Tables*, Boston, Author, 1947.

Fisher, Ernest M., *Advanced Principles of Real Estate Practice*, New York, The Macmillan Company, 1937.

Gray, Alexander, *Development of Economic Doctrine*, New York, Longmans, Green and Company, 1931.

Hoagland, Henry E., *Real Estate Principles*, New York, McGraw-Hill Book Company, 1949.

Kent, Frederick C., *Compound Interest and Annuity Tables*, New York, McGraw-Hill Book Co., 1926.

Kniskern, P. W., *Real Estate Appraisal and Valuation*, New York, The Ronald Press, 1933.

Kratovil, Robert, *Real Estate Law*, 2nd edition, New York, Prentice-Hall, Inc., 1952.

McMichael, S. L., *Appraising Manual*, New York, Prentice-Hall, Inc., 1951.

McMichael, S. L. and Bingham, R. F., *City Growth Essentials*, Santa Barbara, McMichael, 1928.

Marston, Anson and Agg, T. R., *Engineering Valuation*, New York, McGraw-Hill Book Co., 1936.

Mumford, Lewis, *The Culture of Cities*, New York, Harcourt, Brace and Company, 1938.

Murray, W. G., *Farm Appraisals*, Ames, Ia., Iowa State College, 1940.

Orgel, Lewis, *Valuation Under Eminent Domain*, Charlottesville, Va., The Michie Co., 1936.

Prouty, W. L. and others, *Appraisers and Assessors Manual*, New York, McGraw-Hill Book Co., 1930.

Ratcliff, Richard U., *Urban Land Economics*, New York, McGraw-Hill Book Co., 1949.

Saliers, E. A., *Depreciation Principles and Application*, New York, The Ronald Press, 1939.

Slichter, Sumner H., *The American Economy*, New York, Alfred A. Knopf, 1948.

Schmutz, G. L., *The Appraisal Process*, Los Angeles, Author, 1951.

Schmutz, G. L., *Condemnation Appraisal Handbook*, New York, Prentice-Hall, Inc., 1949.

Semenow, Robert W., *Questions and Answers on Real Estate*, New York, Prentice-Hall, Inc., 1952.

Society of Industrial Realtors, *Industrial Real Estate Lectures*, 1948, Author, Washington, D. C.

Thorson, I. A., *Simplified Appraisal System*, Los Angeles, Realty Research Bureau, 1949.

Townsend, Gilbert and others, *How to Estimate*, Chicago, American Technical Society, 1939.

Underwood, G., *Estimating Construction Costs*, New York, McGraw-Hill Book Co., 1930.

Von Mises, Ludwig, *Human Action*, New Haven, Yale University Press, 1949.

Walker, Frank, *Building Estimator's Handbook*, Chicago, Author, 1950.

Weimer, Arthur M. and Hoyt, Homer, *Principles of Urban Real Estate*, New York, The Ronald Press, 1939.

Index